Groundswell

Groundswell: Grassroots Feminist Activism in Postwar America offers an essential perspective on the post-1960 movement for women's equality and liberation. Tracing the histories of feminist activism through the National Organization of Women (NOW) chapters in three different locations: Memphis, Tennessee; Columbus, Ohio; and San Francisco, California, Gilmore explores how feminist identity, strategies, and goals were shaped by geographic location.

Departing from the usual conversation about the national icons and events of second-wave feminism, this book concentrates on local histories and asks the questions that must be answered on the micro level: Who joined? Who did not? What did they do? Why did they do it? Together with its analysis of feminist political history, these individual case studies from the Midwest, South, and West Coast shed light on the national women's movement in which they played a part.

In its coverage of women's activism outside the traditional East Coast centers of New York and Boston, *Groundswell* provides us a more diverse history of feminism, showing how social and political change was made from the ground up.

Stephanie Gilmore is Assistant Professor of Women's and Gender Studies at Dickinson College.

GROUNDSWELL

Grassroots Feminist Activism in Postwar America

Stephanie Gilmore

Routledge
Taylor & Francis Group

NEW YORK AND LONDON

First published 2013
by Routledge
711 Third Avenue, New York, NY 10017

Simultaneously published in the UK
by Routledge
2 Park Square, Milton Park, Abingdon, Oxon OX14 4RN

Routledge is an imprint of the Taylor & Francis Group, an informa business

Library of Congress Cataloging-in-Publication Data
Gilmore, Stephanie.
Groundswell : grassroots feminist activism in postwar America / by Stephanie Gilmore.
p. cm.
Includes bibliographical references and index.
1. Feminism--United States--History. 2. Feminists--United States--History.
3. United States--Social conditions--1945- I. Title.
HQ1426.G454 2012
305.420973--dc23

ISBN: 978-0-415-80144-7 (hbk)
ISBN: 978-0-415-80145-4 (pbk)
ISBN: 978-0-203-87613-8 (ebk)

Typeset in Bembo
by Taylor & Francis Books

Printed and bound in the United States of America by
Walsworth Publishing Company, Marceline, MO.

Contents

Acknowledgments   vii

1. Beyond the Friedan Mystique: The Importance of Grassroots
    Feminism   1

2. In the Midst of the "World-Wide Revolution of Human
    Rights": Creating the National Organization for Women   21

3. Feminist Activism in Memphis: Beyond the Liberal/Radical
    Divide   45

4. Feminist Theorizing, Feminist Activisms in Columbus   69

5. A Liberal Feminist Front of Progressive Activism in San
    Francisco   97

6. Learning from Grassroots Activisms in the Past   127

Notes   139
Bibliography   161
Index   175

Acknowledgments

Let me begin with a bit of a confession: whenever I put a new book in my hands, I turn immediately to the acknowledgments. (If this is your habit too, welcome.) I do so because it is such a lovely reminder that, no matter whose name appears on the cover, the work is accomplished through the energy, time, and love of many. Many wonderful people contributed to the making and actual publication of *Groundswell*. Anything good that comes of it is the result of their generosity and support; of course, any faults that remain are mine alone.

My first and deepest thanks go to the many women who did—and do—the work of grassroots feminism, some of whose voices are chronicled in here. Their activism reminds me that a movement is made up not just of leaders but of everyday people, unsung heroes who devote time, passion, money, energy, and love to themselves, their neighbors, and the larger cause of feminist revolution. For their time in the movement, and for sharing that with me, I am deeply humbled and grateful.

This book began as my dissertation, which I completed at Ohio State University. A most lovely and rigorous committee of Leila Rupp, Susan Hartmann, and Ken Goings kept me motivated with their own exacting standards. They comforted me when life threatened to dismiss any plans I had made for myself. They celebrated when I achieved any accomplishment. I remain impressed by the rate with which they conduct and publish research, especially when I know how much time and energy they have given to their students (me among them) over the years. Like Leila, Susan, and Ken, other faculty mentors at Ohio State, including Birgitte Søland, Judy Wu, Donna Guy, and Ken Andrien, became friends. My graduate-school peers (many of whom were also fellow "Journal Girls") not only kept me on my toes but also kept me laughing at clever turns of phrase, curious observations, and the funnier things in life. Renee Lansley, Heather Miller, Basia Nowak, Charlotte Weber, Anne Collinson, and Susan Freeman were especially important colleagues and friends, and I am grateful that we all still remain friends. Annie especially endured more than her fair share of my grad-school angst, but she did so with love and joy. She can have margaritas at my house anytime!

Since graduate school, I have had the good fortune of working at two fine institutions. Trinity College offered me an intellectual and academic home for two years, and I will be indebted to colleagues there, especially Steve Valocchi, Lou Masur, and Joan Hedrick. My current institution, Dickinson College, is unsurpassed in its academic nourishment, convivial atmosphere, and supportive colleagues, and I remain grateful for all of the intellectual reinforcement I have received there. In the four years I have been there (two of which I served as department chair), my home department of Women's and Gender Studies has quadrupled in number of majors, a testament to the importance of feminism and feminist faculty. I am deeply appreciative of my WGST colleagues Amy Farrell, Susannah Bartlow, Megan Yost, and Megan Glick, as well as a number of other colleagues who have supported and encouraged me along the way: Amy Steinbugler, Helene Lee, Laura Grappo, Vanessa Tyson, Wendy Moffat, Susan Rose, Jerry Philogene, Joyce Bylander, Sharon O'Brien, Ann Hill, Susan Feldman, Dan Schubert, Karen Weinstein, Sarah Brylinsky, Simona Perry, and Barbara Shaw. They make my time at Dickinson a true pleasure, even as—and especially because—they raise the bar for scholarly and intellectual pursuit. Neil Weissman deserves special acknowledgment: I have never met a dean who was more invested in the faculty as a whole, and in this particular faculty member. He and my colleagues have always considered "yes" before insisting "no," a rarity these days.

My students have always been a true source of inspiration, and as I walk into my classrooms every semester, I am reminded that we need feminist histories so that they can build feminist futures. For every student who came to my classes, and especially those who came back for more and even decided to major in WGST, you are wonderful teachers. I appreciate you and I look forward to your own activist endeavors.

Many of my colleagues are also my friends, and their friendship is a real treasure. Dan, Vanessa, Megan, Laura, Amy, Helene, Sarah, Susannah, Simona, and Barbara made time for good food, much coffee, strong drinks, and hearty laughter, and I hope to return tenfold the friendship and generosity they have given to me. Susannah, Simona, and Barbara have been particularly good to me, offering not only friendship but also a sense of home for me in Carlisle.

Routledge is an outstanding press, and I am honored to publish this book with them. Working with Kimberly Guinta and Rebecca Novack has been nothing short of inspiring; their patience and kindness have gone a long way in my book and I appreciate them tremendously. They also worked to solicit five reviewers for this book in its various stages, and for the reviewers' time and help I am grateful and impressed.

I completed this book while on a year-long fellowship at Duke University, where the Women's Studies Program offers a most hospitable place to work. To

Ranji Khanna, Robyn Weigman, Ara Wilson, Kathi Weeks, Kathy Rudy, Jolie Olcott, Marialana Weitzel, Melanie Mitchell, Lillian Spiller, Laura Micham, and Kelly Wooten, I extend my sincere thanks for your encouragement and support. I am simply delighted to call all of you colleagues and friends. Miles Grier, Victoria Hesford, and Shannon Withycombe were also on fellowship when I was at Duke; they are wonderful colleagues, generous people, and excellent drinking and eating buddies. Big "MH" to Miles Grier, who shared joy, pain, passion, television, music, food, and good times with me and made my year at Duke a most enjoyable experience.

Beyond Dickinson and Duke, I am fortunate to call many other friends my intellectual colleagues as well. Each of them has offered help with everything from tracking down a source to working out new ideas, and without them this book would never have seen the light of day. I extend heartfelt thanks and deep gratitude to Ros Baxandall, Eileen Boris, Leslie Brown, Marisa Chappell, Sue Cobble, Judith Ezekiel, Jacquelyn Hall, Susan Hartmann, Nancy Hewitt, Elizabeth Kaminski, Ian Lekus, Nancy Maclean, Lou Masur, Premilla Nadasen, Jo Reger, Leila Rupp, Kimberly Springer, Verta Taylor, Anne Valk, Steve Valocchi, Leigh Ann Wheeler, and Judy Wu. We have enjoyed together good food, conversation, and intellectual and emotional support, and I am a better scholar for your collegiality and a better person for your friendship.

It may be a strange thing to note, but I could never write a word without the dogs in my life. Fred was with me from my first year in graduate school to my first year at Dickinson; I miss him every day and appreciate how very much love he gave to me. (He also listened as I read every word of my dissertation aloud, and did so without complaint.) Raleigh never really cared what I was writing, but he always reminded me to stop everything to rub his belly. Olivia is a beautiful dollbaby of a dog; her own sad story always makes me cry. She is painfully shy around people, but when she thinks no one else is looking, she is downright silly and loving, and snuggles with absolute gusto. She really came out of her shell when she met Daffy and Dodger, who, with Olivia, are the Three Bad Dogs. Dodger gives love without reservation and longs only for pets; he's one sweet dog who reminds me to be sweet too. Daffy is very much her name, and even though she drives me mad and often eats me out of house and home, she makes me laugh out loud in ways that no other dog ever has. Margot, Lucy, and Happy, by contrast, are Three Good Dogs who have me very well trained during my time in Durham, and I'm so pleased at how willing they have been to accept me into the pack. (Ace and Madison round out the Durham bunch, and they're also very sweet pups.) These creatures, individually and collectively, encourage me to be far better than I am and remind me to play, laugh, and love without hesitation or reservation.

I am blessed to have participated in some of the dearest human friendships imaginable, many of which were accompanied by good food, strong drink, hearty laughter, copious tears, and, it turns out, unwavering love. Leila and Verta have been mentors, friends, and family to me; we are separated only by geographical distance but they will always be a part of my life. Susannah, Simona, Betsy, Lori, Steve, and Laz will always have a special place in my heart, as will Laura Gates, the best damn neighbor on the planet. Heather Hindin opened her home to me in Durham, and she has become one of my dearest friends. My sister Suzanne has also turned out to be a very dear friend to me, often encouraging me through her own example to be a better person, daughter, and friend. My parents Jill and Henry also encourage me in the best ways they know how, and, in spite of myself, they love me unconditionally. I think of them all when I imagine my sense of home over the years.

One night after a filling meal with my friend Lori, I opened two fortune cookies. The first fortune read: "You are a lover of words; someday you will write a book." I laughed because I was in the often laborious process of writing it, a process that often brought me to anxious tears. But now as I put this manuscript in the mail, I find a sense of closure—not because I've written the last word but because it is time to finish this book and move on to other projects and facets of my life. This brings me to my second fortune: "You will find great contentment in the daily, routine activities." As I settle back into my own sense of home, and before I dive headfirst into my next book, I will relish time with friends, lovers, dogs, family, and myself, and I look forward to the adventures and activities that await us.

1

BEYOND THE FRIEDAN MYSTIQUE

The Importance of Grassroots Feminism

In April 1970, just before she stepped down as the first president of the National Organization for Women (NOW), Betty Friedan called for a "Strike for Women's Equality." The strike would take place on August 26, marking the fiftieth anniversary of the passage of the 19th Amendment to the U.S. Constitution that assured women's political citizenship through the vote. Proclaiming this strike took the new leaders of NOW by surprise: as Aileen Hernandez, second president of NOW, said, "Betty just announced that this would take place out of the blue. She told the media it would happen and to be prepared, but we had no idea what it would look like!"[1] Rather than coordinate one single, massive demonstration, such as a march on Washington, Hernandez and new members of the national board of NOW encouraged feminists to "do your own thing" in protest of women's unequal status in society.[2]

And they did. Women in communities across the country responded to NOW's clarion call to action in a variety of ways. On that summer day, women in New York City marched en masse down Fifth Avenue during the evening rush hour. By contrast, in Beaver Dam, Wisconsin, Gene Boyer grabbed a bullhorn, a homemade sign, and literature about feminism and marched alone outside of her husband's furniture store.[3] Many media outlets declared the strike to be a "flop" and that the day was marked with "business as usual," but feminists on this day drew critical attention to inequality. NOW chapters around the country reported success with strike activities, which, in many places, brought together feminists, labor organizers, peace activists, civil rights activists—demonstrating not only that these are overlapping categories but also real and potential coalitions that feminists were creating and sustaining in their communities. According to Heather Booth, a founder of the Chicago Women's Liberation Union (CWLU), "it was clear" from the 1970 strike that "this is a movement as opposed to little factional efforts. [The strike] was a take off, and NOW was going to be a leading edge within the movement."[4]

Founded in 1966 as "a NAACP for women," NOW became the largest membership-based, explicitly feminist organization of the post-World War II era. NOW was often at the forefront of feminist issues, dedicating legal and political resources and action on the most pressing concerns, ranging from reproductive rights to pay equity to media images of women. It also boasted strong, charismatic leaders who became spokespeople in the heady days of feminism in postwar America. Scholars and activists alike note the role of NOW as a leading feminist organization of the 1960s and 1970s in books about U.S. feminism's history. Although NOW's leadership was significant and NOW was a leader in many fights, most notably the ERA (Equal Rights Amendment), the history of this organization goes far beyond its offices in Washington, DC.

Indeed, much of what we know about NOW is related to founder and first president Betty Friedan. It is nearly common knowledge that Friedan wrote the 1963 bestsellser *The Feminine Mystique*, a book that, according to Stephanie Coontz, "has been credited—or blamed—for destroying, single-handedly and almost overnight, the 1950s consensus that women's place was in the home."[5] We now know that Friedan misrepresented her own history, masking her own work as a leftist, labor journalist; we know that she was no ordinary housewife, even as she spoke to and for millions who identified with the "problem that has no name."[6] The book and its author are credited with launching the modern women's movement, although "the women's liberation movement doubtlessly would have emerged without the book."[7] Still, it "defined the perspective of a generation" and gave Friedan immediate cachet with the media and vast audiences of women. Three years after its publication, she was founding president of the National Organization for Women. Love her or hate her, Friedan helped change the lives of millions of women and men with *The Feminine Mystique*. But allowing her to stand for the whole of NOW's history, and NOW as the standard bearer for liberal feminism, ignores the realities of the women who comprised the women's movement.

Groundswell explores and analyzes feminist activists and their work to change consciousness and political realities in cities and towns across the country. In Memphis, Columbus, and San Francisco—cities known generally for social movement activism in the postwar era—feminists of all walks of life worked in their communities, through networks and organizations, to respond to injustices and create change toward a more equitable world. Although it is easy—and important—to follow social movement change through the success and/or failure of leaders, the work of social movements takes place among the rank and file. The women's movement is no different, and NOW, its largest organization during the heyday of activism in the 1970s, derived its strength in terms of numbers and financial support from women and men who did the work of feminism in their hometowns around the country. This book, then, is and is not a history of NOW. Although this book utilizes NOW as a connective thread between three sites, it moves past the concept of a national movement and analyzes instead the grassroots feminist activism in distinct communities. Beyond the need to create a usable organizational model, connecting these sites through NOW is practical: by 1971, NOW chapters had sprung up in all fifty states, making the *national organization for women* a geographically correct moniker. But in cities across the country, NOW thrived through local membership, and at the local level, it—and feminism—had localized agendas, issues, strategies, and goals. As such, tethering feminist sites of activism through NOW reflects a reality for many—though certainly not all— women in the 1970s: As one feminist activist and historian shared with me, "you could join a lesbian-socialist-vegetarian-feminist cell only in New York; otherwise you went to the NOW chapter."[8]

Here, this book explores locally based social justice activism in the hands of what John Dittmer called "local people." They were not media stars, nor did they seek to be; their names are not part of a recognized historical record. Indeed, for most of them, their feminist activism was about redress in the face of local struggles, and they did not openly or even necessarily connect themselves with a national move-ment (even if they were part of a national organization). Instead, they created change in their own communities, responding not just to national calls to action but to immediate and local issues that demanded feminists' attention. Their work cer-tainly falls within the temporal boundaries of a national movement known as the "second wave." But feminists in and beyond NOW did more than surf a wave of feminist activism; they created *groundswells* from which this social movement emerged, developed, and sustained itself.

The women's movement for equality and liberation reached a heyday in the 1970s, and because of its effects on politics and culture, it became the farthest-reaching social movement of the twentieth century. Historians and social scientists have written sweeping histories of the women's movement. *Moving the Mountain*, *Tidal Wave*, and *The World Split Open* are probably the three most cited histories of the movement, and notably each bears a title that evokes a literal breaking of ground that was the tremendous shifts in politics and culture brought on by this movement. Within the pages of these texts, scholars Winifred Wandersee, Sara Evans, and Ruth Rosen, respectively, trace the historical roots of this "second wave" of feminist activism, recounting the deeper philosophical and practical roots of the women's movement, emerging from civil rights and new left movements but also connected to a longer history of feminist activism.[9] Each analyzes growing discontent in the immediate post-World War II era, evidenced by growing intellectual and artistic movements, increased mobilization against the war in Vietnam, civil rights movements demanding rights for Black, Chicano/Latino, Indian/indigenous, and gay peoples—and each shows, quite well, how feminism grew up within and emerged as distinct from all of these spaces and places. Furthermore, each notes the conscious use of the phrase "second wave" as a way to build a historical link to feminist foremothers at the turn of the twentieth century. These authors also demonstrate the sheer breadth and depth of this movement across the country, bearing out how this movement changed politics and culture, and each gauges the strength of this movement by virtue of the backlash against it.[10]

These texts are analytic and carefully researched overviews by activist-scholars who participated in this movement, and they give us a rich and usable history—vital at the turn of the twenty-first century. But as we know from other historical movements, as well as our own, sweeping nationally based narratives of a movement cannot possibly capture completely the nuance and texture of feminist activism in this era. We learn as much from grassroots studies that contribute to and complicate, even disrupt and challenge, national narratives, as we have in the larger context of the civil rights/Black Power movements and the lesbian and gay liberation movements. Historians have turned their attention to the "local people" of the feminist movement for equality and liberation; Judith Ezekiel, Anne Valk, and Anne Enke demonstrate the vitality and vibrancy of the movement in ways that move beyond the arc of the "second wave" as it swelled in the late 1960s, crested in the mid-1970s, and crashed in the early 1980s.[11]

Groundswell enters into the fray to move between local and national histories of the women's movement of the 1970s. In this book, I take a grassroots approach to the women (and some men) who identified as feminists (or not) or with feminism in three cities: Memphis, Columbus, and San Francisco. The term "grassroots" often refers to "women out there," suggesting a sort of urbane or elite group of women who are "here" in juxtaposition to ordinary women who are not "here." (Other dyads include non-poor/poor, colonizer/indigenous, and urban/rural, and this kind of "us"/"them" is often familiar in social movement analyses as a way to define activist boundaries and identities.)[12] I use this word to refer to women whose activism was not represented in the dominant sites of activism on the East Coast. Doing so expressly challenges this way of organizing history and activism that often leaves behind the implication that those who are not "here" or part of "us" in our historical narratives or immediate activist consciousness are not relevant or contributory to our movement.

To get to my own historical analysis of this largest, explicitly feminist, membership based organization—a group that, by 1971, was truly a national organization for women—I am borrowing rather liberally from queer theory and methodologies. Queer theory's application has evolved beyond an individual focus on sexuality to interrogate all manners of identification, such as ethnicity and nationalism, and I am suggesting here that we can use it to interrogate feminist identities in the 1970s. As Danielle Clarke has suggested, queer theory can be utilized most successfully as "a method or practice, a set of tools which can help us re-read and over-read historical traces, spaces, and gaps."[13] If we understand the project of queer theory as encompassing the destabilization and radical questioning of all forms of identity that presume themselves to be the norm, we can find utility in this kind of research approach to feminist activism in the 1970s—especially NOW, the organization assumed to be the most normative and mainstream feminist organization of the day. Rather than take for granted the historical existence of NOW, which has served in many ways to set it up as a straw woman, I interrogate its historical past and explore the dynamics of feminist identity and activism within this group.

To do so, I seek to explore and analyze the contexts in which feminists created political and cultural change in different "fields of action." Sociologist Raka Ray develops a sophisticated conceptualization of communities as places where activists mobilize and operate within a political "field," which she defines as "a socially constructed environment within which organizations are embedded and to which organizations and activists constantly respond."[14] She explores this concept to mean not only a geographically bounded environment but also social networks that often originate and thrive within a physical community but can also extend beyond it. Within these fields, people share a common local culture, even as they do not share all aspects of a common local culture.[15] As a result, people in the same local space can have varying, even different levels and routes of access to local and regional sites of power, with the understanding that power can be political, legal, commercial, and/or social. Some strategies, such as seeking political office or opening or supporting a feminist book store or music festival might look the same across fields of protest, but they have deeper nuances that make each strategy more or less palatable or possible in any particular space or time. This perspective allows for an understanding of activism that maps a movement across a national landscape as well as digs deep into movement work among and between networks within a particular community.

To illustrate this point, I take a grassroots approach to feminist activism, which offers a view into the contexts, or, in Ray's terminology, "fields," in which feminists created political and cultural change. Rather than look at NOW from the top down, as political scientist Maryann Barakso does in her work *Governing NOW*, I seek instead to look at how feminists mobilized under the name of NOW in their local communities and in their day-to-day lives. In my analysis, feminism is never just about national and recognized leaders, although many of our histories reflect this preoccupation. NOW is the mainstay representative of liberal feminism, and Betty Friedan, as its first national president, represents NOW. Instead, feminist activism at the grassroots level is, according to Temma Kaplan, "mainly concerned with local issues, with what affects ordinary people every day.[16] I turn to the rank and file of feminist activism in three locations to see how women who never sought to be feminist stars accomplished what they needed to do in their own. Their work underscores how feminism in three different communities can bring to light the various and dynamic ways that activists were able to effect feminist change. By exploring these feminist contexts—and these feminists' contexts—it becomes clear that feminism in the United States, much like the *feminisms* that scholars have discussed in histories of Western Europe, Latin America, Asia, and Africa, is not homogenous and unable to be rendered in an overly simplistic dichotomy.

Following Kaplan, I examine and situate activists within their own local milieu, the political and cultural environment that makes some forms of activism as well as activist goals and strategies more practical than others. As she points out, "the media and public opinion are preoccupied with the spectacular, with the activities of celebrities" and scholars of second-wave feminism often follow suit, allowing nationally recognized figures to represent—positively or negatively—the whole of the women's movement. Such figures are, without a doubt, integral to sustaining social movement work, and key leaders are often integral to establishing and building powerful bases from which to build substantial coalitions. These leaders are also captivating, able to turn a phrase or harness the momentum of, and bring media attention to, a particular issue. Their tireless work is impressive, and the work of recognized leaders is important in explaining and understanding social movement activism.

Yet rank-and-file activists—the people who arguably keep the "move" in "movement"—go unrecognized, and their historical contributions have been elided. By looking to *these* feminists, I seek, following Kaplan, to analyze "ordinary women attempting to accomplish necessary tasks, to provide services rather than to build power bases." In the three sites I examine here, I seek to focus on community activism with an eye toward the small groups dedicated to changing status quo, not in response to a call from national leaders but from the needs of people around them in their day-to-day lives. Mothers, sisters, neighbors, workers, and more, they pursued gender inequality as a barrier to social justice. They often worked, or sought to work, alongside other social justice activists within and beyond liberal establishments and organizations.

Many of the issues they addressed are familiar as large-scale problems, but they are present at the local level, and grassroots activists theorized and actualized solutions at the local, grassroots level. Feminist identity may be integral to creating a feminist "imagined community," but this work examines the face-to-face interactions, bringing a sense of grassroots community to histories of the women's movement. We are starting to see more attention to women's movements in different regions, but I find that scholars who study beyond the United States have made great inroads to understanding the difference that geographical difference makes. In her 2005 book, historian Jocelyn Olcott introduced us to revolutionary women in the "many Mexicos" of the post-revolution era. In her work, which sits at the intersection of gender identity and the rights (and, perhaps, rites) of citizenship, local narratives provide more than nuances to a national story: "Research beyond Mexico City reveals the jerky, stuttering, uneven progress of provincial women's organizing, and the standard periodization falls apart in places where major events in the center ... mattered little in local politics." Moreover, women's activism responded "to shifts in the local political climate" and women took advantage of locally based opportunities and addressed locally based obstacles.[17]

Similarly, sociologist Raka Ray traces the political and cultural circumstances "under which groups of women organize to create and sustain movements to fight for their rights and their self-worth" in Bombay and Calcutta, India. Her comparison yields an analysis of "the circumstances under which movement issues, styles, and strategies come to be selected by participants.[18] As Ray observes, perhaps even to the point of being obvious, Bombay and Calcutta "are two cities in the same country, yet the ways in which activists engage women's issues, the nature of the issues, and indeed the activists' understandings of what constitutes a legitimate women's movement are fundamentally different."[19]

As we all know, calls to "think globally, act locally" have current cultural cache, and can provide a frame of reference to consider grassroots activism in the past. But "merely thinking globally will not result in effective local actions, if one does not also simultaneously learn to think locally as well."[20] For feminists in the heyday of the women's liberation movement in the 1970s, they were drawn to feminism because they were not only acting but also thinking locally. They understood local roots and long-term as well as immediate causes of disempowerment in their own lives as well as the lives of people around them, which compelled them to act—and it is here that we can explore the value and importance of "grassroots" activism and the significance it bestows. Such an approach underscores Ruth Rosen's important point that "*movements are made by people, not simply by ideas.*"[21]

And it is very easy to forget that feminists worked tirelessly to create the world in which we currently live. Indeed, as Rosen reminds us very well, the world before feminism is virtually unrecognizable to women and men today—many people subscribe to the notion popularized by Jennifer Baumgardner and Amy Richards that "feminism is like fluoride. It's in the water."[22] Although Baumgardner and Richards never anticipated that this phrase would be so popular, it is an important statement on how many people think about feminism past and present. So it bears asking how it got there, why it did not affect everyone evenly, and what was the resistance—questions others have certainly addressed in different ways. And, of course, the answers are more complicated than current popular narratives can allow, so this book seeks to deepen and broaden our awareness of this movement.

A focus on local, community-level feminism and feminists sheds light on the activists who changed consciousness and political realities in cities and towns across the country. In doing so, it moves beyond the concept of a national movement and pushes us instead into the grassroots activism of communities as significant sites of feminist activism. This approach offers several important correctives to the telling of U.S. feminist history in postwar America. First, it moves away from the East Coast, where feminist activism is assumed to take hold. Second, it moves away from the liberal/radical divide that dominates the telling of the history of U.S. feminism. Third, it moves away from the standard waves framework that guides the ways that we understand this movement. Finally, it showcases the "local people" who made the movement by shaking the ground beneath their feet, people whose histories are often overlooked in national narratives of feminist activism.

This book is not so grand in scope or intent that it restores everyone's words; it cannot speak to or for all activists everywhere. But it does seek to give rank-and-file feminists a voice in the historical record. It is inherently incomplete: a study of feminist activism in three cities could never encompass the scope and reach of movements for equality and liberation across the United States in the 1960s and 1970s. It cannot even cover all feminist activism in any one city or represent what was happening in any region. But it does offer insights into the formation of feminist identity and activism from the ground up, privileging the voices of ordinary activists rather than movement leaders. As such, it is inspired by Gloria Anzaldúa, Audre Lorde, Vicki Ruiz, Temma Kaplan, and so many others who resist dominant narratives that allow for the erasure of voices. In that sense, then, it hopes to supplement and give nuance to sweeping histories of the postwar women's movement in the United States, providing a "local people" approach to our histories that explores daily, on-the-ground realities of oppression and feminists' work to expose, challenge, and undo it. It also provides a ·usable framework for understanding grassroots activism in the past in the hopes of building a history upon which to continue feminist work in the present and future.

The use of "groundswell" in this work is a response to the continued debate over the "wave" metaphor that scholars and activists use to describe feminist activism in the United States. Historian Julie Gallagher reminds us that "scholars in all fields grapple with the frameworks of analysis they employ," and feminist scholars writing about their—our—movement are no exception. Radical feminists in the early 1970s identified themselves as the "second wave," seeking to build a historical connection with radicals in the past; feminists in the late twentieth and early twenty-first centuries distance themselves from second-wavers but continue the wave metaphor into a third, and even fourth wave of activism. As an activist construct, many are reluctant to eschew the wave metaphor, and, in many ways, it is quite compelling. Be they sound, oceanic, or hand gestures, waves are active and provide a way to demonstrate energy and vitality in a social movement.[23] And as generations of feminists continue to debate over what constitutes our agenda and our most effective strategies to meet our goals, we are wise to note the historical threads that bind our feminist work toward a more equitable and free world.

At the same time, feminist historians are compelled to point out how the wave metaphor has privileged the work of middle-class white women whose work has taken place in the realm of the public sphere. The first wave is marked by the long fight for woman suffrage, although we know that the 19th Amendment effectively applied primarily to white women. A focus on the vote also marginalizes or ignores many other battles that feminists waged or fought, such as anti-lynching, anti-racism, anti-war, educational equity, labor, childcare, sexual liberation, and more—issues that remained meaningful even after suffrage was achieved in 1920. Traditional narrative suggests that women's activism receded until the mid-1960s, with the surge of the second wave. While there is no doubt that feminism experienced a resurgence in the era of postwar fights for equality, freedom, and liberation, the telling of feminist history through the waves minimizes the activism of many women whose work can be reclaimed as feminist. A third, and now even a fourth, wave has insisted that it is different and unique, with a clear focus on race, sexuality, and other facets of identity as they intersect with gender, but feminists today may not have an accurate history by which to measure whether or not their movement is unique or a continuation of feminist work in the past.

In our histories, then, we unintentionally create a disservice to young feminists when we perpetuate feminist waves. Undoing the waves is certainly a hard habit to shake, as Gallagher so rightly notes, but it is to our own peril if we do not attempt to do so. The wave metaphor, while visually appealing and useful in teaching a history survey, elides the important and necessary activism of poor and working-class women, women of color, and those whose work is not recognized or showcased publicly or at the national level. It also privileges those feminists who worked on the East Coast, allowing what happened there to stand for feminist activism across the country. After all, the self-identification of some feminists as the "second wave" came out of a small group in New York City, but it has become accepted as the way to think about all feminist history in the United States. This focus reifies the idea that history moves from east to west, buttressing what historian Vicki Ruiz has criticized as the "hegemony of a U.S. women's history rooted in the lives of eastern elites."[24] Like fashion and culinary trends, feminism and its history start on the East Coast and move inward; like these trends, by the time the powerful feminist waves get to other parts of the nation, they are, well, somewhat watered down.

Here, I assert that feminists across the country may have been a part of a national movement that could be conceptualized as a "wave," but they created and sustained groundswells of feminist activism within their own communities as they addressed issues germane to their own lives. The issues they addressed were part of a larger national feminist agenda, but the goals, strategies, and identities they developed along the way were locally situated. These women had little to no access to national fields of activism; they did not publish widely read treatises and tracts; they did not enjoy a public forum for their ideas and debates. As such, they have been washed aside by the feminist waves.[25] By focusing not on national waves but instead on regional and local groundswells, this book presents the opportunity to examine the work of grassroots feminists, those who moved to activism out of sheer necessity in their day-to-day lives.

Attention to geographic context and differences within the United States offers an important way to explore historically the rise and sustenance of feminism in the 1970s. Indeed, because of its diversity across the country—an attribute rarely acknowledged in histories of social movements generally—this social movement had a significant impact on politics and culture. It did not become the largest movement of the twentieth century in any sort of singular way, but through the strength of difference and diversity of many voices, ideas, and actions.

The history of the United States has been one of cultural, social, and economic fragmentation; understanding these divides, often rooted in geographical differences, is essential to analyzing U.S. history. Scholars have been exploring how the "politics of location" reframes the ways we understand social movement activism in the United States.[26] This phrase takes on particular significance in transnational feminism, which arguably has made the most headway on the connection between geographical location and feminist activism.[27] Feminist philosophers refer to the politics of location as the ways that one's time–space location shapes the effects of one's vantage point, which, although not the precise way I am employing it in this text, is rather significant for thinking about activism in a grassroots context.[28] Even as they may use the language of location differently, geographers, social scientists, and historians alike know that "changing the location of things changes how they interact."[29] Scholars have traced how local political and cultural context shapes a variety of movements, including lesbian and gay liberation, African American civil rights, labor, welfare rights, and anti-nuclear environmentalism. These movements have national significance in part because they create a collective and shared "sense of we" in opposition to political and/or cultural oppression.[30] And while there may be factors that allow for a national sense of oppositional consciousness, local dynamics also shape this development of identity. While feminists were a part of a national movement—and, in many cases, simultaneous movements—local context provides another vital perspective on this movement and allows us to see in what ways and around what issues feminists were able to create and sustain women's movement and feminist activisms.

The politics of location—used here to explore the activist communities and possible strategies and outcomes available to activists in their respective communities—demonstrates that understanding feminism on the ground offers more than a local variant of a national story because U.S. feminism has never had a singular or national narrative. Such an analysis here is built on Albert Hurtado's suggestion that "women's history must be understood in all of its particularity, conflict, and complexity."[31] Part of accepting Hurtado's challenge is recognizing the importance of location. By comparing cities and regions across the country in order to analyze how women defined feminist goals and worked on their behalf; what factors in their political, cultural, and economic milieus constrained as well as enabled their activism; and how their activism operated across a feminist spectrum that includes liberal and radical as well as points between and beyond, I embrace Hurtado's charge. Only through conflict and community at the local level can we really understand the nuances of feminist activism in the 1970s. I build here on Leila J. Rupp's work on the development of transnational feminism from World War I through post-World War II. In this context, Rupp analyzed both conflict and community "not as opposites but as part of the same process by which women came together ... to create a sense of belonging and to work and sometimes live together."[32]

I explore the rise of feminist identity and activism in various cities across the United States—by design of this study, none of them is on the East Coast. By analyzing how feminists came together to create change in their communities and in their day-to-day lives, and by understanding how, at times, these very same feminists faced conflict and internal division, I explore both the feminist communities women built with one another and within their local contexts as well as the conflicts that separated feminists from one another and impeded change. This analysis extends historian Victoria Wolcott's concept of "malleable discourse." Although Wolcott analyzes the ways in which such concepts as "gender" change based upon the social, political, and cultural settings of women's lives, I suggest that we can also see how "feminism" and "activism" change and are changed similarly.[33]

Focusing on NOW chapters as a way to consider and understand grassroots feminist activism was undertaken for a number of reasons, including the reality that entire books can and have been written on various activisms in each city. This work does not forestall other research on feminism in each place; indeed, it openly encourages it, as no one book can possibly answer every question to be asked of the subject matter. NOW chapter status and membership also allows for another practical reason: many NOW chapters, including the three here, archived papers locally, following the national NOW decision in the mid-1970s to archive its papers at the Schlesinger Library at Radcliffe College in Cambridge, Massachusetts. Unlike many other feminist groups of the era that were not organized in a similar fashion or individuals who did not see the value of their individual work, NOW members were often conscious that their organizational (if not personal) papers merited the attention of library archivists.

Turning attention to NOW chapters also has significance and value in terms of scholarship on the women's movement for equality and liberation. Much ink has been spilled to underscore that NOW was a—if not *the*—liberal feminist organization of the 1970s and early 1980s, and despite waning numbers in the first decades of the twenty-first century, it is still referred to as the mainstay of liberal feminism. Founded in 1966, NOW is one of the oldest, explicitly feminist organizations. Because it had a federated structure of national, regional, state, and local chapters and a history of pursuing legislative change on behalf of women, NOW has been identified with—even as—liberal feminism. Almost fifty years later, the organization still has chapters in all 50 states and many states have numerous local chapters. Many in leadership positions still identify the government as the avenue for change, and recognition of women as "the route to redistribution."[34] Indeed, the organization's leadership favors new or amended legislation to enhance the equality of women to men over complete political overhaul, a standard definition of liberal feminism.[35] By contrast, radical feminists argue that women's "rights" as the state bestows them are not very meaningful in a social and cultural milieu that oppresses people based on gender, race, class, and sexuality. Radical feminists historically have pursued feminist issues beyond the confines of the state, using public protest and other cultural strategies to get across their messages of women's liberation. Likewise, many self-identified radical feminists put the word "radical" in their group names. Of course, this does not mean that they were the only radical feminists, and many women whose identities, philosophies, and actions were radical joined

NOW because it was significant in their particular city, because there were not many options, or because the NOW chapter was doing things to get to the root of women's oppression in sexism. At the same time, it is important to point out that NOW never identified as a liberal feminist organization. But as we have seen in various social movement battles, the radical/liberal divide left "liberal" to be a term of derision.

So "liberal" may be more descriptive of a political strategy than a designation of a particular group of feminists. Even still, this "liberal" label takes on the most significance at the national, rather than at the local, level. NOW was the first, and largest, explicitly feminist, membership-based organization of the women's movement. In 1966, when some thirty women gathered at the third meeting of the President's Commission on the Status of Women and, out of frustration with the Commission and the newly formed EEOC, formed NOW, a national women's movement in the United States was moving out of a forty-year era of "abeyance."[36] (Chapter 2 offers more detail on national NOW.) However, this does not mean that women were not active in other social movements or that they were not mobilizing around issues relevant to women's lives and toward a goal of women's equality and liberation. In all sorts of social movements over the long twentieth century, women were often the backbone of social movement work, and though often not visible at the national level, women were gaining important social movement skills and networks at the local level.[37] Furthermore, they were developing and sustaining feminist consciousness.

The terms "liberal" and "radical" as ways to understand feminist activism in the 1960s and 1970s were made popular in 1975, when political scientist and self-identified radical feminist Jo Freeman published her book *The Politics of Women's Liberation*, which conceptualized the movement as composed of two distinct branches.[38] Freeman divided women's organizations into two camps based on age of members, structure, ideology, and style. While the "younger" branch included smaller, grassroots organizations with little or no internal hierarchal structure, the "older" branch consisted of federated, formal organizations with branches at the regional, state, and local levels. The latter group included NOW, Women's Equity Action League, and National Women's Political Caucus, and was, according to Freeman, "liberal," concerned with equality within the existing social, political, and economic systems. The younger and more radical branch sought to overthrow patriarchal structures, damning them as oppressive to women.[39]

Scholars followed Freeman's lead in dividing the movement into two camps, embracing this dichotomy or a related dichotomous framework to explain feminist activism in the 1970s. Whether called "small group sector" and "mass movement," "collectivist" and "bureaucratic," "younger women" and "older women," or "women's rights and women's liberation," the two-branch model has dominated scholarship on the women's movement in postwar United States.[40] This division, coupled with the waves metaphor, all but omits the work of working-class and poor women, women of color, and women in different geographical regions of the

United States. National Black Feminist Organization, National Welfare Rights Organization, and other groups may have put "national" in their title and may have had various chapters around the country, but they move far beyond the liberal/ radical divide and underscore how whiteness and middle-class-ness signify the women's movement—in spite of the historical reality that women of color and poor women bear the brunt of institutional sexism. Many women took what Benita Roth has called "separate roads to feminism,"[41] and their paths and journeys do not fit within these dichotomous frameworks. Indeed, most women did not have the luxuries of time or geography to decide if they were liberal or radical; instead, they were feminists in identification and/or through their own activism. While they debated and tangled over what that meant in ideology and practice, this dichotomy was not salient, and most feminists embraced a variety of strategies and pursued a number of outcomes at the same time. Boxing them into a label ignores and undoes the multiplicity and dynamism of feminist activism in the heyday of this movement for equality and liberation.

Radical feminism and its attributed offshoots, cultural feminism, were anomalous, oppositional, challenging—and have been most interesting to scholars. This may well be the result of the fact that scholars who have studied second-wave feminism academically wrote from their personal affiliations with radical feminism. Self-identifed radical feminists Jo Freeman (aka Joreen), Sara Evans, and Alice Echols produced (and continue to write) well-researched and readable works that have become foundational frameworks through which postwar feminist activism has been studied and analyzed. In their work, they have unashamedly embraced the political roots that gave rise to their academic work, suggesting that the personal is not only political but is also worth understanding historically.[42] This is not unique to feminist history: Black civil rights and radical activists, Chicana liberationists, queer activists, and working-class people who have joined the academy have also penned outstanding scholarly works from their vantage points and embraced their identities as salient to historical perspectives. But, in the case of feminism, when white women scholars divided the movement into "liberal" and "radical," they reduced the movement to the places where these terms originated and operated—namely, the East Coast—and the people who embraced them—particularly white women.

Anyone who has been engaged with social movement activism knows that labels rarely apply in a doctrinaire manner. Yet scholars largely have allowed "liberal" and "radical" feminism to stand for second-wave feminism across the United States, suggesting that feminisms "in the heartland," to borrow Judith Ezekiel's felicitous phrase, in the South, or on the West Coast followed this model. Yet the reality, particularly at the local level, is far less neat than scholarship on "liberal" and "radical" feminism conveys. Rather than stretch essentialized and seemingly distinct conceptions of "liberal" and "radical" feminism to fit over the varieties of feminist activism, I argue that we must understand the women's movement from the ground up, looking specifically at what feminists did, what factors shaped their activism, and how they effected feminist change. We should also understand how they identified themselves. NOW chapters grew up in the late 1960s and early 1970s, prior to any real consensus about what the various philosophical forms that "feminism" (as if it were singular) would take. More to the point, feminists formed chapters in places where feminist activism rarely qualified as "liberal" or "radical." Although some groups explicitly identified as "radical"—New York Radical Feminists or Radicalesbians, for example—as I've noted before, none identified themselves as "liberal." When applied to feminism in the 1970s, the terms "liberal" and "radical" may be theoretically salient, but in practice this dichotomy obscures the variety and dynamism of feminist practices, goals, strategies, and events. So here, using NOW chapters as a common thread, I look at how women in different locations defined and enacted "feminism" for themselves and how it changed over time. By looking at the context of activism in the historical unfolding of this era of heightened and conscious feminist activism, it becomes clear that this dichotomous framework of "liberal" and "radical" limits, rather than enhances, the ways in which we can understand and analyze feminist activisms in the 1960s and 1970s.

In theory, a national organization for women, as NOW proclaimed itself to be, would represent women across the nation. In fact, however, many factors determined the membership and growth of NOW chapters, as well as their relationship to the national board. From the outset, national NOW was a political lobbying group, and its first president, Betty Friedan, as well as many board members, felt it would be most beneficial as such and hoped to continue as a small cadre of feminist activists. However, chapters began to take off, the first in New York City. By 1970, there were over 3,000 women (and men) in chapters across the country, making the "National Organization for Women" accurate, at least geographically. Through its chapters, NOW became much more than a national political force. It also became a site for local political and cultural change, and NOW in different places often reflected local goals, strategies, and outcomes rather than a national agenda.

After the 1970 "Strike for Women's Equality," membership grew at an even faster pace, and feminists in all parts of the country formed NOW chapters in their cities. From its headquarters in Washington, DC (moved from union offices in Chicago in 1968), Betty Friedan announced plans for a strike in 1970 to commemorate the fiftieth anniversary of the 19th Amendment. However, after this pronouncement, Friedan stepped down as national president of NOW; new president Aileen Hernandez and fellow board members were left to organize the strike. In the aftermath of the strike, local chapters took on tremendous significance in NOW.

The national organization responded by creating active task forces on subjects ranging from women's employment and women in the media to rape and violence against women. In so doing, NOW provided a common umbrella under which many feminists organized to help create and sustain the women's movement in the 1960s and 1970s, and, in this way, NOW could bill itself as an organization with something for everyone. Scholars have commonly discussed and analyzed NOW activism at the national level, and recognize that its federated governance structure allowed for flexibility at the local level while also creating a space for it to be a longstanding national organization (in spite of internal conflicts that tore apart other feminist groups or left them to the "tyranny of structurelessness"). But at the local level—where NOW derived its strength in terms of numbers and financial support, and, with chapters across the country, offered a real national presence—NOW made a difference in women's lives. In most cases, it was a positive difference, but many people rejected membership in NOW, abandoning the group after joining or refusing to join at all.

NOW also never attracted large numbers of women of color, and could not always retain the activist interest of those who did join. This was true among national leaders: Florynce Kennedy, a NOW founder, left the organization fairly early on because it was not radical enough; Aileen Hernandez, second president of NOW, left in 1980, devoting her attention to activism among women of color. Women of all socioeconomic backgrounds joined NOW chapters, and chapters did a great deal of work to address immediate and long-term needs of working women. Women of different sexual identities also joined NOW and, for lesbians, Betty Friedan's famous grousing about "the lavender menace" never really meant much because NOW members were willing to talk and act in different ways around issues of heterosexuality and same-sex sexuality. NOW members acted in concert with one another but were also different in tremendously significant ways. I attribute this to geographical difference—there is no singular US feminism, and we must take geographical difference into account. So some issues, such as the ERA, may have united NOW women in that all chapters acted somehow on behalf of the amendment. But other matters took precedence when it came to members' daily actions and to defining and raising feminist consciousness in their respective communities and different local contexts give rise and salience to particular strategies and issues. To understand *how* women came together in their communities to create a sense of belonging and to create feminist change at the grassroots level through salient strategies and goals is at the heart of this study.

I have asked repeatedly in this study why women formed NOW chapters and why women joined NOW. The reality is, for many women, the NOW chapter was the only place to go. Chapter members were likely aware of and sympathetic to NOW's national agenda, and many people reported an interest in the ERA, which by the mid-1970s was national NOW's main, if not singular, focus. But NOW chapters did so much more than work on the ERA; indeed, at the local level, the ERA often took a back seat to other issues that mattered to members. So how did women work through NOW to create feminist change at the local level? What factors shaped their activism? To answer these questions, I look not only at the women involved but also the contexts in which feminism, and NOW, emerged in each city. Through NOW chapters, feminists in Memphis, Columbus, and San Francisco created a way for others to identify and define them as well as a way for them to define themselves—identities that were shaped not only by the women involved but also by the activist and feminist milieus in which women lived. Within feminist communities, some women were members of NOW while others remained outside of the organization. In each location, there were larger feminist and women's coalitions, and NOW was only part of the larger feminist, social justice community.[43]

Thus, to understand feminist activism in each location, I look not just to NOW membership but also to the salient local issues that mobilized feminists (in and, at times, beyond NOW). NOW often worked in concert and coalition with other groups to tackle issues and helped create larger feminist communities in each city; sometimes, they did not. But in all of their activisms, identities, work, and outcomes, they embraced dynamic and multiple ideologies along with accompanying strategies, tactics, and goals to create meaningful feminist change.

Rather than understand women's lives simply as gendered, historians of the U.S. South, Midwest, and West have also been exploring how region has shaped women's lives. In the history of women's and feminist activism, scholars have highlighted the uniqueness of the South as a geographical location as well as differences between and among Southern women. Whether writing about woman suffrage, club activism, slavery, or formal politics, scholars have understood the nuances of Southern women's lives both as a part of and apart from the rest of the United States. The "metalanguage of race" often defines much of this history, and white, Black, Latina, and Asian women have often pursued "separate roads to feminism."[44] The history of woman suffrage makes this point abundantly clear. In Tennessee, the final state to ratify the 19th Amendment, women and men from both sides of the suffrage issue argued their positions often from a position of race, specifically whether or not Black men should have the right to vote before white women or if Black people should be able to vote altogether. The overt racism of some white feminists further exacerbated tensions between white and Black women, offering one of several reasons for the impossibility of a singular Southern feminist voice in the later twentieth century.[45] In the 1960s and 1970s, feminists of all racial backgrounds confronted a host of stereotypes about racialized Southern womanhoods and about feminism. Rather than choose between "womanhood" and "feminism," Southern feminists blended the concepts, talking and marching publicly about issues that "ladies" should not discuss, such as rape, domestic violence, and pornography. They also continued to fight racism, even in organizations often separated in terms of race, making the cause of feminism and anti-racism inextricably linked.[46]

Midwestern women's history is also marked by a uniqueness of region, but rather than confronting a history of cultural distance from the rest of the country, women of the Midwest have lived "at the crossroads" of U.S. culture.[47] Confronting the "stereotype of the Midwest as drab," historian Glenda Riley has offered a different perspective: "modern Americans also refer to the Midwest as the 'heartland' of the United States. Can a region be both things—downright mediocre *and* the essential core of a nation? Apparently so, for many people like to think of a 'heart' as solid, sturdy, and basically obscure. But a heart also provides crucial services; it keeps the extremities of New York and California alive."[48] But beyond being the heartland, the Midwest was home to a number of activists who would become significant leaders in postwar feminism—Betty Friedan, Gloria Steinem, Elizabeth Boyer, Dorothy Haener, Addie Wyatt, and many other feminists came of age in the Midwest but became nationally significant activists who addressed issues of labor, gender, race, and education as feminist issues.[49] Their movement activism is not surprising, given that the Midwest as a crossroads region has been "a region of continuous migration" in which "Midwestern women's efforts were crucial in community building."[50]

The West, by contrast, is hardly "drab." Its dramatic topography—from blistering desert to snow-capped mountains, enormous sequoias and sandy beaches—offers a contemplative scenery unlike any other region of the country. In studies of the U.S. West, the lives of Chicana women laborers, Chinese women in San Francisco's Chinatown, and Native American women all make clear that racial/ethnic communities in the region view "the West" differently from one another.[51] But rather than operate independently of one another exclusively, feminists in the West, San Francisco in particular, often worked in coalition with one another, evincing a public acceptance of, even strength in, difference that is less prominent in other regions of the country.

This study on feminists in NOW in Memphis, Columbus, and San Francisco, then, explores what women were doing and thinking in different kinds of communities: a Southern city, a Midwestern state capital, and a West Coast progressive hotspot. NOW offers a tangible thread to connect these three cities; as a research apparatus and a subject of historical inquiry, NOW provides the opportunity to contrast these activisms. In that way, it serves as a tether between and among these locales as well as a lens into different relationships to feminism in general. I explore the factors that shape feminist activism in each place, understanding that "feminism" will take on different dimensions in each location. These locations cannot represent what was going on everywhere, but they do constitute a range of political, economic, and social contexts. This study, then, offers both geographical diversity and comparative analysis that is often absent in studies of postwar U.S. feminism. It also offers a rejoinder to the East Coast-dominated history of feminist activism and a challenge to the idea that feminism in one place represents feminism everywhere.

These communities also offer different contexts by which postwar feminism, and NOW chapters as one, but not the only, representative of feminist activism, emerged. In Memphis, NOW was the only explicitly feminist, membership-based organization during the heyday of the movement in the 1970s. In this "sleepy little river town," NOW was everything to everyone because it had to be. San Francisco NOW, by contrast, was part of the city's many progressive and feminist forces. Feminists had a variety of organizational options in this "wide-open town"; those who chose NOW did so to be a part of the forefront of feminist coalition building to create social change. In Columbus, however, NOW existed on a political and cultural spectrum somewhere between the Ohio Commission on the Status of

Women (OCSW), organized women with a history of activism within the liberal establishment, and on the fringe of a wide-reaching radical feminist community that coalesced under the umbrella of the Women's Action Collective (WAC). NOW feminists focused on material rights for women in Columbus, blending radical feminist analyses and strategies with liberal feminism in a way that OCSW and WAC could not.

To analyze here how feminism and the three NOW chapters took shape and what NOW feminists were doing on the ground, I explore the malleability of feminism through sociologist Mary Bernstein's concept of identity deployment.[52] Using the U.S. lesbian and gay movement as a case study, Bernstein suggested that context determines how activists articulate and construct their collective identity, either as contemptuous of and a better alternative to dominant culture or as drawing similarities to the mainstream of society. This idea gives further salience to Maxine Molyneux's distinction between practical and strategic gender interests, which posits that practical interests derive from women's position in society while strategic claims involve a necessary transformation of gender relations.[53] Extending this analysis to the women's movement, feminists in NOW chapters often expressed their feminist identity and tailored their strategies and goals to the local context in which they operated, opting to toe a national NOW party line only when convenient and never because of any sort of mandate from NOW officials. In the context of the Equal Rights Amendment, feminists in all three locations often stressed their similarities to men, fostering and mobilizing around an identity that suppressed differences. At other times—or perhaps, more to the point, in response to different issues—feminists embraced radical strategies and actions. In doing so, they cultivated an identity that celebrated women's differences, both from men and in contrast to the region in which they operated.

Membership in NOW provides a useful element of continuity and a solid basis for comparison, but in some ways it is only by virtue of being affiliated with NOW that these feminists share common ground. Some of the issues they confronted were the same but the strategies available to them to pursue feminist goals were driven by the context in which they operated. Rather than explore feminism as "liberal" (which one has come to expect when talking about NOW) or "radical" (the perceived alternative), I look instead to their activism—motives, strategies, goals, and outcomes—as it was affected by the local contexts in which they lived as feminists. In their actions, the boundaries between "liberal" and "radical" become less significant. What emerges as salient is the ways in which feminists acted within the context of their cities, how they confronted region-based stereotypes, how they worked with other activists within and beyond the women's movement, and how they achieved (or why they did not) their outcomes.

This project is grounded in feminist research, which implies "a perspective … in which women's experiences, ideas, and needs are valid in their own right."[54] In conducting research for this book, I have relied on a variety of sources, all of which illuminate feminists in their communities, and all with both possibilities and limitations. I interviewed and have had conversations with over forty women involved with NOW at the national and local levels, locating the names of national leaders and rank-and-file members in the archives. Through what social scientists call the "snowball" method, I found names and sometimes contact information for some members during the interviews I conducted. Collecting oral histories has its own risks in research, as oral history can shift perspective from the movement to the individuals being interviewed, and relying upon them incurs the risk of recording and analyzing selective and non-representative memories (and careful omissions). Still, interviews give insight into events that may not be recorded in organizational records; answer questions about happenings mentioned in passing in such records; or offer a different perspective or behind-the-scenes information about notable events. Such research offers a richer picture of the complex conflicts, struggles, and negotiations that take place among activists. As a feminist historian, I also think it is vital to capture the lives and words of individual women who pursued social justice as movement footsoldiers because the cause hit close to home. They made important gains for themselves and for others in their day-to-day lives—and that work matters.

To supplement interviews and oral histories, I have utilized chapter newsletters, minutes from meetings, and other archival sources, as well as documents and ephemera in activists' possession. Like other historians who work in archival documents, I have been limited by what chapter newsletter editors, recording secretaries, journalists, and others documented. These records, along with media coverage, do help create a sense of what issues sparked feminists to action and what strategies they employed to remedy undesirable situations. These resources, along with secondary sources, have helped me piece together how women created feminist communities in their hometowns and how they interacted with one another and within the larger environments in which they lived. But, of course, these resources leave me with necessarily incomplete stories. I find it valuable, even comforting, to confront this reality, knowing that this book offers (I hope) new insights as well as questions for other scholars to explore.

Groundswell is comprised of three case studies. To provide some backdrop for the use of NOW chapters as a tether between these studies, chapter 2 offers a historical analysis of NOW in the early years, starting with its organization in 1966. It is surprising that, to date, there is only one monograph, *Governing NOW*, and a handful of articles on this organization and its chapters, especially when we consider that it was as large as it was (and that it is still in existence, though with wavering efficacy since the 1980s). But it is also surprising, given that, in the perpetual narrative of the radical/liberal divide, only radical feminism and self-identified radical feminists have set the agenda for the way feminism in the 1970s is remembered historically. As radical feminists wrote their own stories and histories, they set the terms of the narrative—despite challenges and refutations from feminist, historical perspectives. Chapter 2 does not promise to give that complete history, but it does suggest that many NOW feminists, the documents they produced, and the stands and actions they took are much more complicated than dominant narratives can suggest.

Local conditions matter, though—and there is no *national* organization for women without chapters and rank-and-file activists. Chapters 3, 4, and 5, then, are the case studies of Memphis, Columbus, and San Francisco, respectively. Each provides different origin stories to understand how NOW chapters emerged, struggled internally and externally, and did the explicit work of feminism in each city. At no point do I mean to suggest here that NOW activism is the *only* lens into feminist activism in each place. Instead, the focus on NOW chapters provides a way to tie these case studies together and to compare and contrast feminism's different expressions and iterations as they mattered in different places. But beyond the focus on NOW as a way to tie together three case studies, it also suggests how complicated feminists and their activisms were in different locations. The conclusion draws out the distinctions between these chapters but also highlights similarities among them. It also invites us to reconsider dominant narratives and considers how historical research and analysis offers useful ways to move beyond them. If we are to have a feminist future, we need a feminist past upon which to stand and build. *Groundswell* helps contribute to a deeper understanding of our feminist past.

2

IN THE MIDST OF THE "WORLD-WIDE REVOLUTION OF HUMAN RIGHTS"[1]

Creating the National Organization for Women

> We, men and women who hereby constitute ourselves as the National Organization
> for Women, believe that the time has come for a new movement toward true
> equality for all women in America, and toward a fully equal partnership of the sexes,
> as part of the world-wide revolution of human rights now taking place within and
> beyond our national borders.[2]

On October 29, 1966, the National Organization for Women was officially
organized; these words open its statement of purpose. With the goal of "bring[ing]
women into full participation in the mainstream of American society now, exercising all the privileges and responsibilities thereof in truly equal partnership with
men," NOW became the largest, explicitly feminist organization in the second
wave of the women's movement. This chapter sketches a history of NOW as an
organization, but also the context in which NOW emerged in the mid-1960s,
in the midst of an era of "world-wide revolution of human rights." It also explores
the early years of NOW, the time in which NOW carved out a place for itself in
the women's movement and set the course for the organization, both nationally
and locally. Rather than offer a complete history of NOW, I seek here to
contextualize the rise of this organization within the women's movement and
explore the development of chapters within the organization. I turn attention onto
this mainstream feminist organization, looking specifically at issues that challenged
the organization as well as emboldened chapters. The historical arcs discussed
and developed in this chapter move us beyond "the Friedan mystique" and into
NOW's "world-wide revolution" within the larger history of the U.S. women's
movement.

"Beneath Those Charred Bras Revolution Smolders": The Cultural Context

In a March 1970 *Washington Post* article, journalist Mary Wiegers opined, "to those who have had their fill of radical movements, the reawakening of a strident women's rights movement is about as welcome as finding out that coffee causes cancer. But reawakening it is."[3] Had people "had their fill" of social movements by the beginning of the 1970s? Were they ready for a return to normalcy and to turn the world, or at least the United States, "right side up"?[4] While Weigers' article, "Beneath these Charred Bras Revolution Smolders," turns its attention to women's liberation groups in a specific sense, it refers "to a gamut of organizations, from the work-within-the-system reformists like Betty Friedan's National Organization for Women (NOW) to the radical W.I.T.C.H. (Women's International Terrorist Conspiracy from Hell)." In order to make sense of NOW, it is crucial to understand the cultural context of revolution and upheaval in which it emerged.

Wieger's article suggests that, by 1970, there were two distinct branches of the women's movement—reformist and radical. The historical narrative supports these two distinct tracks in which second-wave feminism emerged as a movement, "radical" feminism from radical elements of contemporaneous social movement activism and "liberal" feminism from confrontations within the liberal establishment. Liberal feminism, according to basic feminist theory, is about the pursuit of equal rights for women and men; its strategies are often legal and political in nature and goal. By contrast, radical feminism rejects political status quo, particularly the sex/gender system that is the foundation of women's oppression. Political strategies are insufficient because the legal system is built on a hierarchy that subordinates and oppresses women as a group.[5] Such a trajectory has firmly entrenched NOW—its roots and its historical development—in the liberal establishment. While this is not completely wrong, it is also not universally right. With all of the revolutionary ferment in the long decade of the 1960s,[6] it would be impossibly myopic to suggest that the feminists who founded NOW were merely the products of conflict with the liberal establishment. The founding of NOW was, instead, a response to confrontations both within and beyond the postwar liberal establishment. Its roots, identifiable through its founders, included people with histories in civil rights activism, union organizing and activism, government agencies, and religious structures.[7] NOW's history has been bounded by a singular narrative of women's movement activism that ignores the many aspects of U.S. culture that gave way to NOW, second-wave feminism in general, and broader cultural and political change.[8]

The 1960s represents in many ways a time of redefining culture in the United States. Although some see the decade as an aberration, historians Maurice Isserman and Michael Kazin offer a different perspective, one that examines the decade as an integral part of American history. They reflect importantly upon the realities of the era, suggesting that "the insurgent political and social movements of the decade—including civil rights and black power, the new left, environmentalism, and feminism—drew upon even as they sought to transform values and beliefs deeply rooted in American political culture."[9] The 1970s, similarly, was a decade, too, in which people pursued deep activism in and among revolutionary movements—which makes sense, as it was the heyday of feminist activism, among many other radical movements.[10] As people advocated social change through pacifism, class equality, democratic politics, and sexual freedom, they built upon a celebration of difference while simultaneously drawing upon common values and beliefs in American culture.[11] As a society, people in various racial/ethnic communities were situated in an unequal hierarchy in this time of general postwar prosperity. Black and Chicano communities saw the rise of a postwar middle class, but it was an incomplete process, one that people sought to remedy through social movement protest. At the same time, some students on college campuses advocated pacifism, invoking their constitutional right to free speech. Increasing entrenchment in an undeclared war in Vietnam raised a host of cultural questions ranging from the United States' role in global imperialism to who, if anyone, should fight this, or any, war. Women were involved in these overlapping movements; from their experiences and interests, they also developed a feminist framework through which to understand these issues as well as those affecting women uniquely or differently.[12]

This context shapes the formation and rise of the National Organization for Women. Its founders advocated both liberal change and radical overhaul—as activists in various ways both prior to the founding of NOW and through the organization itself. While it is impractical (and impossible) to trace the background of each individual involved in NOW, it is unrealistic to believe that as feminism developed among women in NOW, it obliterated their other concerns or disconnected them from contemporaneous social movements.[13] Instead, founders and members brought a host of issues, tactical repertoires, and goals, all of which they manifested through the National Organization for Women. Before turning to NOW's organized activism, I discuss the 1966 founding of the National Organization for Women and some of the women who led this new feminist organization. Looking at NOW's earliest members and documents suggests that NOW was both liberal and radical from the outset. I then turn to early chapter activism to explore the framework through which NOW feminists expressed themselves and pursued feminist change.

The Feminist "Underground"

Although feminist activism had been underway—especially within the liberal establishment—the federal government helped set the stage for social movement activism in general and feminism in particular.[14] Women in the twentieth century had protested inequalities on the basis of sex, but when the federal government stepped in, especially with important presidential orders, court cases, and legislation specifying equality under the law, there were undoubtedly greater opportunities for success.

In 1961, President John Kennedy attempted to stave off support for the passage of the Equal Rights Amendment by creating the President's Commission on the Status of Women (PCSW). Appointing Eleanor Roosevelt as honorary chair of the commission and selecting various women from the Women's Bureau, labor department, and Democratic Party to serve on the PCSW, Kennedy charged it with a fact-finding mission on the experiences of American women. After two years of work, the commission presented its report, *American Women*, to the president on October 11, 1963 (Eleanor Roosevelt's birthday; she died in 1962). This report documented widespread job discrimination against women and recommended guarantees for equal treatment, including a cabinet post to monitor discrimination and offer solutions and an executive order tying equal opportunity for women to companies receiving federal funds. Commission members had been selected in part because of their opposition to the Equal Rights Amendment (ERA), and *American Women* argued that a separate amendment was not necessary since equality was already afforded to women in the equal protection clause of the 14th Amendment. The report optimistically suggested that the courts would affirm such an interpretation and urged women to file discrimination grievances in the courts. Furthermore, the commission mandated that each state convene commissions on the status of women at the state level. Although critical, *American Women* was ultimately optimistic in suggesting that the problems of sex discrimination could be remedied.[15]

In 1963, Kennedy signed the Equal Pay Act, which endorsed the principle of equal pay for men and women doing the same work but did not mandate equal access to jobs. As sociologists Myra Marx Ferree and Beth Hess suggest, this legislation was not simply the result of the PCSW recommendations but was perhaps, more to the point, a reflection of "union concern that employers not hire women at a lower rate of pay in order to replace men or to drive down male wages."[16] The following year, the pending Civil Rights Act was broadened to include "sex" in the act's Title VII, which concerned equal employment opportunities. Some suggest that the addition of "sex" was an attempt on the part of a Southern congressman to defeat the act altogether, but once it was in, a small group of members of Congress and feminists in the National Woman's Party lobbied for it to stay. Congress passed the act—as amended—in 1964, although President Johnson signed it at a ceremony where no women were present and with no mention of equal rights for women.[17]

The Civil Rights Act also created the Equal Employment Opportunity Commission (EEOC) and charged it with handling complaints brought under Title VII. Although a high proportion of complaints that came to the EEOC were charges of sex discrimination, the EEOC decided not to deal with sex discrimination cases and handled nearly exclusively complaints of racial discrimination, guaranteeing that the Commission would not take women's rights seriously. So when the state commissions on the status of women convened in June 1966, many women joined Representative Martha Griffiths in charging the EEOC with a failure to take its mandate seriously. It was one thing to recognize that the EEOC had little power to enforce its decisions; it was another thing altogether to make open jokes about sex discrimination and deny claimants with legal recourse—both of which some EEOC commissioners did.

With legislation in place, then, the federal government unwittingly laid the groundwork for further social and political protest. State commissioners were often appointed for the same reasons that Kennedy appointed women to the PCSW—repaying political debts to women who had helped governors win campaigns.[18] But there were many unintended consequences that resulted from the state commissioners' meetings, including many state commissions pushing for state Equal Rights Amendments. The state commissions, which represented networks of community and political leaders at the state and local levels, also created a "climate of expectations that something would be done."[19] At the third meeting on the state commissioners, something rather unexpected happened.

Many scholars gloss over NOW's founding, often suggesting it was the result of the work of one woman—Betty Friedan—and do so to point out the direct line of descent from actions on behalf of women in the formal political arena to the founding of this organization. Giving Friedan the lion's share of the credit, many note that she called for a covert meeting of women who were angered that the 1966 meeting leaders would not condemn the EEOC for its failure to take sex discrimination charges seriously. After this now-famous meeting in her hotel room, she scribbled on a napkin the words "National Organization for Women" and called for an organization that would lobby for women the way the NAACP lobbied on behalf of African Americans. While these events did in fact take place, they are not the whole of the founding of NOW. Indeed, as the PCSW and state commissions—as well as important secondary scholarship—indicate, a broad network of feminists and sympathetic organizations existed well before NOW's founding, and the organization drew heavily from this network for its founders and early members.[20] Even in the doldrums and in a time of feminist "abeyance," organizations proliferated, including the National Federation of Business and Professional Women's Clubs (BPW), American Association of University Women (AAUW), League of Women Voters (LWV), National Woman's Party (NWP), and Women's International League for Peace and Freedom (WILPF).[21] In addition to such organizational presence, women who would become NOW founders and early members were also in positions of power in the Women's Bureau, the state commissions on the status of women, and the EEOC. Understanding the breadth of leadership among the founders of NOW sheds necessary light on the many different women who were instrumental in founding and leading this longstanding feminist organization, allowing us, finally, to move beyond the Friedan mystique.

"The problem lay buried, unspoken, for many years in the minds of American women. It was a strange stirring, a sense of dissatisfaction, a yearning." So go the first sentences of Friedan's landmark text, *The Feminine Mystique*. This opening paragraph articulates what she called "the silent question—'Is this All?'"[22] Much of what we do know about NOW is tied to Friedan—the book, of course, but also her reported grousing about lesbians and the lavender menace. Of course, Friedan warned about "the homosexuality that is spreading like a murky smog over the American scene" in *The Feminine Mystique*, a depiction that "sounded more like something that would come out of the mouth of a right-wing televangelist than a contemporary feminist."[23] But this lavender menace episode (discussed below), which prompted a takeover of the second Congress to Unite Women in 1970, is often the extent of NOW's appearance in our histories of the women's movement. So, again, her question "Is this All?" takes on a new significance as the impetus for this book and its reconsideration of NOW's history and the history of the women's movement in postwar United States.

Although it is impossible to trace the biographies and activisms of the two dozen founding members—much less the 300 women and men who would attend NOW's organizing meeting in October 1966—a glimpse into a select few provides a sample of the backgrounds of the activists who founded NOW. NOW did have initial support from some of the state commissions on the status of women; in fact, NOW's first Chairman of the Board, political scientist Dr. Kathryn (Kay) Clarenbach, also chaired Wisconsin's Status of Women Commission.[24] But most of NOW's support came from other and diverse avenues. Aileen Hernandez and Richard Graham were EEOC commissioners, both of whom had been pushing against the majority to hear cases of sex discrimination with the legal support of EEOC lawyer Sonia (Sonny) Pressman. Caroline Davis was director of the women's department of the United Auto Workers; Dorothy Haener was also an important union leader; and Hernandez had been a labor organizer in San Francisco. Communication Workers of America representative Catherine Conroy was another founding member from the Midwest; she later went on to become the first woman appointed to the Wisconsin AFL-CIO. Muriel Fox was a public relations executive who, along with television newscasters Betty Furness and Marlene Sanders, gave important media image and "spin" to the nascent civil rights group.

Other individual women had been making a name for themselves through publications and activism. Dr. Pauli Murray, along with Mary O. Eastwood, published an article in the *George Washington Law Review* entitled "Jane Crow and the Law," which examined the effects of Title VII on women's rights. Shortly before the article appeared, Murray had addressed the National Council of Women of the United States, where she condemned sex-segregated want ads. The *New York Times* reported that Murray urged protest: "If it becomes necessary to march on Washington to assure equal job opportunities for all, I hope women will not flinch from the thought."[25] Betty Friedan was similarly feisty, encouraging women to resist "the problem that has no name" and find themselves in spite of the feminine mystique that defined (white, middle-class) women's lives. Although Friedan is probably most well-known for her landmark book, prior to its 1963 publication, she was also a freelance writer who wrote about union organizing and issues. Her contacts and her left-wing associations were invaluable resources for NOW's early organizing efforts.[26]

Giving credit for the formation of the National Organization for Women to Friedan alone elides the participation of these different, and differently influential, women. Friedan herself even acknowledged the broad and diverse group of women and men who founded and joined NOW, indicating that it came to fruition largely because of the feminist "underground" that recruited and cajoled her.[27] Although Friedan pushed for creation of a new feminist organization, she was also pushed into it by such women as Eastwood and Davis, who feared losing their positions of power in the Labor Department and UAW (United Auto Workers), respectively. As "suffragettes, dauntless old women now in their eighties and nineties who chained themselves to the White House fence to get the vote" called upon Friedan to "do something about getting Title VII enforced," they also pushed her into heading up a broad-based civil rights organization.[28] She and other NOW founders felt a sense of disdain for the state commissioners and recognized that such groups as BPW and AAUW (of whom some founders were members) were not particularly interested in broadening their political base to become a civil rights group for all women. At the June 1966 meeting of state commissions on the status of women, they founded NOW.

The feminist "underground" avoided the spotlight, pressuring Friedan instead to hold a press conference to publicize the EEOC's lackluster handling of sex discrimination cases. Friedan was a likely candidate to do so—in addition to her fame (perhaps notoriety) after publishing *The Feminine Mystique*, she was in a unique position at the meeting because she used a press pass to attend.[29] Since she did not have official business as a commissioner, she was able to charge the government with laziness on sex discrimination. She met with commissioners and other interested people who wanted to bring a resolution to the floor of the meeting, demanding enforcement of Title VII and calling for Richard Graham's reappointment (Graham was the only one of the four male appointees who was sympathetic to women's claims). When Esther Peterson, chair of the PCSW, informed the women that they could not bring the resolution to the floor, the founders of NOW set out to plan their new organization. Thinking of organizing conference four months later, they embraced the reality that "such a group would be free and act … and be free to speak out unhampered by official connection with the government."[30]

Over 200 people (almost one-third of who were from the state of Wisconsin)[31] attended the organizing conference in Washington, DC in October 1966. These women and men—members of government agencies and departments, labor organizers, political party activists, members of such groups as BPW, AAUW, and the National Association of Women Lawyers (NAWL)—provided not only revenue at the early, critical stages but also feminist networks. In addition, they brought with them personal experience and differences; they had employed a variety of strategies to draw attention to feminism from outside the formal political system as well as within it. Their networks offered political depth and insight as well as media and professional contacts. Within six months of NOW's formation, the newly appointed board of directors—chaired by Dr. Clarenbach and filled out by women from labor unions, religious orders, and universities—held press conferences to broadcast its "targets for action."

Documenting NOW's Feminist Philosophy

At that first meeting in October, organizers elected Betty Friedan president and adopted a Statement of Purpose.[32] Because of founders' backgrounds in liberal agencies and structures, scholars have (pre)determined NOW's liberal feminist mission and appellation. With such key phrases as "true equality for all women in America" and purporting to "take action to bring women into full participation in the mainstream of American society ... in truly equal partnership with men," it seems that NOW was less concerned with radical overhaul of American politics and culture. However, this document also suggests the seeds of feminist revolution and should not be read exclusively as the documentary broadside of liberal feminism.

In the "Statement of Purpose," NOW affirmed its commitment to "action, nationally, or in any part of this nation, by individuals or organizations, to break through the silken curtain of prejudice and discrimination against women in government, industry, the professions, the churches, the political parties, the judiciary, the labor unions, in education, science, medicine, law, religion, and every other field of importance in American society."[33] Aware again of the environment around them, it states that "enormous changes taking place in our society make it both possible and urgently necessary to advance the unfinished revolution of women toward true equality, now."[34] By comparison to self-defined radical feminist groups that eschewed partnership with men or identified men as the natural and cultural enemy of women, NOW proposed to work with men, seeing them as "victims of the current half-equality between the sexes."[35]

But NOW founders did not reject those issues that radical feminists would soon be credited with bringing to the forefront of American cultural and political debate, particularly the need to change fundamentally the social structure in order to bring about an egalitarian culture. For example, Friedan later suggested that she was rather uncomfortable with the analogy between NOW and NAACP, indicating that the NAACP model was not quite radical enough: "We were talking about a *revolution*, and though the NAACP fought for black people (not like those women's organizations so afraid of being called 'feminist'), the NAACP was not considered a radical organization at all."[36]

Some scholars have read the Statement of Purpose solely for the demand to become a part of the mainstream and to have input in decision-making, seeing NOW as uninterested in fundamental social change. However, I suggest that this was not exclusively the case. The Statement of Purpose repeatedly acknowledged, for example, that marriage and motherhood have placed the greatest constraints on women's lives: "it is no longer either necessary or possible for women to devote the greater part of their lives to child-rearing; yet childbearing and rearing—which continues to be a most important part of most women's lives—still is used to justify barring women from equal professional and economic participation and advance."[37] Further, it stated, "we do not accept the traditional assumption that a woman has to choose between marriage and motherhood, on the one hand, and serious partici- pation in industry or the professions on the other." The solution as NOW proposed it: "True equality of opportunity and freedom of choice for women requires such practical and possible innovations as a nationwide network of child-care centers, which will make it unnecessary for women to retire completely from society until their children are grown, and national programs to provide retraining for women who have chosen to care for their own children full-time."[38] Radical and socialist feminists issued similar calls, suggesting that such patriarchal institutions shackled women.[39] Parsing this document, then, suggests that the organization, even in its early years, defies strict categorization or, at the very least, cannot simply be used as a substitute for "liberal feminism," given that it offered cultural critiques and solu- tions to problems that would require a complete overhaul of American society.

Having established itself with a Statement of Purpose, NOW issued its Bill of Rights for Women at the 1967 national conference. As adopted, the Bill of Rights included the following demands that embodied the principles laid out in the Statement of Purpose: 1) the ERA; 2) enforcement of laws banning sex dis- crimination in employment; 3) maternity leave rights in employment and social security benefits; 4) child day-care centers; 5) tax deductions for home and child- care expenses for working parents; 6) equal and unsegregated education; 7) equal job training opportunities and allowances for women in poverty; and 8) women's unqualified control of their reproductive lives. The membership accepted six of the eight "rights" without controversy, but when the subjects of the Equal Rights Amendment and the call for repealing anti-abortion and anti-contraceptive laws came to the floor, sides formed. When the two controversial measures were passed, a number of members departed from the nascent feminist organization.

By 1967, the majority of union women in NOW supported the ERA, but the unions to which they belonged did not yet support it. Many labor women, including NOW secretary/treasurer Caroline Davis, who also belonged to the UAW, lobbied their unions to drop their anti-ERA stances, but to no avail. When NOW came out in support of the ERA, some women left NOW; others retained membership but shied away from overt activism. Indeed, the UAW, through Davis's office, had been subsidizing NOW's early printing and mailing costs. When NOW supported the ERA, it had to leave behind its UAW office space. (The irony, of course, is that the UAW became the first major union to endorse the ERA.)[40]

The fight for reproductive freedom proved an even more contentious issue than the ERA. NOW leaders took a big risk coming out in favor of repealing abortion laws, a decision that cost them numerous members. Some, including founder Elizabeth Boyer, an Ohio lawyer, founded the Women's Equity Action League (WEAL). NOW might have retained these members had they called for reform instead of complete repeal, but it did not. However, NOW also lost radical members as a result of its stance on abortion. In 1968, members of NOW's first chapter, New York NOW, proclaimed that NOW was corrupted by its own bureaucratic and centralized structure and called for greater egalitarian decision-making. Led by Ti-Grace Atkinson, those making this call were defeated when the measure to change the chapter's structure was brought to a vote; as a result, those who preferred less structure left NOW and founded The Feminists. An interesting sidebar to this story, however, is that The Feminists also believed that because NOW refused to confront churches' oppositions to abortion, especially the Catholic Church, they were simply reformist, a position some women were starting to reject.[41]

These issues caused the greatest dissent within the organization—and, depending on one's vantage point, NOW was either too conservative or too radical. But the greatest struggle surrounding the ERA and reproductive rights emerged outside of NOW, as these issues became important legal and cultural ways to separate pro-ERA and pro-choice activists as feminists, from anti-ERA and anti-choice activists as anti-feminists.[42] When the ERA passed both houses of Congress in 1972, state ratification seemed a foregone conclusion. A strong and vocal opposition grew up from the grassroots, challenging the threat to "traditional" gender roles that enhanced differences between women and men; in the process, it solidified the conservative ascendancy in the United States. Conservative activist Phyllis Schlafly became the spokesperson for the anti-ERA campaign and used the amendment as a symbol of all that had gone awry in postwar America. She and many people around the nation felt that "equality" would threaten the "natural," God-ordained (which also meant "white" and "heterosexual") order of society.[43] Through her organization Eagle Forum, she mobilized thousands of Americans to work to defeat the ERA. By 1977, after thirty-five states ratified the amendment (thirty-eight states made up the necessary two-thirds of states needed to amend the Constitution), grassroots volunteers had mobilized into a highly organized force to ensure that no more states would ratify. As I recount in detail in later chapters, some local NOW chapters fought this growing opposition, albeit in different ways, when the amendment moved to the states for ratification. Pro-ERA advocates, including NOW chapter members, secured a Congressional extension in 1979, but to no avail; in 1982, the ERA failed.[44]

Abortion and reproductive freedom also became volatile issues in the United States and, like the ERA, one's position in support of or opposition to abortion and reproductive rights determined one's alignment as a feminist. After the Supreme Court affirmed the right to privacy, and in the process a woman's right to abortion, in *Roe v. Wade* (1973), "right-to-life" organizations sprang up, focusing their attention on the single issue of abortion and mobilizing hundreds of thousands of people from across religious, cultural, racial, ethnic, and class backgrounds to defeat the "feminist agenda," of which reproductive rights was the most egregious example. Their organization has also been successful—in part, owing to overlapping membership in anti-choice and anti-ERA groups; in addition to mobilizing masses of people and politicizing the language of the debate ("baby" vs. "fetus," for example), they have supported and applauded the gradual erosion of the *Roe* decision.[45]

After 1973, the Supreme Court remained an important force in the struggles over reproductive rights, and NOW, especially through its separate Legal Defense and Educational Foundation (LDEF) in the mid-1970s, issued *amici curaie* in every case potentially affecting *Roe v. Wade* that came before the Court. Despite NOW's pleas to retain or extend the reproductive freedoms granted in *Roe*, the Court issued important challenges: *Maher v. Roe* (1977) upheld a Connecticut ban on abortions funded with public monies, while *Harris v. McRae* (1980) upheld the Hyde Amendment, legislation that prohibited use of federal Medicaid money for elective abortions. In 1989, the Supreme Court case *Webster v. Reproductive Health Services* upheld a Missouri law prohibiting the use of public employees and public facilities for the purpose of performing abortions that were not medically necessary. In *Planned Parenthood of Pennsylvania v. Casey* three years later, the Court upheld many restrictions on accessing abortion services, including requiring parental consent, anti-abortion counseling, and a mandatory waiting period. The Court did invalidate spousal notification for abortion, but many pro-choice advocates, including many NOW members, viewed *Casey* as a near-evisceration of the *Roe v. Wade* decision.

Beyond the courts, however, abortion was also an important cultural barometer during the 1970s. During the television "sweeps" month of November 1972 (prior to the 1973 Supreme Court decision), the CBS television character Maude had an abortion after birth control failed her. (On the show, when Maude's husband Walter found out she was pregnant, he blurted, "The gismo! Why weren't you using the gismo?!" She replied, "I was. It didn't work.") Producer and creator Norman Lear pointed out that television shows often deal with once-taboo subjects, "but only with outsiders. A pregnant neighbor or one of Dr. Welby's patients or a stranger wandering into the series might consider an abortion. But the star of a series herself—never! It's never done." Rather than stick with the first draft of the script, which had a pregnant neighbor of Maude's consider an abortion, Lear and the show's writers decided to have Maude contemplate and ultimately decide to have an abortion.[46]

Organizational and individual support for and opposition to abortion emerged, which demonstrated strong divisions among Americans on the issue and foreshadowed the ways that abortion would become a bellwether for feminism. Although Maude openly and comically discussed her situation as a pregnant, divorced woman, many complained that there was nothing funny about this sitcom's handling of the issue. For example, John McDevitt, chief officer of the Knights of Columbus, indicated that he and the organization he represented did not see abortion as "a laughing matter." Public pronouncements indicated the gulf of

opinion separating pro-choice proponents, such as NOW, and anti-choice advocates, including the Knights of Columbus. McDevitt stated, for example, "Should
the advocates of permissive abortion desire to dispense their inducements to bar-
barity, they should not be given the medium of a popular television program at a
prime children's viewing hour."[47] When, in Champaign, Illinois, the CBS affiliate
announced its refusal to air the episode, the local NOW chapter filed a class-action
suit seeking an emergency injunction requiring the station to air the show. The
circuit court judge denied the case because the chapter failed to demonstrate
necessary urgency, but the group continued to fight, seeking an order from the
Federal Communication Commission to require the affiliate to air the show. Local
station manager James Fielding invoked both his own personal feelings and his
interpretation of the law regarding this volatile issue: "We don't think abortion is a
proper subject for treatment in a frivolous way in a comedy program. Moreover,
the handling might be in violation of Illinois law," referring to an Illinois state law
that forbade advertising or advocacy of abortion.[48]

Such issues as the ERA and reproductive rights defined "feminism" in the public
eye; NOW's unqualified support for both, then, marked them as a leading feminist
organization throughout the 1970s. NOW was not alone: according to the oft-cited
1972 Virginia Slims American Women's Opinion Poll, "feminist thinking is gaining
strength in virtually every demographic group of American women."[49] The ERA
and reproductive rights were most often played out in the formal political arena, but
it would be erroneous to suggest that the founders and early directors of NOW
were attuned only to these areas of activism. As the first "Invitation to Join" stated,
the founders sought to build upon the "ripe" political environment: "With so many
Americans consciously concerned with full participation of all our citizens, and with
dramatic progress at many levels in recent years, the time is ripe for concerted,
directed national action."[50] Founders also committed themselves to activism,
"not ... limited in its targets for action or methods of operation by official proto-
col."[51] As political scientist Maryann Barakso has noted, "independence and activism were the two hallmarks of the group from its inception," quoting from a letter
from Alice Rossi to potential members that NOW was created out of the "conviction that there is a pressing need for an independent organization, free of involvement with political organizations on the state and federal level, which can move
quickly to apply pressure when and where it is needed."[52]

From its origins in June 1966 to its first meeting four months later, founders
wrote numerous letters to others who might be interested in joining. Although
Friedan debated about whether the group should remain small or whether it should
be a mass-based organization, it would become for many a grassroots group that
held much sway in many locales as well as at the national level. Rossi and Clarenbach encouraged Friedan to direct attention to increasing NOW's membership as
it offered the greatest flexibility. Rossi wrote to Friedan in August 1966, "I do not
think ... that such an organization should be a tiny group of elite persons, since
there are so many situations in American society in which what will be politically

and socially effective is not just direct personal influence, or quotes from prominent women, but the pressure represented by numerical strength."[53] Friedan replied: "My stress against a 'big bureaucratic organization' did not mean I want a small select group, but rather an organization directed to action and not to perpetuating its own bureaucracy in the fashion of most women's organizations, all of which it would seem to me to be completely ineffective, and none of which dare to tackle the problems we want to tackle."[54]

A National Organization for Women—Early Chapter Activism

This correspondence represents some of the early discussions about developing a mass base for the National Organization for Women. But what it also suggests is that, from the beginning, NOW sought to be an action-based organization that would target problems women faced. Like the founders, NOW members also reflected many different ideological positions and strategies and targets of feminist activism, and represented, to varying degrees and based upon location, labor unions, business and professional women, leftist activists, women of color, younger women, and lesbians. Even when such women might not have been official members of NOW or one of its chapters, NOW feminists at every level often, but not always, grappled with their (overlapping) concerns.

NOW hoped to represent "all women in America ... as part of a world-wide revolution of human rights," but when it came to the realities of women's lived experiences and philosophies, being everything to everyone was clearly impossible. Many scholars have made this point, often to assert the whiteness and relative conservatism of NOW. To be sure, NOW was composed largely of white women, but this should not suggest that NOW members concerned themselves exclusively with feminist issues only as they affected white women. From its founding in 1966, NOW addressed poverty, racism, and inequality, issues and realities that many feminists in the organization witnessed, lived through, identified with, and understood.[55]

Attention to NOW's activism on a broad range of issues may be absent from scholarly analyses of second-wave feminism in part because of what sociologist Benita Roth calls historical "white-washing"—the history of second-wave feminism is generally told from the vantage point of white women's activism; in this representation, women of color are assumed to have articulated different feminist positions only in response to white women's feminism. The media further whitewashed the movement by focusing nearly exclusively on white spokeswomen, especially Betty Friedan and Gloria Steinem. Scholars adhered to this model of centering white women and assuming that feminists of color responded to them by embracing or rejecting their feminism instead of tracing feminist activism among women of color. This model also assumes that white feminism happened first, which, according to rich scholarship on Black feminism, simply is not true.[56]

In this project, I recognize that, relative to its overall membership, few women of color joined NOW. However, I also assert that it is not simply because women of color were hostile to NOW's issues, agendas, and membership (although some certainly were). Women of color were involved in their own organizations and issues, feminist and otherwise.[57] Indeed, the 1972 Virginia Slims poll indicated that "women's liberation" had a more positive meaning among Black women than among white women and that "Black women express dissatisfaction with their lives as women as well as members of a racial minority."[58] NOW membership may not have been the vehicle through which they expressed their feminism, but it does not follow that women of color were not feminists or that they were overtly hostile to NOW as white women's feminism. As Roth states, "Feminists of color saw themselves as belonging to a different movement than white feminists did, a self-perception that should be taken seriously."[59]

In light of this perspective, NOW sought to reach as many people as possible and address as many issues as members deemed important. The most important way they did this was through the formation of chapters. Chapters were officially incorporated into the organization's bylaws in 1967 but their potential importance was not immediately recognized: "It was agreed that NOW will basically function as a national organization of individual members, with provisions, however, for setting up local chapters where desired."[60] Although membership grew rapidly in the first four years of its existence (3,000 members in ten chapters by 1970), "local chapters have sprung up almost incidentally, usually through the efforts of local people, not national organizers."[61] Jo Freeman has noted that there were tremendous communication gaps between national officers and local chapters, and members were often unable to get basic material about NOW actions and goals; "other people wanted to start NOW chapters, but could not find out how to."[62] Such board members as Alice Rossi treated membership recruitment as a high priority, but the national organization lacked serious efforts to recruit members. Much of this is likely due to the loss of office space in 1968 along with the reality that NOW relied on volunteers, many of who worked full-time and/or were mothers or caregivers who also worked "the second shift."[63] Whatever the reason, national board members "feared that momentum and enthusiasm are being lost when there is a delay."[64]

In 1967, Board of Directors chair Kay Clarenbach suggested that "local chapters … may turn out to be the major action vehicles as well as the route to membership involvement."[65] A key way to encourage membership in NOW was through its numerous task forces, ranging in subject from women in the media to religion to child care.[66] All task forces had a chairperson and issued statements that outlined NOW's action agenda and philosophy on particular issues. Because "task force statements are basic documents of philosophy and will only reflect total NOW thinking when they become the products of many minds," Clarenbach insisted on membership participation in the task forces.[67] However, she recognized that many women could not travel easily in order to meet face to face to generate statements and action policies. Still, it was vital to get word to existing chapters, and the members of the board of directors grappled with how to do so.

In addition to losing the office space (and the gratis postage) at the UAW offices, NOW operated on a shoestring budget and on the volunteer efforts of its members. NOW's official office moved from Chicago to New York City to Washington, DC, often making interim stops in people's living rooms.[68] Moving boxes of files was costly, especially in light of other expenses—court costs, mimeographing, postage, and other necessities that accompany organizational life. In a *NOW Acts* article entitled "Dollars and Sense of Revolution," the board reminded members of their tremendous expenses in fighting court battles, maintaining communication among NOW members, and staging demonstrations: "any organization needs three things in order to be effective: meaning, members, and money. We have the first two but very little of the third ... the real struggle, the work stage, is still very much with us."[69]

In spite of difficult starts on the part of the national board, chapters were growing, bringing women into the fold of NOW, feminism, and the "world-wide revolution of human rights." Over time, NOW became an important first stop for women who moved from one place to another, offering an immediately familiar space for feminism. As members moved, they brought with them their own issues, styles, and tactics, offering greater organizational dynamics among members on the ground than would be reflected on the national board. As the national board implored members to give as much as they could, then, it also had to grapple with the myriad ways that members gave to NOW. As a national feminist community of chapters developed, so did internal diversity and, sometimes, conflict. This was most apparent in the national board's conflict with its first and largest chapter, New York City NOW (NYC NOW).[70]

NYC NOW grew quickly, its presence enhanced by its location in a city that is a national center of activism and politics. This chapter experienced a number of internal conflicts over strategies, structure, and goals. In 1968, for example, one faction within the chapter objected to the formal hierarchical structure the local (and national) leadership attempted to impose. Because some members abandoned the chapter for other groups, NYC NOW leaders quickly introduced and embraced such non-hierarchical philosophies as consciousness raising (CR) within the organization.[71] CR focused on the social construction of women's problems and their relationships to and in society, and it became widespread among chapters in the early 1970s. As Jo Freeman argues, it was initially the members who demanded CR in their chapter meetings, "It was with great reluctance that many NOW chapters set them up to 'cater' to the needs of their newest members. The idea ... was contrary to NOW's image of itself as an action organization."[72] However, for many members in New York City and across the country, CR was a necessary action and wholeheartedly supported it.

Although NYC NOW overcame some differences by merging various feminist styles of organization under the umbrella of NOW feminism, other issues divided the New York chapter and the national organization. The "lavender menace" episode is perhaps the most noted episode in NOW's early history. Although there had been lesbians among the national founders and earliest members (including Dolores Alexander, a NOW secretary who did not come out to Friedan until years later[73]), it was not until NYC NOW began to discuss lesbianism that Friedan started muttering about the lavender menace—although the issue quickly became significant among women across the many chapters.

In 1968, NYC NOW leader Ivy Bottini organized a CR session to address the question "Is Lesbianism a Feminist Issue?" Bottini claims that, because she brought lesbianism to the table, she was purged from the group through an active campaign to prevent her reelection to chapter office. She moved to Los Angeles and started many CR groups there, including some in NOW. But unrelated to Bottini's West Coast activism, other lesbians started raising questions about lesbians' issues as feminist ones. Daughters of Bilitis founders Del Martin and Phyllis Lyon recalled when they joined NOW: "It was 1967, and we heard this wonderful woman, Inka O'Hanrahan, talk on the radio about feminism and this group she'd helped to start called NOW … We sent in our money to join, sight unseen, and became members of NOW at the national level. It was not until the next year that we joined Northern California NOW."[74] When it came time to renew their memberships in NOW, they decided to do so at the national level—for a reason. At this time, NOW offered discounted memberships to married couples—defined explicitly as husband and wife. Martin and Lyon, who had been together fifteen years, sent their membership forms to Inka, who was a national officer at the time, with a note:

> I am sending these application forms to you as national treasurer inasmuch as I suspect this is a rather unusual request. However, as a matter of principle, we feel that if you are going to allow a discount for husband and wife memberships, you should also allow the same for Lesbian liaisons. Phyllis and I have been together for fifteen years. As a couple or partnership we are denied tax breaks, but in the case of a civil rights organization we feel this courtesy should be extended.[75]

O'Hanrahan replied: "There is no reason why we should not allow the husband and wife reduction to apply to any other form of living together or homosexual liaison. I suppose the board will approve … Unless you hear to the contrary your joint membership fees are accepted as paid up for 1968."[76] Martin and Lyon did not hear to the contrary, but in 1969 NOW dispensed with the joint membership altogether, and the issue has not come up since.

The question of whether or not lesbians would threaten NOW's political clout, however, came up repeatedly, and more people within NOW were aware of Friedan's unease with the "lavender menace." In 1970, Friedan issued a memo to NOW chapters encouraging coalitions with "all groups seeking equality and other vanguards of the human revolution." Martin pleaded with Friedan directly to encourage NOW to embrace lesbians as members, sisters, and comrades in the feminist struggle. Writing in a letter to Friedan, she suggested that "Fear of the Lesbian taint and refusal to cope with it is what can be disastrous to the women's movement. It is an issue that cannot be denied, and NOW should take the lead in getting it into proper perspective before it gets out of hand." Ending her letter with a realization that lesbians and feminists share concerns about sex discrimination, child care, protections on the job, and many other issues, Martin stated, "this is not an unholy alliance."

Martin also raised the issue of personal freedom in the context of sexual orientation with the NOW board in 1970. She beseeched Kay Clarenbach to support sexual autonomy for women, including decriminalizing same-sex sex. In response, Clarenbach, a NOW founder and board chairperson, wrote to Martin:

> it is my serious conclusion that to amend our position statement at this time on rights of control of reproductive life to add 'and sexual life,' and to take a stand on 'repeal of all laws penalizing sexual activity between consulting adults in private' would be a disastrous blunder. I believe it would provide the ammunition not only to destroy NOW, but indeed to destroy the decade of advance in the women's movement. The struggle is to be taken seriously, to persuade both women and men that women are second-class citizens has at least been successful. To present gratuitously a sure-fire weapon to the wavering or to the opposition would be foolhardy.

Even more telling that the issue of lesbianism was causing tremendous concern to many on the NOW board, Clarenbach went on to suggest that "such a step would be carte blanche to any NOW chapter which so elected to address itself primarily to this cause. This would be every bit as deflective from our reason-for-being as an organizational position against the war or in favor of environmental control … NOW is committed to bringing women into the mainstream; this organization is not a vehicle for the homophile movement."[77]

When Martin and Lyon set about writing their landmark book, *Lesbian/Woman*, they encountered tension among NYC NOW members, especially individual fears that talking about lesbians in the movement would lead to an exposé. Martin and Lyon intended to address homophobia within the women's movement but "as members of NOW who have worked closely with the political scene, batted out press releases and handouts for the picket lines, we certainly have a stake in preserving the image of the organization as a whole."[78] While they—and many others— were lesbians, they were also feminists working on a variety of issues, suggesting that "us" and "them" within NOW as a social movement organization was not always clear.[79]

For others, however, inclusion under the rubric of "feminist" was too difficult, and they publicly challenged NOW's—or, more to the point, Friedan's—position on the "lavender menace." In response to this epithet, forty lesbians, many from

NYC NOW, stormed the stage at the 1970 Congress to Unite Women—a meeting that NOW co-sponsored to bring feminists from different groups together. The protesters wore purple shirts bearing Friedan's words and insisted that lesbians' rights were women's rights.[80] This powerful public display was also a moment in which Friedan and others had to recognize that the "lesbian issue" would not simply disappear.

But it was not only internal dynamics that challenged feminists to embrace or reject lesbians as a part of the movement and of NOW. In 1970, *Time* magazine featured a story on author Kate Millett, who, while discussing her recent book, *Sexual Politics*, had disclosed her sexual identity as bisexual. This article created a media frenzy, prompting NOW and other organizations to defend Millett's decision to come out and linking issues of sexual orientation to feminism. NOW president Aileen Hernandez, elected to office in 1970, issued a press release on December 17, 1970, to be read at a public event supporting Millett at Washington Square Church in New York City. In it, she stated that, while NOW had no formal statement on lesbianism because "we do not prescribe a sexual preference test for applicants," members worked "for full equality for women and … they do so in the context that the struggle in which we are engaged is part of the total struggle to free all persons to develop their full humanity."[81] After condemning "frightened, unethical individuals in the media" for "linking all its leaders to lesbianism (and all that word connotes in the minds of the public)" as "despicable and diversionary," she addressed the greater issues facing both NOW and society as a whole: "Let us—involved in a movement which has the greatest potential for humanizing our total society—spend no more time with this sexual McCarthyism. We need to free all our sisters from the shackles of a society which insists on viewing us in terms of sex."[82] (Friedan later suggested that lesbians promoted "sexual McCarthyism" by making lesbianism a feminist issue.)[83]

In this context, then, it is not surprising that, just two years after Friedan's grousing about the "lavender menace," NOW passed a resolution acknowledging lesbians' rights as women's rights. Taking "the struggle seriously," as Clarenbach suggested to Martin, became a matter of recognizing lesbians and the different issues they faced as such within the organization while respecting the organization's national structure. In 1969, the Los Angeles chapter of NOW passed a resolution supporting lesbians' rights. Members then used NOW's federated structure and procedures to support lesbians' rights as women's rights, moving the resolution to the state chapter, the western regional conference in early 1971, and then to the national conference. When it passed by an overwhelming majority, the resolution and NOW members formally acknowledged "the oppression of lesbians as a legitimate feminist concern."[84]

Its success likely prompted some people to leave NOW. It encouraged at least one former member to rejoin NOW: "I have recently experienced a wonderful confirmation of my lifelong faith in women … I was a member of NOW in 1969 and 1970, but dropped my membership in disgust with its prissy, lily-heterosexual policies." Because of NOW's "momentous about face" with the 1971 resolution, she wrote, "I would like to rejoin NOW and join your vigorous [LA NOW] chapter."[85]

Implementing inclusivity, of course, was another matter altogether, and in the three NOW chapters I study here, each grappled differently and to different results with issues of sexual orientation and what constituted feminist sex. But recounting this episode in detail here sheds necessary light on one of the most important and oft-cited moments in NOW's history. Scholars have used the "lavender menace" in a variety of ways—to expose NOW's conservatism and homophobia, to trace an important step in the rise of lesbian feminism, or to provide an early example of dissension among feminists and further support for the narrative of feminism's decline. But I posit a different interpretation: it illustrates how NOW's history is not just one of the national board members. Instead, chapter members from different locations worked diligently to discuss lesbianism in a feminist context, to advocate on behalf of their friends and fellow feminists, and to topple the notion that Betty Friedan represented and spoke for the entire organization.

NOW members, however, were largely unsuccessful in keeping the media, and consequently other feminists and scholars who study second-wave feminism, away from Betty Friedan as the spokesperson of NOW and feminism in general.[86] Her influence was important—in reference to the 1970 Women's Strike for Equality, Susan Brownmiller noted, for example, "let's face it, if any other woman had called a strike press conference, she would have been talking to herself. Without the name of Betty Friedan, the strike would never have happened."[87] And Friedan's presence was legendary. She captured the media's attention with such seemingly radical ideas as the fact that, as she wrote in *The Feminine Mystique*, women did not have orgasms waxing the kitchen floor, or that women should demand nothing less than full equality with men. She held press conferences in her Victorian-style parlor, decked out in suits with fur-lined collars, and after talking openly with her African American maid about the evening's dinner, she turned to the press to insist upon women's full and equal place in society.[88] She gave tough interviews; her agent at Norton, Tania Grossinger (who worked with her to promote *The Feminine Mystique*), recalled: "I can remember her confronting Virginia Graham on 'Girl Talk' and screaming, 'If you don't let me have my say, I'm going to say orgasm ten times.'"[89]

With just a couple of examples, then, it is clear to see how and why Friedan captured the media's attention. But one must wonder if this attention becomes part of the reason that NOW has been portrayed so conservatively, even negatively, in scholarly work on second-wave feminism. When Friedan called for the Women's Strike for Equality on her way out of office as NOW president, she could not have predicted its success (despite many media outlets' suggestion to the contrary). It drew attention to local activism and the fact that feminism was emerging from coast to coast. After leaving office, however, Friedan stated that feminists should not be so concerned with public protest and demonstration; instead, they should focus on electing feminists (especially women, but also feminist men) to office. With this goal in mind, she joined Bella Abzug, Gloria Steinem, and Shirley Chisholm in founding the National Women's Political Caucus in 1971. She never really stayed out of the media spotlight, and sometimes in ways that promoted damage and dissent in the women's movement, such as charging Steinem and others with "female chauvinism" and sexism, indicating that lesbians came to NOW with the explicit purpose of seducing her and sabotaging the movement, or suggesting that the Watergate scandal and efforts to defeat the ERA were linked.[90] But as she discouraged the "feminist" mystique that glorified careers for women in the same way that the "feminine" mystique glorified family life for women, she continued to call for more attention to formal politics and maintained her insistence that women and men must work together for feminist change. NOW never abandoned these goals nationally or locally, but they focused on a variety of issues and engaged in a variety of strategies and tactics to meet their goals.

Although this book charts and explores the activism of three NOW chapters, chapters across the country fomented feminist revolution wherever they saw fit. National NOW set the tone for demonstration and protest when, in 1967, it challenged the EEOC to do away with sex-segregated help-wanted advertisements in newspapers. After setting December 14, 1967 as the "National Day of Demonstration against the Equal Employment Opportunity Commission," Friedan and leaders of the national board encouraged members to join demonstrations against the EEOC in Washington, DC, New York, Chicago, Atlanta, and San Francisco to protest the Commission's inattention to their demand. In a letter to board members and chapter conveners, she stated that in "areas where we have active chapters but no EEOC regional offices, such as Wisconsin, might send delegations to join the demonstration in another area," encouraging cross-chapter collaboration and recognizing the potential strength of members in various locations. Moreover, she encouraged "you all to be imaginative in deciding what form the protest in your city should take. Efforts should be made toward maximum effectiveness and maximum publicity. ... Try to get as many NOW members and sympathizers as you can to take part in the demonstration; but even if you have only 10 members, a dramatic protest with clearly visible signs carrying out our message can have an impact, especially as it will coincide with other NOW demonstrations around the country."[91]

Whether intentional or unwittingly, the Board encouraged feminists in NOW to take charge of their own situation and to protest creatively. In Washington, DC and Chicago, NOW members marched with placards protesting EEOC policies; in San Francisco, Aileen Hernandez joined Northern California NOW members, who presented EEOC regional director Frank Quinn with a large basket of red tape and "the scissors to cut through it." In Worcester (Massachusetts), Dallas, and Pittsburgh, NOW members contacted the local media to register their complaints.[92] In New York City, NOW members from three states carried bundles of newspapers to the regional EEOC headquarters, but, perhaps as to be expected, twelve members (who, in a dramatic display, chained themselves to typewriters) also used this opportunity to suggest that "women's roles" as wives and mothers amounted to little more than "a sort of socially acceptable whoredom."[93]

Such divergent actions likely led NOW leaders to debate and pass a "Public Relations Guidelines for NOW Members and Chapters." This 1968 document, passed after the EEOC pickets, indicated that "the press does not always take the trouble to differentiate between the official positions of NOW and the personal views of NOW officers as individuals." The solution, according to this document, was simple: "NOW officers or official spokesmen [sic] may not publicly express views which they know to be contrary to NOW policy. A NOW official who disagrees with NOW policy should resign from his or her position before publicly expressing views on the subject."[94]

Although the National Board of Directors attempted to quell dissent within the ranks of the organization, the reality was that members used a variety of tactics to pursue feminist change. The Board continued to sanction street protests: NOW orchestrated pickets against Colgate-Palmolive in 1968 for discriminatory hiring and promotion practices. NOW also supported the Poor People's Campaign "Fast to Free Women From Poverty" day in May of that year. Although NOW did not openly support the Miss America Pageant protest in Atlantic City, the protest clearly garnered media attention—from this event, feminists were dubbed "bra burners" because protesters threw lipstick, girdles, and other instruments that represented "the chains that tie us to these beauty standards against our will."[95] Sometimes confrontations over dramatic protest style resulted in leaving NOW altogether, as Ti-Grace Atkinson did in 1968, when she and other dissidents organized "the young, the black and the beautiful" into the October 17 Movement.[96] Atkinson's irreconcilable differences with Friedan over organizational structure and style as well as salient women's issues—abortion, marriage, family, oppressive class structure—meant, to her, that she could not accept NOW's policies and, following the directive, she resigned. Many other times, however, NOW members stayed in the organization, embracing a variety of tactics—from letter writing to sing-ins and speak-outs—to protest the issues most salient to them as individuals and members of a local (as well as a national) feminist community.

For example, San Francisco NOW (SF NOW) member Mimi Kaprolat promoted a sing-in at local newspaper offices of the San Francisco *Chronicle and Examiner* building. In further protest of sex-segregated want ads and support of a recent judicial decision that upheld the illegality of sex-segregated classified under Title VII, she offered revised lyrics to Christmas carols to bring attention to her December 19 action, including (to the tune of "Jingle Bells") "Jingle Help, Jingle Help, Help, Help, All the Way. Oh what fun 'twill be to read, Help Wanted— Equal Pay" and (to the tune of "God Rest Ye Merry Gentlemen") "God Rest Ye Merry Gentlemen, let something you dismay. Remember 'Title Seven' was meant for no delay. To save us from the presses' power when they go all astray. Oh tidings of fairness is joy."[97] In New York City, NOW chapter members held a "death

watch" outside of the New York headquarters of the American Newspaper Publishers Association, which filed an appeal to reverse the recent judicial decision
determining sex-segregated want ads were illegal under Title VII. Women dressed
in black veils and carried coffins, tombstones, and signs protesting the "murder of
the 1964 Civil Rights Act."[98]

In other places, NOW members demonstrated against overt sexism. In Beverly
Hills, for example, members held a sit-in at the Polo Lounge bar of the Beverly
Hills Hotel, where management prohibited women from drinking. Although the
women were served without incident, they made important statements about per-
ceptions of women, including the prevalent notion that unescorted women who sit
at a bar "are prostitutes coming into the bar to solicit." Of course, they encountered
other women who felt that the demonstration was frivolous. As one patron said of
the protesters, "This is the most ridiculous thing I have ever seen. It's really rather
degrading. Why would a woman want to sit at a bar? I'd say it's because she's
looking for something." Another woman commented, "I don't think a woman
would want to go into a bar unescorted." But the male maitre d' offered no complaints: "the more girls I have, the more sunshine in my heart."[99] In another
example, NOW members in Atlanta, Chicago, New York, Pittsburgh, and Syracuse
joined a "Freedom for Women" week that culminated in an anti-Mother's Day
Protest. In Los Angeles, members tied "mother's day" to other examples of
exploitation and demanded living wage for all women, equal pay for equal work,
free child-care centers, rehabilitation programs for imprisoned women, ending
"special oppression of black and brown women," and "a world without wars."[100]
These examples, just two of many, illustrate how NOW members were creatively
targeting episodes of sexism, merging them with other forms of oppression, and
demanding full equality for all people. Whether or not the NOW board dis-
approved of or supported these actions is unclear, as there is no record of official
board response. However, it is clear that NOW members spoke both for themselves
and for their chapters, and they may have been less concerned with pleasing and
appeasing the national board as they were fighting sexism on the ground.

Restructuring NOW

By 1970, chapters were affiliated with the national organization, but there were
breakdowns in communication from the local affiliates to the national board of
directors. The national board could pass demands regarding press coverage, but it
could not stop the local chapters from pursuing their own goals and tactics. To
promote intraorganizational communication (and increase financial solvency), the
national board restructured the organization in 1970 along regional lines and
appointed regional directors from the South, East, Midwest, and West. These
directors, along with vice-presidents for fundraising, public relations, legal activities,
and legislative activities, made up the new Executive Committee.[101] Some of this
restructuring was clearly a result of poor management of an organization that was

attracting thousands of members. However, external cultural and social factors, including the waning of the civil rights movement, increasing violence in the anti-war movement, and the influx of feminists from a variety of social movements and philosophies, also shaped the organization. In 1969, for example, organizers of the Atlanta conference in 1968 raised questions about modeling the women's movement after the civil rights movement:

> NOW's struggle, particularly in the areas of protest, legislation and litigation, has leaned heavily on the experience of the black civil rights struggle ... [W]e in NOW must realize that the black struggle has accomplished no real revo-lution, that in some ways it is only discovering itself, that we must not be trapped in the same pitfalls, and that we are at a point of departure from it and from all others. Thus, the need to develop new, more effective strategy.[102]

Part of this "new, more effective strategy" was to strengthen internal communica-tions; it also involved coalition building with other feminist groups, which led to inevitable overlap in style, strategies, and goals.

NOW members also embraced protest politics and coalition building, most evi-dent in the groundswell of support for the 1970 Women's Strike for Equality. This strike commemorated the fiftieth anniversary of the 19th Amendment but, at the grassroots level, brought women from a variety of backgrounds and neighborhoods together, if only for a day, to consider the cause of women's rights. From the Strike, NOW membership grew and chapters sprung up across the nation.[103] Some national NOW board members also saw women's liberation as the "competition": "If we in NOW are to stay in the vanguard of this revolution, we are faced with the responsibility of developing an ideology for the future. Our task is to venture beyond that 'primitive' stage, break new ground, formulate unprecedented policy: visionary [and] undogmatic."[104] Such a statement suggests that the overlap between "liberal" and "radical" feminism was quite dynamic. Some of the ideas that new liberationist groups advocated were partially embedded in NOW's Statement of Purpose and Bill of Rights. Moreover, NOW's protest politics were already a part of the group's tactical repertoire,[105] often making quite public displays about gender segregation and women's relative disadvantages to men.

By 1971, NOW boasted between 4,000 and 5,000 members in approximately 150 chapters. With little communications infrastructure and no educational program in place, chapters and members were often left to their own devices and forged feminist space in their own cities. Chapters toed the national NOW line and worked on the ERA and electing feminists to political office, but in very different ways and to purposes beyond conforming to national directives and agendas. More often, they directed their energies toward issues in their own communities, con-fronting the local environments in which women lived, worked, raised children, faced sexual harassment and job discrimination, were victims of myriad forms of abuse, and found common ground with other feminists. In doing so, they altered NOW locally to fit their needs and to respond to their own communities rather than simply reflect the national organization.

It is not surprising, then, that when members disagreed with the board, such as the Memphis NOW delegates to the national convention in Philadelphia in 1975, they continued to make NOW their own rather than conform to national style or disaffiliate from the national group. Chapter president Carole Hensen indicated that "mindless block voting" (a reference to NOW's organizational design of nominating an entire slate of officers to fill all board positions rather than nominate individuals for each office) "was a grave disappointment [that] cost me a great deal of respect for the women and men in NOW who claim to be independent thinkers." Member Holly Peters made clear that the issues were greater than the structure of voting for the national board: "we see an ongoing quest for sisterhood that can overcome political power plays. And we see specifically in NOW's history, tension between national and local priorities." Rather than dividing and polarizing chapters from the national, Peters suggested self-empowerment: "we must take responsibility as feminists for the future of our organization … Once we lose perspective and follow patriarchal political models we endanger not only the future of NOW nationally, but the creative thrust of the entire feminist movement." She suggested that chapters should question the conservativism of the national board, whose actions, in her view, did not always match its rhetoric. Moreover, chapter members should develop a sound feminist philosophy to "provide a theoretical base for our choices."[106] If national leaders of NOW did not align its actions with its rhetoric, rank-and-file members clearly felt empowered to do so.

In October 1966, Betty Friedan reflected on the founding of NOW; indeed, just three months after the Third Conference on the Status of Women, the organization had over 200 charter members in states across the nation. In her reflection, she wrote, "Many people have asked how NOW got started. The real question is why it didn't happen 20, 40 years ago. The absolute necessity for a civil rights movement for women had reached such a point of subterranean explosive urgency by 1966, that it only took a few of us to get together to ignite the spark—and it spread like a nuclear chain reaction."[107] Understanding NOW at the national level provides a sense of national politics and resonance; I have offered little more than broad strokes here and look forward to more scholarly research placing national NOW in the fuller context of the culture in which it emerged. But the local contexts in which chapters grew up also shed important light on the ways in which feminists set out to create feminist change in different locations. Whether the chapter was the only explicitly feminist, membership-based group in town, a liberal feminist flank of a large and varied progressive community, or a group that operated between and beyond pre-existing liberal and radical feminist organizations, these chapters, when studied in depth and analyzed together, illuminate the vitality of NOW and the dynamics of second-wave feminism from a grassroots perspective.

3

FEMINIST ACTIVISM IN MEMPHIS[1]

Beyond the Liberal/Radical Divide

Under the banner "Opening Up a Can of Whup-Ass on the Patriarchy," the first Southern Girl Convention was convened in Memphis, Tennessee on July 31 and August 1, 1999. An event designed "to celebrate the unique culture and experience of southern females," Memphian Robin Jack and her co-organizers Jennifer Sauer, Victoria Brough, Michelle Parra, and Kimberly Mitchell invited convention-goers to see a variety of bands, participate in and see a drag king show, and attend a variety of workshops at the University of Memphis' University Center and sponsored by the city's Women's Action Coalition.[2] The idea of a girl convention was not unique to Memphis: the first, in Washington, DC in 1992, was the Riot Grrrl convention, a gathering tied historically to punk and do-it-yourself (DIY) feminism and third-wave feminism.[3] At the Southern Girl Convention, the 100 attendees could explore what organizers called "D.I.Y. cosmetology" to basic car maintenance; other workshops covered topics such as race and class in the South, how to survive sexual abuse, sexism in the activist movement, and body image.[4] From Memphis, Southern Girl (later Girls) Conventions took place in cities across the U.S. South until the last one in Gainesville, Florida in 2008; over the ten years of its existence, it became an annual grassroots meeting for networking, organizing, educating, agitating, and activism, devoted to empowering women, girls, and transfolks in the South, and to furthering the struggle for social justice in the South and across the United States based on the understanding that Southern feminism, anti-racism, and justice work would embrace the same causes as this work did in other places, but also took on a unique dimension in the South.[5]

Thirty years prior, Memphis was also home to a thriving feminist community that sought, in many ways, to "open up a can of whup-ass on the patriarchy" by creating and articulating a kind of feminism that was Southern in many ways. Some of the issues may look familiar as part of a national feminist movement, but the impetuses and responses are distinct. At heart, though, is the sense that, for Memphis feminists, all feminism was radical because it challenged the core of Southern gender structure as it intersected with all facets of Southern life and livelihood. But feminists in Memphis often negotiated how they would deploy this Southern identity as well as a feminist one, and adopted liberal as well as radical strategies and goals. Whether bringing domestic violence and rape to the forefront of political and social awareness, addressing the Equal Rights Amendment (ERA), or confronting lesbian identity, feminists used Memphis NOW to attempt to be, in a feminist sense, everything to everyone. Of the three chapters under study in this book, it most explicitly moves beyond the liberal/radical divide.

The Memphis chapter of NOW, or Memphis NOW, sought to be everything to everyone from its inception. In November 1970, chapter members called for a "reorganizational meeting" to take place the following month. This "crisis!" is rather unusual: the chapter was only two months old and, clearly, it was not doing what members needed or wanted. The very first meeting in September 1970 promised an in-depth discussion of day-care centers and the possibilities of establishing a committee on "the Abortion issue" as well as a discussion of the ERA, defined in the chapter as "the political scene."[6] But, were these issues Memphis feminists wanted to address in 1970, or over the course of the decade? This second newsletter calling for reorganization pleaded with local feminists:

> If you really care about equal opportunity for women in Memphis, *please* come to the *reorganizational meeting*. If you find meetings boring, say so. If you just want to 'rap,' say so. If you want a specific goal or project to work on, say so. EACH INDIVIDUAL should decide what steps she wants to take (if any) to end discrimination. Whether you want a stronger or more flexible structure, speak out at this meeting![7]

Perhaps this move was a nod to NOW's "Do your thing" motto for chapters to follow on the heels of the Women Strike for Equality. Perhaps it was a call to work with members who sought to work on formal political policy as well as to engage in consciousness-raising sessions. Whatever the reasons for this early reorganization, it is clear that, from its first days, Memphis NOW was an organization of its members. Indeed, the local chapter rarely communicated with or about national NOW politics. Instead, the focus was on feminist work in Memphis. Even when chapter conveners Mary Sullivan, Sally Mace, and Linda Cowden offered the program for the December meeting—Peg Cherry led a group on the subject "Sexists: Are you one too?"—they hoped it would "serve as ground work or a starting base for a general discussion on what *you* want to do—as a group or as individuals."[8] Of course women can also be sexist, but the provocative question in the heady days of feminist consciousness raising invited women to join in the conversation about what this group would mean and how it would interact and intervene in local feminist politics as well as politics related to women's lives.

This chapter explores the growth and development of Memphis NOW from this rocky start in 1970 until 1982, when the chapter lost many members over social and political tensions. Memphis, once characterized as a "sleepy little river town," has a unique past as a hotbed of civil rights activism.[9] However, as this chapter demonstrates, it also has an interesting feminist past, one that many scholars have overlooked, in part because the South as a region and Memphis as a major city in it have been defined historically as a place to see other social and political tensions unfold in U.S. history.

Forming a feminist organization and coming into a feminist identity in Memphis occurred alongside and in the wake of the civil rights movement; sustaining one meant interacting with a less-than-sympathetic political and religious culture. Historian Dewey Grantham once observed that "Southerners continue to be profoundly conscious of their regional identity,"[10] no doubt a factor of their political, economic, and cultural history, all of which intersects with the histories of race relations, social rights and justice, and political conservatism in the United States. The political and religious conservatism that defines the region has been buttressed by racialized deployment of womanhood and the need to protect Southern white womanhood through attacks on and murders of Black men and rape and physical violation of Black women. This racial and racist concept of "Southern womanhood" exacerbated political disunity among Black and white women and men. But "womanhood" is also constructed in a heterosexual way, and challenges to heterosexuality often resulted (and still do result) in cultural and political backlash. As Southern women openly embraced feminism, they confronted this kind of backlash as well. Understanding feminist activism and identity against this backdrop helps explore and analyze how women maneuvered around and grappled with these histories and realities and, at times, deployed this identity of Southern womanhood. Cultivating feminism behind "the Magnolia Curtain," then, was not an easy venture.[11]

In a contemporary cultural and political context of a growing discourse about race, discrimination, and equality—and using both legislative means and street protests—feminism emerged in the Bluff City. In some instances, white and African American women organized for themselves as women together. For example, the Memphis Volunteer Women's Roundtable formed in the early 1970s as a group of Black and white women who worked for "women's rights, the fight against racism, *and* black/white unity."[12] Similarly, an interracial group of women formed the Panel of American Women (PAW) in the aftermath of King's assassination to talk freely about racial tensions in Memphis. PAW organized panels with representatives from the Jewish, Catholic, and Protestant faiths, with at least one African American woman among them. The women presented panels at churches, city council meetings, school board meetings—anywhere they could get a platform from which to speak.[13]

One PAW organizer, Jocelyn Wurzburg, was also an early member of Memphis NOW, demonstrating the overlap between social movements in the city. Although she, a white Jewish woman, linked her feminist activism directly to the cause of

African American civil rights, many African American women in Memphis were not necessarily drawn to local feminist organizations. Most politically active African American women in the city focused their political energies on issues of race; if they focused on women, it was specifically and explicitly for African American women, forging a "separate road to feminism."[14] Several scholars have highlighted the national tenor of racial divides among feminists,[15] but it also resonated locally in Memphis and would continue to resonate in the NOW chapter.

Race and Feminism in Memphis

In Memphis and across the South, feminist activism was caught in the local political "protection" of Southern womanhood, a racialized code for ensuring social and cultural distance between white people and African American people. This code is also a powerful example of how the "metalanguage of race" operates in people's daily lives.[16] The image of Southern womanhood was not lost on NOW members in the South. The first Southern Regional Director, Judith Lightfoot, addressed this image as something with which NOW women in the South grappled and sought to overcome. Realizing that "nowhere else in the country" has the "pedestal image … been so forceful and so false," Lightfoot encouraged NOW members to revamp the image of the Southern woman into a strong feminist. She invoked such examples as Lorena Weeks, "that genteel, brave little woman who defied and defeated the mighty Southern Belle," to encourage "those who scorn us or take us lightly" to "look beyond the false image" because "it is ill-advised to be our enemy."[17] Moreover, she noted that "Southern women know how to organize for church, League of Women Voters, against pollution, for civil rights. This time we are organizing for ourselves."[18]

Early in the chapter's history, NOW simply was not attractive to many African American women because of their overt suspicions of white women.[19] That NOW had an African American national president held no sway with Black women in Memphis; as one African American housewife commented, "I really don't think black women will ever be treated the same as white women are treated."[20] For her, equality was less an issue of sex and more an issue of race; quite likely, personal experience indicated that, as Toni Morrison wrote in 1970, "racism is not confined to white men."[21] And if newspaper columnist Art Gilliam is at all representative, Black men in Memphis agreed. In comparison to being black, Gilliam suggested in 1971, the exclusions that women face are minor.[22]

Rather than join a feminist agenda that white women in NOW set for themselves, African American women created and sustained their own organizations and spaces for feminist activism.[23] For example, Dot Smith and Helen Duncan, directors of the Southwest Mental Health Center, offered a six-week workshop on "Problems of Being Black and Female" in 1978. Both for and by African American women, this workshop addressed African American women's history, family issues, and images of beauty. One group, United Sisters and Associates (USA), formed with the intent of addressing Black womanhood in Memphis and nationwide. In attempting to establish unity among African American women, resist the exploitation they suffered, and provide an arena for emotional and spiritual development, USA directed its energies toward Black femininity and beauty. To this end, it worked with *Essence* magazine to develop the Miss Essence of Tennessee beauty pageant, bringing "national attention to Black women, to the city of Memphis and by example present an image of Black womanhood in a manner that renders more respect and appreciation."[24]

The evidence does not indicate whether or not the local NOW chapter took issue with USA's promotion of beauty standards for women; what is clear is that many African American women felt that they did not have much to gain by affiliating with the local NOW chapter. Some women felt that they had little to learn from white feminist consciousness raising. Although Memphis NOW's minority task force leader Merle Smith applauded NOW for its activism on behalf of feminism and women's equality, and stayed with the organization "to keep black women visible in the movement," she also understood why many women of color would not be attracted to NOW. Drawing fundamentally different cultural distinctions between white and Black women in the South, Smith stated, "you see, we come from a strong matriarchal society and were raised to be feminists, something white women found out about later."[25]

The civil rights movement clearly affected both white and Black women, but they tended to organize separately and concentrate on different issues. Women forged alliances across racial lines within feminist organizations when local issues demanded them—PAW is one important example in Memphis.[26] Sustaining alliances, however, was increasingly difficult—the reality was that race had everything to do with capturing the ear of local political leaders. The mostly white membership of Memphis NOW would always have more political voice than African American women in the city.

This reality was not lost on Memphis NOW members. Although chapter membership, more often than not, was all white, local NOW activists sought to address complexities of race, class, and gender in the city as they related to feminism—and to question racism among themselves. In a 1974 contribution to a running newsletter feature, "One Woman Thinking Things Through," Memphis NOW member Martha Allen implored her sisters to realize that "it is [not] divisive to have uppermost in our minds the fight against racism in everything we do. Rather, it provides a basis for unity with our black and minority sisters." She warned: "By being out of touch and not relating enough to our black sisters, misconceptions are developed, even about groups where black and white women work together."[27] She respected that Black women pursued feminist goals through different organizations and suggested that Memphis NOW work through their own group as well as in concert with other organizations to create feminist change in their city.

Moreover, white women in the NOW chapter were aware that racial "protection" hindered their own feminist gains for an equitable society. In January 1976, for example, Mary Jo Cowart opined that the connections between sexism and racism were all too real in local women's lives: "The Belle on her pedestal *might* be crying out for her life, but she has been so well protected from You Know Who by her white man that she no longer recognizes her own voice." Rejecting this imagery that perpetuated discrimination across race and gender in the South, Cowart urged women across racial lines to work together for change. After all, "what good is [our liberation] if a majority of our sisters still have the man's foot on their neck?"[28]

Some members clearly were aware of and sympathetic to the realities of how racism and sexism operated simultaneously in women's lives. But their awareness, which they shared with the larger group through the newsletter, did little to alter the fact that Memphis NOW was a white women's group in both perception and reality. In March 1976, the chapter hosted a program on the "Status of Black Women in Memphis."[29] Memphis NOW members faced difficult and important questions: When one NOW member asked why more Black women were not involved in NOW, moderator Andrewnetta Hawkins Hudson retorted with "how many of you go to PUSH [People United to Save Humanity] meetings?" Leathia Thomas, director of Women and Girls Employment Services (WAGES) in Memphis, commented that she did not join NOW because "I view [NOW] as first being white and therefore suspect. Black people have been used to gain benefits for white people, so I don't think black women are going to be found flocking to chapters of NOW or anything that is primarily trying to do something for women."[30]

The chapter was aware of its whiteness, a point Nancy Clayton made in the November 1979 newsletter: "Look around you at the next N.O.W. meeting. Is this a middle class white women's movement? It certainly appears to be so." But she continued, as others before her had, to reiterate the fact that, however unevenly, all women faced discrimination: "The issues that concern us do not pertain merely to white women. Discrimination in education and employment opportunities is not limited to white women … We are working for all women regardless of race."[31] Memphis NOW sought to reach out to Black women in the city, but rarely found themselves showing up for Black women at their meetings and events. White and Black women alike operated within a complex racialized political and cultural system that did not encourage them to stand together simply as sisters united for the same cause. Many white women in Memphis NOW did not challenge that system. Some suggest that such an example may prove the exceptionalism of the South, but as many women of color across the country challenged the whiteness of NOW nationally and the women's movement in general, they illustrated how race is not a matter of Southern exceptionalism but rather one of national experience.[32]

Getting off the Ground

After its reorganizational "crisis," Memphis NOW was underway with twenty-five attendees at the December 1970 meeting at the Half and Half Coffee House. The group embraced a less rigid style and format, building "study groups" to discuss "concrete issues." Again, the plea went out: "Whether or not you have a particular interest area, please come; join a group, start one, or just 'float'. We hope this structure will provide an efficient exchange of information as well as a basis for organizing feasible projects." And they decided—most likely by consensus, based on the wording of their newsletters—to focus on abortion and day care, two of the main issues from the very first meeting.[33]

Early members ranged in age from 23 to 53, included men and women, and involved people who were affiliated with other local groups in town. The slate of nominees for council membership (which is how the chapter first referred to its officers) included Mike Adler (27, a land officer with the Memphis Housing Authority who was also enrolled in law school); Peg Cherry (29, an assistant sociologist with the Memphis Regional Medical Program); Linda Cowden (23, technical biologist at Dobbs Research Institute); Olgie Deason (30, substitute teacher); Peggy DiCanio (41, assistant professor of sociology at Memphis State University); Marion MacInnes (53, retired Air Force major); and Tanya Miller (23, manager of Carolyn Lacy, Ltd.). In addition to being affiliated with other local groups, each of them held different types of jobs in education (K-12 and higher education), retail, the corporate world, and the city.

With built-in contacts and initiative, the Memphis chapter would become a formidable presence in the city and would tackle many of the problems they identified in their community. They addressed issues that were directed from the national board—the ERA and electing feminists (women and men) to political office. They also grappled with problems women across the country faced—rape, domestic violence, job discrimination, sexuality differences, reproductive rights, and more—that were not necessarily at the top of NOW's national agenda. NOW certainly endorsed their work on these many issues, which is clear from the breadth and number of resolutions passed at the national meetings. But the way Memphis NOW grappled with these issues differs in style and tactic from the national board. By the early 1970s, the national board turned its attention to formal politics; the national protests of the early days of NOW were eschewed in favor of more dignified tactics. However, the local chapters did not always follow suit. Both the locals and the national were freed by this division of labor—the national board could focus directly on the formal aspects, and the locals could take it to the streets as needed. Each fulfilled a function in the politics of feminist activism, both in the name of women in the United States and under the name of "National Organization for Women."

Here I turn to look at the issues that Memphis NOW addressed. Across the board, whether working for the ERA or addressing local issues, the chapter always conducted itself in ways different from the national board. Their interest in feminism and feminist change was generated not from national NOW but from local women who needed help or who wanted to create feminist change. This organic approach to issues offers insight into how local context shaped chapter members' activism—and what changes their activism created in their cities.

Memphis NOW and the ERA

Many scholars use the ERA as the most prominent example of "liberal feminism": the broad language of the amendment that would secure *equality* for women—that neither Congress nor any state would pass a law that would abridge or deny equality for women—did not seem to thwart cultural and social gender roles. But in the South, this amendment did challenge gender roles directly.[34] In pursuit of this amendment, Memphis NOW, as did other chapters, utilized the federated structure of the organization, and many of its early actions on behalf of the ERA reflected a firm commitment to equality without attention to regional distinction. But when anti-ERA activists justified their disdain for the amendment through the trope of "Southern womanhood," Memphis NOW members also employed stereotypes of southern women's identity to buttress their pro-ERA cause. Although the ERA was a major issue for the national organization, once Congress ratified the amendment it became a local cause and people fought—for and against—with whatever images they could conjure to create support for their respective sides.

When the ERA finally passed the House of Representatives and the Senate and went to the states for ratification in 1972 (nearly fifty years after it was first introduced into Congress), the women's movement, and NOW, was in full swing. Memphis NOW was one of 150 chapters of the organization, and its members, like people across the nation, were certain the amendment would be ratified in short order. Indeed, Hawaii passed it on the same day it went to the states; twenty-two states passed it by year's end.

Tennessee was one of those states, helping set the tone of apparent support for the ERA by ratifying it in April 1972. In fact, within two weeks of Congressional approval, the Tennessee House voted unanimously in favor of the ERA, followed by overwhelming support in the Senate.[35] With such tremendous support, Memphis NOW seemingly had nothing else to do for the ERA and turned its attention to many other issues that women in the city faced. NOW members did not expect strong and organized resistance after the amendment's state passage. They were unprepared for a groundswell of opposition, or they did not take it seriously until it was too late. As a result, they watched their success unravel.

In Tennessee and other states across the nation, Phyllis Schlafly's Eagle Forum launched STOPERA campaigns, which, supported by other groups sympathetic to this cause, grew up from the grassroots to block passage of the ERA. At bottom, they clung to gender norms that enhanced differences between women and men, charging that the amendment violated women's rights to be mothers and wives and forced women to reject their biological and cultural difference from men.[36] In Tennessee, former Miss America Barbara Walker Hummel led local opposition to the ERA through Memphis-based AWARE (American Women Are Richly Endowed). Walker Hummel was a local icon, having won the pageant in 1947. Rather than embark on a potential career in movies or theater (she was offered roles in both venues), she returned to Memphis State University to complete her degree; she said, "I had no ambition to be Miss America when I entered the contest. My interest was in the scholarship to continue my studies."[37] After completing her degree (and marrying her husband), she launched a successful career in local television, hosting Memphis' first local daytime television show, *Miss America Matinee*, in 1953 and the following year hosting *The Lady of the House*.[38] After these shows went off the air, she became active in many social clubs in Memphis; by 1972, she—a white, Protestant, college-educated "lady"—had the social cachet to be taken seriously in her opposition to the ERA.

AWARE women defined themselves as housewives and mothers who supported the notion that men and women were essentially different; the "equality" that the ERA offered would jeopardize the privilege and protection that women, in their opinion, currently enjoyed. To defend their rights, they presented an anti-ERA skit on the floor of the Tennessee House of Representatives. Upon its completion, Representative W.K. "Tag" Weldon, a Republican from Memphis, asked the General Assembly to rescind the amendment's ratification. The debate over whether or not the state could revoke its support of the amendment raged for two years.

Memphis NOW's response to the rescission measure reveals both the chapter's and the national organization's sentiment toward efforts to rescind and the seemingly laughable notion that the ERA would not succeed. Memphis NOW members waged a letter-writing campaign to state representatives in support of the ERA.[39] When individual representatives debated the rescission measure in their home communities, Memphis NOW participated in these town meetings, but their contributions spoke more often to the perception that the ERA was a foregone conclusion. In one public forum, members carried signs stating "Case by Case is too slow" and "1776 was for Women Too" to articulate support for the amendment.[40] When they spoke, it was with a sense of frustration that they had to reiterate what they thought to be common sense.[41] NOW members wrote letters, organized petition drives, and lobbied—time-honored strategies to support the ERA. These actions ultimately reflected their perception that the ERA just could not be taken away.

This is not to suggest that Memphis NOW lacked creativity in addressing the effort to rescind the ERA. Members, for example, literally gave their blood for the ERA and encouraged others to do so as well in a 1973 chapter-sponsored blood drive to raise money for the NOW Emergency Fund for the ERA.[42] When state representatives from Shelby County met with the public at a Jaycee-sponsored town meeting the following year to discuss the resolution to rescind the state's support for the amendment, NOW members hosted a small demonstration. In an attempt to attract local media attention, one member dressed in a gorilla suit to highlight a parallel between the mentality behind rescission and that of the infamous Scopes "monkey trial." Although some members found this particular protest in poor taste on the grounds that the Scopes trial was a sensitive issue in Tennessee, member Jeri Blake defended the action by pointing out that the ERA, not the gorilla, was the subject of the media coverage received: "Its *sole* purpose was to draw the attention of the media to an *issue*, and in this it succeeded exceptionally well."[43]

Although the Memphis "gorilla girl" succeeded in drawing media attention to the ERA issue, anti-ERA activists were ultimately successful in bringing down the ERA in Memphis. Their creative strategies consisted of skits and performances, including one at the General Assembly of the Shelby County Delegation. At this meeting, designed for legislators to canvass their constituents' sentiments, AWARE members presented an anti-ERA skit that involved a full rendition of "I Enjoy Being a Girl," complete with piano accompaniment. Evoking popular affectations women supposedly enjoyed—a world of lipstick and hairdos, flowers and lace—AWARE women also used Peggy Lee's rendition of this popular Rodgers and Hammerstein song to reinforce their idea of womanhood: "I'm strictly a female female/And I hope that my future will be/In the home of a brave and free male/Who'll enjoy being a guy having a girl like me."[44] Through this performance, AWARE underscored the idea that "equal rights" for women meant that they had to give up being traditional "girls."

Anti-ERA advocates often put pro-ERA activists in a defensive position, and Memphis NOW members were no exception. Carole Hensen, Linda Etheridge, and Lou Farr, the Memphis NOW representatives who attended this meeting, had "no designs of speaking on the 'dead issue,'" but were forced to offer arguments in response to the demonstration. AWARE women argued that, under ERA, women would have to supply one-half of the family income, pay alimony, and subject to themselves to the draft and communal bathrooms. Farr rebutted with "logical, truthful, and fact-oriented arguments," stating that courts could not designate who provides family income; the draft was a moot point since it was not in force; and that everyone uses communal bathrooms in certain situations, including airplanes, but that, as a result of the recent Supreme Court decision *Roe v. Wade* (1973), the 5th Amendment protected an individual's right to privacy. On the issue of alimony, Farr conceded that, in divorce, a woman would have to pay alimony if she was able to do so financially, but argued that, for the first time, marriage would be seen as an equal partnership between individuals under the law. Farr and the others in attendance were concerned by AWARE's "apparent success" but only encouraged their sisters to write "at least one more letter" in support of the ERA instead of offering more pro-ERA demonstrations and a visible presence.[45]

Following the national board's lead, Memphis NOW also pursued the amendment to the exclusion of other laws that would grant women equality in particular realms. These stopgap measures seemed to the Memphis chapter to take focus and energy away from the full recognition of women's equality granted by the ERA, but ultimately AWARE women seemed more willing to work with politicians for piecemeal legislation to alleviate specific problems women faced. For example, Hummel reported that her organization supported two national bills sponsored by Republican Senator Bill Brock that would make it easier for women to obtain credit in their own names. Memphis NOW did not endorse these bills; as a result, they and other NOW chapters around the state and country appeared rigid, unwilling to endorse this or any other legislation in favor of the broader amendment.

In the state legislature, post-ratification debate over the ERA—ultimately a debate over womanhood—culminated in rescission, which finally passed in February 1974. When the measure came to the House of Representatives, legislators debated the issues of the ERA from restrooms to religion in front of "500 sign-waving and baby-toting women" divided on the measure.[46] At the end of the deliberation, the house rescinded its ratification by a vote of 56 to 33. That the state Attorney General's office ruled that the resolution was unconstitutional became a sidebar to this story in Memphis and nationally. At bottom, Memphis NOW could not compete with the idea of protected traditional womanhood couched in Southern fears of federal encroachment on states' rights, and they did not work very hard to do so.

After this setback, Memphis NOW abandoned the ERA until 1977, when Congress extended the amendment's ratification deadline. At this time, national NOW concluded that the ERA could not be ratified by its March 22, 1979 deadline, and support from all levels of the organization emerged to fight for an extension. In July 1978, 100,000 activists marched on Washington to illustrate both continued and renewed support for the ERA. Memphis NOW sent ten members to the march and engaged in yet another letter-writing campaign to their legislators urging their support for House Joint Resolution 638, the measure that would extend the life of the ERA campaign. Their efforts were again countered by anti-ERA forces, many of whom drove from Memphis to Washington to meet with their representatives directly and give them homemade bread, a symbol of woman's appropriate place in the home.[47] Pro-ERA forces were able to win what would become a moot victory, though, with the extended date of ratification set at July 30, 1982.

When Eleanor Smeal, president of the National Organization for Women, rallied the troops with the call that "women should be outraged that there must be a vote to determine whether there will be equality for women," Memphis NOW responded. They raised money—specifically, the newly minted Susan B. Anthony dollars—for the ERA through parties and flea markets and pushed for ratification in neighboring Arkansas and Mississippi. Chapter president Betty Sullivan encouraged Memphis NOW members to join the national ERA Message Brigade, a nationwide computer bank service that notified members when a state legislature was scheduled to vote on the ERA. The brigade reinforced the political tactic of letter writing, something Memphis NOW had practiced since the beginning of this debate.

Memphis NOW also took the message of the ERA to the local airwaves. For example, on June 30, 1981, the day signifying one more year to ratify the ERA, Memphis NOW broadcasted a series of public service announcements on the necessity of the amendment and held a press conference on the importance of the ERA for women nationwide. In addition, members gave the ERA increasing attention on their radio and public access cable television shows, *Women NOW*. Former member Lynda Dolbi recalled one experience on the talk radio show. After speaking for a short time, she fielded questions from the radio audience. One man called into the show, voicing his opinion that supporters of the ERA amounted to "a bunch of lesbians who wanted to go to the bathroom with men." According to Dolbi, this call was the one she was waiting for: "I said, 'you know, what strikes me as odd is that you would even say that. Think about it. Why would a lesbian want to go to the bathroom with a man? Don't you think lesbians would want to go to a women's room?" Answering this man's challenge was "one of life's high points" for Dolbi.[48]

In many instances, however, high points would be the exception to the rule. As time wore on, women were spurred to increased activity as it became more and more apparent that the ERA was losing ground. In a desire to see the ERA become the law of the land, the Memphis affiliate sent delegates when NOW hosted demonstrations in Illinois and Florida, states with the greatest possibility of ratifying the amendment. Outside of the South, they invoked powerful stereotypes of the South. In Chicago, "a busload of Memphis women [promised to] bury the image of the helpless, stay-in-your-own-backyard Southern belle." Carrying a banner proclaiming "The South Will Rise and Ratify," thirty-seven women from Memphis NOW joined a sea of thousands of ERA supporters in a lakefront march urging Illinois legislators to ratify the amendment.[49] Two years later, members of Memphis NOW geared up for the final ERA battle in Tallahassee, Florida. Forty-one members made the overnight trip to the Florida capital for the rally. One member recalled the high emotions and desperate zeal of the participants:

> Memphis NOW was one of the last groups to move out marching the "last mile" to the Capitol so we were able to count and feel the fervor and grass-roots power behind equality for women. Marching ten abreast, each unit with its gold, purple, and white banner in the lead, the chanting line stretched down the valley and up the hill to the Florida Capitol a mile away. No media report or picture yet has captured the intensity of those women, men, and children.[50]

At the height of passion for the ERA, Memphis NOW carried its struggle to the bitter end, but no amount of commitment could save the amendment. Just months before the deadline, Florida, like Illinois, failed to ratify the ERA. Despite the letter-writing and public demonstrations of NOW women at every level, the ERA died on June 30, 1982.

Although it replicates much of the literature on the fight for the ERA, Memphis NOW's story provides nuances and different voices to the national story. These subtleties illustrate how the Memphis chapter followed the national lead, utilizing the federated structure to the best of its abilities. But the Memphis chapter also forged its own way with creative protests and demonstrations to fight the statewide rescission efforts. At bottom, its members were no match for the AWARE woman, but it is less, in some ways, about the actors involved. At stake, on both sides of the issue, were sex and gender roles; debates throughout the country centered on the new roles women would have and how they would affect men.[51] In the South, and beyond the walls of Congress in Washington, DC, the trope of Southern womanhood shaped the debates about the ERA. Southern women such as Walker Hummel and her AWARE comrades fought alongside one another and with anti-ERA women around the country to retain their status as different from and not "equal" to men. That it was a position only white women could possibly enjoy, irrespective of wealth, did not factor into their verbal presentations and actions; it did not have to be addressed because the Southern womanhood they invoked had always been reserved for white women. Because AWARE women shaped the debate locally, Memphis NOW members not only had to defend the amendment but they also had to deny categorically associations with their Southern heritage. When Memphis NOW did summon images of the South, it was to "bury" them in favor of a region, and nation, that supported equal rights. When faced with AWARE's appeals, many politicians and citizens in Memphis were uncomfortable with the idea of relinquishing the Southern womanhood that had "protected" them. This southern identity, then, not only intersected with the struggle over the ERA but also provided a framework for this debate.

Although NOW nationally sought to elect feminist leaders to office, the Memphis chapter devoted relatively little time to elections and the individuals seeking political office. In fact, only once during the 1970s—March 1979—did the chapter host a meeting program that addressed "local politics and women" that featured local politicians currently in or seeking office.[52] The chapter newsletter listed local politicians usually in the context of the ERA—to acknowledge early support for the ERA, to discourage rescission, and to express disdain for the 1975 rescission resolution. Memphis NOW's inattention to formal politics, especially relative to the national board, may be a result of the fact that the NOW chapter shared overlapping membership with the Memphis Women's Political Caucus (MWPC), which formed a short-lived chapter in August 1972.[53] With MWPC keeping members abreast of local political primaries and general elections, the NOW chapter was free to focus on issues as they related not to voting day but rather to women's daily lives.

Feminism among the People

Debate over formal political issues—the ERA is the most salient example in Memphis—took shape in the context of Southern identity. But local women's concerns and needs did, as well. Such volatile issues as rape, wife abuse, and pornography entered the public discourse as a result of feminists' insistence that "the personal is political"; in the South, they stayed there because the rhetoric of "protection" offered them necessary leverage to create change on the ground.[54]

Most scholars write about the origins of rape crisis centers and domestic violence protection shelters as the projects of radical feminists, many of them self-defined.[55] In Memphis, however, it was women who did not outwardly define themselves as "radical" who brought these issues to the fore of local politics. This suggests that "radical" and "liberal" are context-specific descriptions of feminism, unique to the major urban centers in which they emerged and less appropriate in a Southern regional context. Rather than categorize Memphis NOW as "radical" or "liberal," I argue that NOW locally took seriously the opportunity to be everything to everyone who joined. Such an organization is certainly what chapter conveners and early members wanted, and they spent little time debating modifiers; they were "feminists."

By the mid-1970s, such personal issues were politicized around the country, and Memphis NOW followed suit. However, women in the city also publicized their individual experiences, bringing necessary local attention to crises that were rarely discussed prior to Memphis NOW's existence. After the *Roe v. Wade* decision in 1973, NOW feminists in Memphis rarely discussed abortion and reproductive rights. In January 1973, the chapter raised money for a woman who wanted to have an abortion but could not afford one. When the woman changed her mind about the abortion, the chapter donated the money to their ERA fundraising campaign.[56] Beyond this example, information and actions related to reproductive rights appear very sporadically in the chapter newsletters, suggesting that any pro-choice activism in which chapter members engaged spread by word of mouth. It may well be that they thought of the chapter newsletter as a public document; one did not have to be a member of Memphis NOW to receive it. As a result, newsletter editors may have elected to avoid "advertising" where they escorted women seeking abortions into clinics or to draw unwanted attention to their pro-choice activities as NOW members. The documentary evidence does not support a firm interpretation of the chapter's pro-choice activism, but NOW members throughout the 1970s volunteered their time as clinic escorts and many were also members of various pro-choice coalitions in the city.[57]

The chapter, however, discussed rape and wife abuse openly in the newsletter and any public venue they could secure. They also generated facilities for women through the assistance of an umbrella structure of women's organizations, the Women's Resource Center (WRC).[58] Founded in 1974 by Memphis NOW, the local YWCA, and city chapters of Planned Parenthood, Girls Club, Church

Women United, Federally Employed Women, and the League of Women Voters, the WRC dedicated itself to "serv[ing] the varied needs of women in the Greater Memphis Metropolitan area not currently met by existing social service agencies and/or local, State, and Federal Government programs."[59]

Over its eight-year existence, basic funding came from its membership organizations, but other sources of revenue included federal Comprehensive Education and Training Administration (CETA) program funds and a grant from the United Methodist Church. Throughout its tenure in the Bluff City, WRC offered a laundry list of community services, including assertiveness training, financial educational programs, and other seminars "contributing to a new perspective for women of our area" as well as support groups for women experiencing the emotional trauma of divorce.[60] It also provided a speaker's bureau, a job bank and training program for women seeking employment outside the home, legal counsel, a library of books on women's history and feminist issues, and programs "designed to focus attention on the changing needs and interests of women as they become more visible and vocal."[61] Because the WRC was working within the necessary political channels to secure funds for facilities for raped and abused women, NOW women could adopt a more radical approach and actually utilize both liberal feminist and radical feminist tactics. Although members never stated it explicitly in their feminist statements, literature, or other extant sources, they were also able to manipulate the well-documented and racialized notions of womanhood and protection of women's bodies.

Although NOW passed national resolutions in favor of stronger rape legislation and protection for women's bodies, the issue of rape took on a personal tone as women confronted their city's reputation as "the rape capital of the nation." In 1973 alone, 534 rapes were reported with victims ranging from 18 months to 84 years. Since contemporary FBI statistics relied upon self-reporting and asserted that only about 10 percent of rapes were actually reported, the numbers were likely closer to 5,000.[62]

Frustrated, angry, and determined to confront women's sense of helplessness in the face of such a crime, Memphis NOW sought to address women's concerns about rape. NOW member Pam Hazen coordinated People Against Rape to solicit the larger community's aid in exploding myths about rape and pursuing legislation. In her speeches, Hazen decried Memphis's "badge of infamy" and chastised judges and prosecutors for "totally and unethically ignor[ing] the victim," contending that women were doubly victimized by the perpetrator and the justice system.[63]

By the end of 1974, the crisis seemed to be escalating: Memphis women reported 607 rapes and attempted rapes. What was most shocking, though, was that only 14 percent of the crimes ended in an indictment, and only 19 percent of those resulted in a conviction. Not content simply to work within local institutions, NOW women raised the stakes by taking their cause of protection and safety for women to the streets. Commemorating the fifty-fifth anniversary of women's suffrage, approximately thirty-five NOW members protested rape in their city with a "Take Back the Night" type of demonstration in which local activists in NOW marched around the thirteen-block perimeter of Overton Park in midtown Memphis. Organizer Gail Adkins stated that she chose this location "because of a recent gang rape in an adjacent parking lot and because one of the bars features topless dancers," asserting the radical feminist connection between rape and the commodification of women. Chanting "Stop rape now" and carrying placards bearing such slogans as "Rape Laws are Made for Rapists" and "Dismember Rapists," these feminists heightened the city's awareness about rape and protested the notion that, according to participant and NOW officer Marion Keisker, "women are only as safe as civilized man allows."[64] This action exemplified their commitment to radical feminist tactics and the philosophy that linked rape to the commodification of women.

Their radical efforts raised political awareness about rape and propelled the Memphis Police Department to form a Comprehensive Rape Crisis Program and a Sex Crimes Squad. They hired more women to work as counselors, extended their hours into the nighttime, and began using unmarked cars to go to victims' homes in an attempt to protect privacy and anonymity. Hospitals also worked with the police by providing speedier care for rape victims, examining women in private hospital rooms instead of more public emergency rooms, and processing and upgrading physical tests to obtain evidence for the prosecution of criminals.[65] At the same time, Memphis NOW established the city's first rape crisis hotline, staffed with volunteers and managed by the WRC. Mayor Wyeth Chandler appointed chapter president Julia Howell to serve as the director of the city's first Rape Crisis Program. Under Howell's direction, the program shifted from a CETA-funded operation to a component of the city government on July 1, 1978, ensuring the longevity of public support for the program. Because the chapter both used radical tactics and took advantage of institutional structures in place, what began as Memphis NOW's grassroots response to a local problem had become "an integral part of the city government" in the space of five years.[66]

Since violence against women was not limited to rape and sexual assault, Memphis NOW also addressed the problem of wife abuse. While the national organization acknowledged wife abuse as a violent act against women, the impetus for the formation of the local task force did not come from a national directive. Rather, chapter member Angie Russo initiated the effort. In August 1975, she relayed to her fellow chapter members a story of a friend who told her about the latest in what had become a series of fights she had with her husband, which, in this instance, resulted in a broken arm, concussion, and black eyes. Devastated and angry that this woman felt she had to stay with her husband out of fear because she had nowhere to go, Russo convinced the chapter to take action against wife abuse and established a public forum to confront the concerns of local women involved in abusive relationships with husbands and boyfriends.[67]

Through the new task force, Russo generated a series of lectures and panels to raise community awareness about wife abuse. Disgusted by the fact that local law enforcement coded wife abuse as regular assault rather than a separate crime, Memphis NOW recognized that women could not turn to the police for help.

Operating outside of this restrictive situation, the chapter opened the city's first wife abuse hotline in September of 1976. The chapter financed the line and volunteers staffed it for three hours daily.[68] In addition, members from Memphis NOW and WRC-sponsored support groups converged to provide immediate counseling and helped abused women find therapy and temporary shelters.[69]

As part of their September meeting, Memphis NOW held an open panel discussion for the larger community entitled "Wife Beating: The Crime That Goes Unpunished." Member Edie Sewell told the story of Marie G. Hamlin, shot to death by her husband after years of abuse. Police knew that Millard Hamlin made threats against his wife twice before that month, but they failed to follow up. Sewell then cited FBI statistics to illuminate the seriousness of the crime: in 1974 alone, 1,285 wives were murdered by their husbands. Other abuse victims on the panel admitted to losing confidence in themselves, feeling "emotionally shattered" to the point that "the damage that was done … is irreparable."[70] Before long, like self-identified radical feminists in other cities, the chapter decided that a hotline was not enough and set out to design a shelter for abused and battered wives that would give women relief from dangerous situations and safeguard women during the long legal process.

Under the auspices of the WRC, Memphis NOW organized a Wife Abuse Crisis Service in June 1977. Under Russo's direction, the service opened a temporary shelter in August 1979, the first step en route to a more permanent facility.[71] The shelter offered women safety as well as a separate space to think and discuss options. Moreover, the shelter gave women a community of support and care, things evidently missing from their home life. After 1982, the YWCA adopted the Wife Abuse Crisis Center and funded additional and more permanent shelter space. To celebrate the opening of this new and more secure shelter that was seven years in the making, Memphis NOW hosted "An Evening of Feminist Theater" by bringing the Rhode Island Feminist Theater (RIFT) to town. RIFT presented *Internal Injury*, an original play about an abused wife. Integrating feminist theater with alternative, feminist institutions to help women, Memphis NOW demonstrated that they were not an exclusively liberal organization.

Memphis feminists recognized that abused women often lacked financial resources to enable them to leave, so NOW and WRC established the "Women's Crisis Loan Service of Shelby County" in June 1978. The loan program began with a $2,000 contribution from WRC-affiliated organizations, but through donations it gradually accrued funds to empower eligible women to leave abusive situations and start a new life. So great was the need that the fund quickly suffered serious depletions.[72] Memphis NOW raised another $2,000 at a fundraiser for the loan service, but funds still fell short.[73] It is ironic that so many women utilized this service that the WRC was forced to shut down the loan auxiliary the next year. Still, the program illustrates the understanding that a woman's disadvantaged economic situation perpetuated abuse; economic uplift offered a route to freedom from it.[74]

This service demonstrated how NOW and the umbrella group in Memphis generated alternative institutions at the grassroots level to alleviate women's suffering. Although they could not sustain the loan service, the chapter continued its educational activities, joining with other women's groups to extend awareness of domestic violence to the greater community. In November 1978, NOW, along with several other local organizations such as the Democratic Women of Shelby County, WRC, and the National Conference of Christians and Jews, hosted a workshop on "The Problem of Wife Abuse." This two-and-one-half-hour assembly illustrated that spouse abuse was not just a domestic problem but rather one of the family and the community. It also spotlighted the shelter for battered women, soliciting financial support and underscoring its importance for Memphis. NOW members also worked to change the current legal system that favored the abuser by placing the entire burden of physical proof on the often reluctant victim without attention to the husband's prior arrest record, previous calls to the police for other instances of wife abuse, or the woman's testimony.[75]

At a public hearing of the Judiciary Committee of the Tennessee legislature, Memphis Legal Services attorneys and chapter members Sherry Myers and Bonnie Ragland discussed the dismal situation of legal recourse for abused women. Family violence in the state was considered a misdemeanor; accordingly, police were unable to make an arrest until the victim produced a sworn warrant for the arrest of the abuser. By defining abuse in these narrow terms, most victims were unable to process immediate complaints because the department would only issue warrants on weekdays from 9:00 a.m. to 5:00 p.m. Given that the majority of domestic violence episodes occurred at night or on weekends, most women were forced to wait hours or days to seek any legal recourse, leaving plenty of time for their husbands to apologize or to continue to beat them. Furthermore, police still often refused to intervene because they regarded domestic violence as a "family matter." Myers and Ragland insisted that male judges and police officers often minimized wife abuse and humiliated victims through mockery or scorn after they testified. The Tennessee legislature passed a bill in January 1979 that would alleviate this situation by allowing an arrest without a warrant and by not requiring women to file a formal petition. Nine months after the law went into effect, Myers and Ragland urged the legislature to encourage enforcement of the new laws.[76]

Memphis NOW's efforts to combat rape and wife abuse evince its commitment to employ whatever tactics were necessary to effect change. The same was true in the struggle against pornography. When the most egregious example of the genre, *Snuff*, premiered in Memphis in 1976, lurid advertisements boasted that it was "the bloodiest thing that ever happened in front of a camera!! The film that could only be made in South America—where life is CHEAP!" The finale of this film was a woman's murder. Members of Memphis NOW attended the movie on its opening night. The next day, several members walked through the rain in front of Towne Cinema II, the film's host, with picket signs, protesting "violence against women [and] a film that advocates killing women for entertainment."[77] The chapter picketed the theater and circulated a flyer calling for an end to sexual violence in the media: "Violence for sexual pleasure is portrayed in crime and magazines, TV, police shows, [and] slick publications such as *Playboy* and *Penthouse*. 'Snuff' films are the missing link between media violence against women and actual violence that women experience daily." NOW members also expressed outrage at the racist attitudes of "a society which says the lives of non-white people, particularly women, are less valuable and more available for exploitation than European and American women."[78]

The ensuing controversy over pornography and the degradation of women prodded Towne Cinema II owner George Miller to defend the movie as being "no worse than *Texas Chainsaw Massacre* or a lot of other violent films." What seemed to anger him the most was white feminists demonstrating at his theater, which historically catered to an African American audience: "People see these white women in front of my theater and they just know they don't want to be in the middle of it. I have been harassed from the beginning and now I got white folks picketing me."[79] Chapter president Jackie Cash denied that the picketing was racially motivated against him in particular, insisting that the inherent and violent racism and sexism of the movie he chose to show demanded their actions. Although no member ever explicitly stated so, it is likely that the ability to take advantage of racist notions of protections Southern (white) womanhood figured into their tactics and the ensuing fear that the movie owner faced if he "threatened" white women. Memphis NOW was the only organization that protested this movie; any objection among African American women was not recorded in any of the local newspapers. The chapter's efforts were successful: within days, Towne Cinema pulled the film.[80]

Such activism on issues of rape, wife abuse, and pornography illustrates the impossibilities of understanding Memphis NOW as either liberal or radical; instead, it was both. They worked both within the system and beyond it to make significant change in women's lives. Their seemingly radical efforts—creating an umbrella structure through which feminist groups in town could help women themselves rather than forcing women into the current and inadequate welfare and human services systems, taking back the night, speaking out publicly about rape and wife abuse, zap actions at the Towne Cinema II—were never defined as such, nor as "liberal"; they were survival strategies. They understood violence as a pillar of patriarchy and sought to create alternative institutions to help women and to live out a feminist commitment to women's safety. At the same time, they also provided social services and pushed existing civic institutions and local government to accommodate feminist demands for protection under the law. Memphis NOW members responded to local needs through whatever means necessary. By turning their rape crisis activism into an institutionalized component of city government and changing laws to protect women from husbands who physically abused them, they permanently altered local structures—government, hospitals, and aid agencies—and provided a safer city in which women could live.

Dividing the Chapter

The standard national picture of lesbians in the women's movement is one of separate activism, typically associated with radical feminism. Moreover, lesbians supposedly either left or avoided NOW in the aftermath of Betty Friedan's infamous stand against the "lavender menace."[81] When, in 1971, NOW adopted a national resolution recognizing lesbians' rights as women's rights, the lesbian issue was theoretically resolved. However, it was not, and exploring the struggle over inclusivity in NOW chapters offers a different dimension by which to understand interpersonal politics in the Memphis chapter of NOW. Without lesbians and straight women in the chapter, they had to address their own feelings about lesbianism face-to-face.[82] Fear that lesbians would take over the chapter and damage the public image and political reputation of NOW reverberated through Memphis NOW, especially in the late 1970s and early 1980s. Rather than abandon the organization in light of these tensions, however, lesbians remained loyal to Memphis NOW. It may be that lesbians had no other feminist choices; NOW was the only explicitly feminist organization in town and some lesbians clearly did not want to separate their lesbian identities from their feminist ones. As Daneel Buring has suggested, there would not be much room for lesbians' particular concerns in a formal political setting; thus a lesbian feminist organization that would have had many members and political clout in San Francisco or New York City would not have found a comfortable home in Memphis.[83] Lesbian and heterosexual women had little choice: work together in NOW or surrender local feminist activism. It was not until 1982 that another option emerged.

Almost four years into Memphis NOW's history, new member and lesbian Johnette Shane penned a letter to the newsletter editor complaining that the previous NOW meeting made her feel "alienated and put down." She asserted that "it is important for us to realize that the whole of women is a diverse group and we must allow everyone to have her place. There are many areas of need and interest." Furthermore, limiting chapter activities to issues of rape or employment discrimination made her feel as if her concerns were incompatible with NOW's goals.[84] President Carole Hensen responded with an expression of understanding and concern: "I regret your alienation at the May meeting—alienation happens too much on the outside—we don't need it at NOW meetings." While time, commitment, and money forced the chapter to narrow its scope to "the greatest good for the greatest number," Hensen explained, "this does NOT mean that any endeavor, interest, or need will ever be deliberately discouraged." Moreover, she wrote, "this is your organization—it exists to do what you or any other member wants it to do."[85] Encouraged by this overture, Shane, Mary Jo Cowart, and other members of the group followed the national example and created a "Sexuality and Lesbianism" task force, publicly merging the identities of "lesbian" and "feminist" in Memphis and shaping NOW to fit their needs. They planned an inclusive environment in which all women could examine their "own sexuality in a supportive, non-threatening atmosphere" and provide consciousness raising as well as address the legal and political issues surrounding same-sex sexuality.

This task force recognized the need to have a space for women outside of the mainstream of the organization, and response to their efforts was "heartening" because the group attracted "an encouraging number" of new members.[86] Between thirty and sixty women attended its monthly consciousness-raising group on sexuality and lesbianism. One participant recalled that, although lesbians were in the majority to begin with, "the percentage [of lesbians] increases even as the number of women in CR stays constant."[87] This situation made straight women increasingly uncomfortable, especially considering what some viewed as the implication that the only true feminist was a lesbian. Still, lesbians in Memphis NOW reported feeling a "sense of one-ness rather than the division of 'us' and 'they'" and felt welcome in the chapter during the 1970s.[88]

The task force was also a social and cultural liaison between NOW and the local gay and lesbian community.[89] In addition to sponsoring gay picnics and women's dances at Memphis State during gay pride weeks, the task force opened Memphis's first Gay Switchboard, a telephone line that served as a crisis intervention line and also offered information about lesbian and gay community activities, in 1976.[90] Through fundraisers and parties, Memphis NOW sponsored the switchboard until 1979. With the departure of key members, management of the Gay Switchboard was turned over to the Memphis Gay Coalition.[91] By the end of the decade, Memphis NOW secured its public identity, at least in part, as a vital part of the lesbian and gay community.

But it was the formation and popularity of a softball team, with its suggestion of informal lesbian solidarity, that caused tensions over sexuality to rise.[92] As Daneel Buring has discussed in her book on gay and lesbian community in Memphis, softball was an important feature of community development among Memphis lesbians in the 1970s and 1980s. In the mid-1970s, the NOW chapter, as well as the women's bookstore Meristem and the delicatessen Bread and Roses, sponsored softball teams that played in city leagues.[93] A former chapter president credited the softball team with "growing the chapter for several years," and indeed many women, lesbian and straight, joined the softball team and ultimately NOW.[94] While NOW members, straight and lesbian, were involved in a variety of political issues—the ERA, anti-rape activism, awareness about violence against women, abortion rights, and more—one team member noted that the team "provided an outlet, other than going to meetings or doing political acts, for us to meet and become friends and create a very strong network."[95]

Members stood together when external homophobia pressured the organization. From 1974 to 1976, NOW held its meetings at the First Presbyterian Church in downtown Memphis. When, in July 1976, church leaders told NOW officers that the Sexuality and Lesbianism task force could no longer hold its meetings at the church, members decided to stop using the church for all NOW activities.[96] Yet the softball team became a source of contention internally, a symbol of the growing tension surrounding the reconciliation of lesbianism and feminism. In late 1981—a full ten years after the national organization formally acknowledged lesbians' issues as feminists' issues—some members called a special meeting to discuss problems openly. Instead, the assembly created "a discernable split ... within the chapter between lesbian and straight members."[97] One member recalled that this rather benign meeting took on a hostile tone when one woman stood up and announced that "she could not stand NOW being represented by a bunch of dykes."[98]

At that point, conversation gave way to conflict. Whereas lesbians wanted to talk about issues they faced in a forum where they felt safe to do so, some straight women thought the overt emphasis on same-sex sexual identity sidetracked their concerns about family, women's safety, and the ERA. They also decried the image of NOW as a lesbian organization. While the softball games were fun and promoted a sense of camaraderie, they were also an avenue for local lesbians to meet and interact. One member recalled that, in her opinion, "softball was the excuse for people who were getting uncomfortable with the fact that those of us who were gay were starting not to be so quiet about it."[99]

Many straight women left Memphis NOW and founded their own organization, a second incarnation of the Memphis Women's Political Caucus, where members focused solely on such formal political actions as elections and public forums. One former member of Memphis NOW and a founding member of the Memphis Women's Political Caucus felt that "NOW never recognized their limitations, trying to be everything to everyone. They were not politically savvy and could not help progressive women or men run for office because they did not know what to do. And I did; so did others."[100] Some women sought this sort of political activity, and the split in the NOW chapter prompted such activists to create their own political network.

That Memphis NOW split apart in 1982 over the "softball" issue gives more evidence to support the idea that the 1971 resolution ultimately resolved very little. But it also offers an opportunity to step back and see what the "softball" issue was really all about. Without a doubt, some women in this NOW chapter were homophobic; others likely felt that the number of lesbians in the chapter had reached the tipping point by 1982. NOW was a "lesbian organization," a label they resisted. If they wanted to retain political voice in the city and continue to effect political change, they had to distance themselves from NOW. Some members in this chapter had been traveling to ratification states to support the ERA. They spent their time, money, and physical energy to work for an amendment that ultimately failed, leaving many women feeling disenchanted and dismayed. In the face of defeat, some women likely turned their disappointment and anger inward, and members conflated the ERA's failure with fears of public association of feminism and lesbianism. Others undoubtedly pursued more formal political actions. As hopes for the amendment diminished, they realized how vital the formal political process was—they sought to elect feminist women and men to office and pursued more concrete political gains. The "lavender menace" that may have been shameful in 1970 was all too real in 1982. When tied to the defeat of the ERA, it becomes impossible to disentangle cause and effect, but it is clear that some NOW members became estranged sisters, abandoning NOW for the MWPC.

Understanding Memphis NOW

As the only explicitly feminist, membership-based organization in the city during the heyday of second-wave feminism, Memphis NOW was everything to everyone, or at least tried to be. It embraced multiple organizational structures, tactics, and issues. From the outset, chapter members opposed a rigid, hierarchical structure; throughout its history, they took the lead in creating an organization to fit their needs or to respond to the greater community. In various ways, they both claimed and confronted images of Southern womanhood.

Rather than pigeonhole this organization, it may be more to the point to understand them on their own terms. At bottom, it matters less if they fall under the category of "liberal" or "radical"; on this continuum, they fall somewhere in between. Memphis NOW created an oppositional community, offering both physical space to challenge normative cultural and political practices and a collective identity that engendered a "sense of we" in direct opposition to those who sought to maintain the status quo.[101] In doing so, they embraced, rejected, and contested local and regional identity.

What emerges from this historical analysis is a group of dedicated feminists who changed the community in which they lived; as one member put it, "I came to NOW to bitch and stayed to join the world."[102] But this analysis also reveals the ways in which location shaped their activism. In the ten-year battle for the ERA, Memphis NOW members rejected "Southern womanhood" and the protections afforded to women based on this idea. Although they rarely publicly called attention to the racism inherent in this trope, members eschewed this model, preferring instead to create a new notion of womanhood that would offer freedom from the pedestal and guarantee civil protection. Indeed, the only time NOW members embraced their Southernness was when they challenged the South to "rise and ratify" the amendment. This same group of activists fell back on the notion of protecting women's bodies, relying (however silently) on local and regional fears of rape and desires to protect women from harm. NOW members built their feminist activism around local political and social conditions—rape and violence against women were not contested in part because these concerns allowed Southerners to protect, rescue, and save women, in spite of the fact that it also meant addressing feminist issues. Even though it cannot possibly stand for all southern feminism or feminism in the U.S. South, this NOW chapter was most explicitly in conflict with its location and regional identity as Southern. San Francisco NOW did not identify in the same ways as "Western" nor did Columbus NOW as "Midwestern," although each chapter's activism reflects the local context in which the chapter and feminism emerged. The context in which feminist activism took place in Memphis, then, was both shaped by and shaped regional identity, suggesting that location plays a more significant role in understanding feminism in the South than fixed, dichotomous models of defining feminism.

4

FEMINIST THEORIZING, FEMINIST ACTIVISMS IN COLUMBUS

In April 2009, President Barack Obama designated the month of April as sexual assault awareness month; the National Sexual Violence Resource Center directed a month-long campaign (as well as year-long programming around violence awareness and prevention) to draw attention to the realities of rape, assault, and other forms of sexual violence. But in Columbus, Ohio, a group of feminists marked the occasion by graffiti-tagging the words "someone was raped here" on sidewalks around Ohio State University. According to Feminist Avengers, a group that denied responsibility for the action (which was credited to a secretive group of feminists), "People have long used physical markers to remember tragedies past, from crosses and flowers at the intersection of a tragic car crash, to memorials at sites of disasters and violent crimes."[1] Spray-painting sidewalks where women reported being raped, the group asserted, allowed for a radical and public response to the realities of rape and sexual violence in Columbus and Franklin County. At 676 reported rapes in 2006 alone, "rape increased in Columbus by more than 12 percent" and "Franklin County led the state in the number of forcible rapes" that year.[2] A local independent newspaper, the *Other Paper*, noted, "radical feminism is back in Columbus."

Bringing rape to the forefront of feminist discussion and political debate is a legacy of radical feminists, which in Columbus has been traced historically in Nancy Whittier's *Feminist Generations*. But of particular interest here is the legacy of radical feminist activism and the nuances between the liberal/radical divide in the Columbus chapter of NOW. The "someone was raped here" tagging on campus seems new, and is identified as a radical act, but in Columbus, NOW feminists in the 1970s undertook such dramatic and public demonstrations, sometimes known as "zap" actions, to draw attention to the realities of rape in local women's lives.

On the morning of February 4, 1979, five women from the Columbus chapter of NOW (Columbus NOW) met one another at 5:30 a.m. at the "Great Wall of Gahanna," a mile-long noise barrier on the east side of Interstate 270. Armed with paintbrushes and buckets of paint—and an intense anger over the continual rapes of women in the city—these five women painted anti-rape slogans, including "Dismember Rapists," and pro-feminist slogans on the wall. The local newspaper published a story about the incident only when the women were officially fined for their actions, and the story ultimately diminished the women's action as silly "fun." "The women wanted to have a good time. They planned the painting a week beforehand, over dinner," the story reported. And Mary Mosley, chapter president, was quoted as saying: "When people ask me 'why did you paint the wall?' [I tell them] because it was there. And because it was fun."[3]

The women were arrested, charged and found guilty of disorderly conduct, and fined $250 each; Betty Powell, who was charged in Gahanna Mayor's Court, was also given a three-day suspended sentence.[4] The incident became "cause célèbre" among Columbus NOW members and an example of how the local NOW chapter was, in some ways, as radical as the Women's Action Collective (WAC), a local radical feminist organization in the city.[5] For participants, the action was not radical simply because they defaced property with anti-rape slogans. In the words of one local NOW member and one of the "Gahanna Five," "The rapes were not being addressed. No one took them seriously. And here all of these women were being raped, beaten, and hurt."[6] Feminists had been working to confront the crime of rape in the city. In 1973, NOW chapter members joined some members of WAC and other interested individuals to form Women Against Rape (WAR) and, through this group, pursued a variety of strategies both within and beyond the formal system for women who had been raped.[7] Gretchen Dygert, a WAC member, reported that WAR had a "rape squad" that would follow men who were charged with rape, documenting and publicizing their actions, and "basically harass this guy, letting him know that feminists were watching him because the system wouldn't."[8] And it certainly seemed to be the case: in 1971, the Federal Bureau of Investigation (FBI) reported that the rate (per 100,000 population) of rape in Columbus was 35.3; in the decade from 1970 to 1980, the number of reported forcible rapes in the state went up, from 1,700 to 3,696.[9] With reports of rape on the rise across the state, and contemporary analysis that only about 10 percent of rapes were reported, feminists in Columbus pursued extra-legal means to confront the issue.

Rather than continue the watches that WAC started or continue to work within the system, the "Gahanna Five" took up the issue through graffiti. "The issue was public signage. We spent a great deal of time thinking this through. We wanted public notice. Men wrote on bathroom walls that Susie was a good lay. We wanted men to know that we were not going to take it any more. The issue was about making a public display, public signage. So we made our own public signs." Moreover, "it was completely theory driven, our perspective on rape and our decision to take this action."[10] Lanna Harris suggested that the action was a statement "for a lot of women. One of the reasons this is threatening is we are bringing home to Columbus that the [feminist] revolution has begun. If middle-class women are taking to the streets in Columbus, it will be happening all over the country in the near future."[11]

That the middle-class white women who made up the "Gahanna Five" took up the issue of rape in a very public, outside-of-the-system sort of way is illustrative of how NOW women in Columbus embraced radical feminism through action and theory. Their action seems aberrant in the historical narrative of second-wave feminism because NOW has not been affiliated or identified with this sort of action (although national NOW never formally condoned it, either). Moreover, by 1979, national NOW's main focus was the Equal Rights Amendment (ERA) and the extension campaign. But in Columbus, it makes perfect sense. For some feminists—radical, radicalized, or otherwise—Columbus NOW was the place to undertake radical political strategies and express radical political perspectives.

In this chapter, I begin with the development of activism in general and feminism in particular in Columbus, looking briefly at the rise of feminism in the city. I then turn to the NOW chapter, highlighting its members' activism and analyzing their theoretical analyses of women's lives. According to sociologist Nancy Whittier, the radical feminist collective WAC emerged as the strongest local second-wave feminist force in Columbus. WAC formed in early 1971, bringing together women's liberation activists from Ohio State University and other, mostly younger, radical activists in the city. The only other organized feminist group was the Ohio Commission on the Status of Women (OCSW), a group of older, moderate women who emerged in response to the governor's resistance to creating a formal commission on the status of women in Ohio.[12] NOW in Columbus fell between these two groups. It shared membership with OCSW and with WAC, but it maintained a separate identity. The Columbus chapter was not the only game in town (as Memphis NOW was), nor was it a local political force, like its San Francisco counterpart. However, it was the only NOW chapter of the three that openly embraced radical feminist theory and practice and outwardly eschewed a focus on national issues, such as the ERA, for the bread-and-butter concerns of local women. Thinking about this particular group of feminists invites a consideration of what happens when a NOW chapter exists beyond a pre-existing liberal/radical divide within a vibrant feminist community.

From Abeyance to Activism: Feminism in Columbus

Although feminist women's liberation has been associated with radical politics of the era, most feminist activism grew up in a more complicated cultural and political milieu. Indeed, Columbus boasted its own history of women's and feminist activism. Over the course of the twentieth century, women in Ohio maintained a strong commitment to social movement activism, including but not limited to feminist activism. Ohio women worked in the General Assembly to secure the right for married women to control their own property, to vote in local school board elections, and to sue or be sued in city and state courts.[13] In 1920, the year that women secured the right to vote, the Ohio chapter of the National American Woman Suffrage Association officially became the Ohio League of Women Voters, following the national trend. Feminist activism moved into an era of "abeyance" in which the women's movement did not cease altogether but instead was "elite-sustained."[14] Women's activism in Columbus subsided, but did not go away completely.

In the years between suffrage and World War II, many Columbus women faced a poor economic situation. By 1920, 18 percent of the city's workforce was female, mostly working in homes, factories, and offices.[15] Although more and more women had migrated to the city, their incomes did not afford them adequate money to live independently. In Columbus, as in cities across the nation, the local YWCA offered a solution, providing day nurseries for children, educational and recreational opportunities for women, and a place to live.[16] By 1920, the YWCA operated a separate local branch, the Blue Triangle, and a separate residence hall for African American women. Within the next ten years, the YWCA became an advocate for women laborers, seeking to overhaul state labor laws, working to keep married teachers on the job, and establishing formal job training programs.[17] The Y also led the way in terms of ending segregation in Columbus: it integrated its board of directors in the 1930s and, by 1953, it integrated its Downtown swimming pool. In the early 1960s, it closed its segregated branches, joining other civil rights groups in pursuit of racial equality and becoming a local model for integration and interracial advocacy.[18]

While the YWCA was a vanguard advocate for women in the city during the "doldrums," other women's organizations also grew up at this time and maintained a women's, if not explicitly feminist, presence in debating contemporary issues. For example, Zonta International, which had been formed in Buffalo, New York, in 1919, formed a chapter in Columbus in 1929. According to Harriet Bracken, a former Zonta member, the organization provided a women's network within the city, offering "contacts with other women in business, professional women. We were able to talk to each other. It enlarged our perspective. We didn't know the word then, but we were networking."[19] More than networking, however, Zonta members also engaged one another and other women's organizations on such issues as the status of women in the workplace, world peace, and the atomic bomb.[20]

Bringing these and other women's groups together in Columbus was the Ohio Federation of Women's Clubs. An important coalition and evidence of the entrenched network of women in the city, the Federation addressed such local issues as public libraries, juvenile courts, and fair labor legislation.[21] Members also engaged in philanthropy and public works programs tied to the Columbus Symphony, Children's Hospital, and other charities. The Federation thrived into the 1960s, but the rise of various identity-based social movements changed the organization—"fewer meetings. Shorter, more casual conversations. More than anything, fewer members."[22] By the early 1970s, the second wave of the women's movement engulfed feminists in Columbus. Joining women across the country, Columbus women moved from civil rights, anti-war, and women's activism into self-professed and self-identified feminism.

One group that emerged was the "self-appointed and self-anointed" Ohio Commission on the Status of Women.[23] This group of women from Ohio branches of national religious, civil, and service organizations came together in 1964 to create a governor's commission to study the status of women, following the national lead of the President's Commission on the Status of Women.[24] Republican governor James Rhodes refused to form such a commission, suggesting that his philosophy of "limited government did not jibe with the federal activism of Democratic presidents Kennedy and Lyndon B. Johnson."[25] In response to the governor's obstinacy, Columbus women from the League of Women Voters, AAUW, National Council of Jewish Women, YWCA, BPW, and the Ohio Federation of Women's Organizations came together as the Ohio Status of Women Commission, Inc. to "maintain pressure on state government to formulate policies on women's issues," particularly economic issues.[26] In 1971, they turned their attention to the passage of the ERA in Ohio. By this time, the NOW chapter had formed, but OCSW members reportedly felt that the NOW chapter was too radical. For example, NOW and the "lib movement" commemorated the fiftieth anniversary of woman suffrage by staging a "theatrical protest of the midi skirt" followed by a "teach-in on the status of women;" OCSW marked the same date with a fashion and style show featuring the popular midi and miniskirts and advocated "political solutions to ending discriminatory practices against women as alternatives to NOW's 'dramatic' tactics."[27]

If NOW was too "dramatic" for some, it was far too liberal, even conservative, for others. The "most notable women's group" of the 1970s was the Women's Action Collective (WAC), which was a coalition effort of women's liberation and radical feminists in Columbus.[28] In this decade, WAC represented the core of feminist activism in the city of Columbus. Formed in late 1970, WAC grew out of women's liberation groups at Ohio State University, but quickly involved many women from the city. Its members' commitment to radical feminism meant that, according to one former member, sexism was the primary form of oppression, social revolution was pursued over social reform, and separatism was an instrumental part of feminist consciousness raising.[29] It brought public attention to a host of feminist issues, including domestic violence (often called "wife abuse" at the time), rape, violence against women, and abortion, but more than just bringing the personal into the realm of the political, WAC also created numerous alternative institutions for women in the city, including a battered women's shelter, women-only "take-back-the-night" demonstrations, and a feminist bookstore, Fan the Flames. WAC was also instrumental in the founding of Women's Studies at Ohio State University, and many members of WAC were students and faculty at OSU. Some of their efforts, such as the battered women's shelter and the Women's Studies department, have been incorporated into city and state operations; Women Against Rape (WAR), which operated under the umbrella of WAC (and, in many ways, was the heart of WAC),[30] but was a separate institution, still operates in the city, working in local hospitals and with city police to help prosecute and convict rapists. Other elements of this organization, such as Fan the Flames, have vanished from the city's activist horizon (the bookstore was unable to compete with the major chain bookstores and closed in 1997).[31] However, as sociologist Nancy Whittier has demonstrated, WAC altered the city's political and cultural landscape and formed the mainstay of feminist activism and community in the city throughout the 1970s.[32]

It is in this feminist environment, then, that some women formed a local chapter of NOW. By accounts of members of WAC and NOW, Columbus NOW in the 1970s and 1980s existed in the midst of the feminist community that was OCSW and WAC. Part of the reason, according to one former Columbus NOW member, is that NOW nationally "looked" mainstream: "The national leaders were very well dressed, very middle class, mostly white. And you could have put them in front of any camera. They were not radical types."[33] For some women, looking and being "not radical" by working through formal political channels was essential for creating and sustaining feminist change in the city and the state; for many other women, radicalized by anti-war, civil rights, and feminist activism, looking "mainstream" was less important, so many feminists turned to the alternative, which was WAC.[34] When some Columbus women formed NOW in late 1970, it fit somewhere in the middle of this feminist spectrum between OCSW and WAC, a feminist force in the city but one that belies neat categorization as either liberal or radical.

As membership rosters for OCSW, WAC, and NOW make clear, many members shared their commitments, at least on paper, to two or three of these groups at the same time. Other women (and men) went only to the NOW chapter. For some, age and sexual identity were the lines separating these local organizations. The older women in OCSW looked "old ... and here we [NOW members] were, young and rather green in terms of political activism. We wanted to be active, and they were much more politically savvy."[35] By contrast, the women in WAC were of the same age as many NOW members, but, as one NOW member put it, "my impression of them is that they were lesbian. We weren't."[36] Indeed, by all accounts, lesbian identity and lesbian community networks were the dividing line between WAC and NOW.[37] In Columbus, the NOW chapter undertook many of the same issues and actions and employed the same strategies as both OCSW and WAC. As a separate organization, however, it did offer some feminists an organization through which to engage in local feminist protest and a range of feminist analyses. However, for some—never more than 100 or so over the course of the 1970s—NOW was a feminist home, even if on the outskirts of a larger, self-identified radical feminist community. They certainly engaged in activism, but only around material issues of job discrimination (their ERA work is interesting in the context of local politics but paled by comparison). But, unlike other case studies here, Columbus NOW developed and articulated feminist theoretical analyses of women's discrimination.

Emerging from "Behind the Scenes"

In January 1972, Columbus NOW published its first newsletter, entitled "Right NOW." In it, chapter president Judy Bell chronicled her own move into the women's movement, recalling how she had seen her mother raise her four children after her father was paralyzed at age 38: "She did it on a so-called woman's job [as a baker at a local bakery], actually a man's job with woman's status and pay attached to it." By May 1969, when Bell "first heard the phrase 'women's lib,'" she recognized that many were "boldly saying publicly what I had been thinking most privately. I could hardly wait to join!"[38] Some fifteen months after Bell identified consciously with women's liberation, the NOW chapter was formed: "until this time, the only feminist organizations that existed in Columbus were on the OSU campus." Bell listed various things that NOW had done or been involved with, mostly presentations about feminism and NOW's goals to local business groups, classes at local high schools and OSU, and women's groups. Because "we have been working behind the scenes for months," the chapter did not start a newsletter until January 1972. With it, Bell hoped that "everyone who's been looking for us … should now be able to find us."[39]

For those who were looking, NOW offered a place where feminist women and men engaged in a variety of issues and employed a mix of strategies to create feminist change for women locally. Early on, the chapter drew a mix of women across class lines and of different ages. Janet Burnside, for example, joined when she was in her early twenties and commented that she looked "like a women's liberation woman" with her long, straight hair and no makeup.[40] However, she attributed her later political success as a lawyer and, later, Ohio Supreme Court judge, to her political activism in NOW. Likewise, Barbara Wood joined NOW in 1972, when she was in her early twenties and "working at the state welfare department, which was a radicalizing experience in itself … I'd been reading anything I could about women's lives and class issues and the like, and then I found the NOW chapter and got active."[41] By contrast, Ruth Browning, who was a founding member of NOW, was considerably older than women such as Wood or Burnside. She came to NOW after a career as an ordained Methodist minister (she was ordained in 1947) and was at the time head reference librarian at the Upper Arlington Library. In the mid-1950s, however, she left the Methodist church because "the church treats its women as second-class citizens … it was a hard choice after having been ordained and after having given so much of my life to it." She moved into the Society of Friends (Quaker) church because it "has a history of treating persons, including women, with equality" and she identified as a lifelong pacifist.[42] Browning was also a member of the OCSW and the Ohio Women's Political Caucus. Anne Saunier was also an early member of Columbus NOW who, like other members, was quite interested in forming local coalitions and bridges with women's groups in the city. By 1977, Saunier was a self-described "feminist mini-celebrity" as a representative to the IWY Conference in Houston; she later moved to Dayton and joined the Dayton Women's Center.[43] In the early 1970s, she and many other women were "looking for" NOW and, as these few examples suggest, found mostly white women who came from different socioeconomic backgrounds, organizational backgrounds and networks, and activist experiences.

Like its counterparts across the country, Columbus NOW joined with others to form a coalition to advocate for the ERA; it also fought violence against women by speaking and acting publicly against rape and domestic violence and sought to address women's economic and social inequality in the city through a variety of demonstrations and actions. However, even when addressing issues on a national feminist agenda, this chapter focused nearly exclusively on women in the city of Columbus. If somewhat provincial, the chapter maintained a strong commitment to grassroots issues and organizing, never comfortable with toeing a national NOW line or conforming to its appearance as a liberal feminist organization. That it was not the mainstay of the feminist community in Columbus gave this chapter an interesting flexibility and allowed its members to explore the dynamics of feminist activism.

"Are You a Serious Feminist?": Columbus NOW and the ERA

When Columbus NOW formed, the OCSW was already in existence, and it represented a wide variety of women's groups and communities in the city. OCSW's president, Mary Miller, who also joined the local NOW chapter in the early 1970s, drew upon OCSW's seven-year history in the city and created the Ohio Coalition for the ERA.[44] At age 63, and in her capacity as chairperson of the Columbus YWCA's Public Affairs Committee, Miller brought significant clout and presence to the office of president of the Ohio Coalition for the ERA, a "collaboration of generations within the pro-ERA movement—made up of women 'representing all walks of life.'"[45] Unlike Tennessee, where the ERA sailed through the state House and Senate with hardly any dissent until the successful rescission movement, and unlike California, where labor marked the only opposition to the ERA, pro-ERA Ohioans faced a two-front battle with labor and a strong STOP ERA.[46]

In Columbus NOW, members identified the ERA as the "most important" issue facing feminists in the chapter and women in the city and state.[47] In April 1972, chapter president Judy Bell recognized that having the amendment move out of the U.S. Senate was only the start of the battle for Ohio feminists—and the major opponent was organized labor: "Rumor has it that the AFL-CIO is concentrating on sixteen states to block ratification," Ohio one of them. And the NOW chapter had reason to suspect that the powerful federation of labor unions, with its origins in the city, would block the ERA vigorously in the state; on March 15, 1972, the

Ohio Supreme Court struck a blow to labor when it ruled that protective labor laws were unconstitutional "because they were inconsistent with the principles set forth in the Civil Rights Act of 1964." According to Bell, the union did not originally favor repeal of "female labor laws (men are their prime constituents)" but it "apparently decided that some protection might be desirable for everyone—men and women. This, of course is the position NOW was taking long before repeal of Ohio's antiquated laws."[48] But local leaders were looking to hold back legislators' support for the ERA.

By June 1972, the nascent ratification effort was stalled in the Senate Rules Committee. The House State Government Committee planned "numerous marathon hearings" on the amendment but no one expected that the committee would vote on it in the 1972 session. More rumors suggested that "the representatives' mail is running anywhere from 5 to 40 to 1 against [the ERA]" and the chapter's leadership encouraged members to write letters in support of the amendment to local legislators. Unlike its Memphis counterparts, who also engaged in letter-writing campaigns for the ERA, Columbus activists knew that "fears and emotions are powerful forces not easily dismissed" and testimony before the House elicited "emotional, fearful projections of 'possible' interpretations the amendment 'might' have. They [testifiers] hardly bother to debate the legal reality of the law."[49] Thus, the chapter was aware early of the importance of framing the debate, and members were encouraged to reiterate how the amendment was positive for women, families, and employers.

On June 28, 1972, the chapter agreed on a "plan of attack" and aligned with the Ohio Commission on the Status of Women, which coordinated the efforts of organizations who made up the Ohio Coalition for the ERA.[50] NOW members signed on to meet with the various groups in the OCSW, engage in precinct-by-precinct petition campaigns, hold personal meetings with state representatives and senators, and continue flooding legislators' mail with pro-ERA letters.[51] Bell reminded her fellow NOW sisters that "all of the above require the strong bodies and sharp minds of *all* feminists in Ohio," recognizing the strength of coalitions for such endeavors and likely recognizing that NOW could not go alone on the ERA—and did not have to. Interestingly, Bell defined one's commitment to feminism around the ERA: "If you are not willing to work for the ERA, you are not really a feminist."[52]

Women in the coalition came from a variety of organizations—NOW, YWCA, AAUW, WAC, Women's Liberation—and unaffiliated feminists joined them to work on behalf of the ERA. Leading this coalition was Mary Miller, who had a history of working through city women's organizations as an advocate for women.[53] OCSW women, Miller among them, thought of themselves as "moderate," and more militant activists pejoratively labeled them "liberal."[54] Among NOW members, the coalition was the best approach to work for the ERA—and Miller was integral to the coalition's strategy. According to one former NOW activist, "there were boundaries on how far you would go. And Mary Miller—she was an older woman who was very proper—she was a front person for us, the face of the ERA. For the younger of us, we would have been seen as radicals, bra burners, and all of that. So we fronted a lot of ERA stuff by Mary Miller because she was this lovely, elegant, gray-haired grandmother."[55] And Miller took control of the image of the ERA and its supporters. In an interview, she recalled that young homemakers often went to the statehouse to speak to representatives, but if they were wearing jeans Miller insisted that they leave and return wearing dresses; the younger women complied because looking "the part" mattered. When Coalition women met with legislators, they looked very similar to anti-ERA activists.[56]

Although NOW members continued to work individually for the ERA and updated the chapter via the newsletter about what was going on, the work of the ERA largely fell to the Coalition. After linking with the Coalition, some NOW members joined the local League of Women Voters and participated in a four-part radio series on the ERA on local public radio station WOSU; they also set up a public education booth at the 1972 Ohio State Fair. Member Dorothy Geiger prepared an ERA information packet for legislators to peruse before the fall election. Janet Burnside, who had been an early member of Columbus NOW and led its legislative task force from 1972 to 1974, was instrumental as a liaison between NOW and the Coalition. The chapter took up many other issues, but for Burnside, the

> ERA was all consuming, the most important thing and overshadowed everything we did. It caused a bunch of different organizations to come together, and we met and worked with so many women … [Through the ERA ratification effort] we made it our business to get to know the mostly men and a couple of women in the legislature, and a couple of women in the legislature did counsel us on how to do this and what would work and what wouldn't.[57]

Through this work, "we got into politics and we met people and we learned to go talk to legislators and found out that they were by and large pathetic. They weren't classy people or particularly smart and yet they were legislators who made it a point to support or defeat the ERA." At the heart of the fight in the legislature, according to Burnside, was labor. "The linchpin in this effort [to defeat the ERA] turned out to be head of the state AFL-CIO Frank King. I don't have a clue why the legislators ceded so much power to this guy but they did."[58] Laughing at her own naiveté at the time, Burnside continued: "At the time, I was just stupid enough not to wonder what's in it for this guy. He'd have all of the say on this issue, and many people said that until Frank King said it was ok, the ERA was not going to pass in Ohio."[59]

In Ohio, the collective strength of labor and the anti-ERA activists mandated that passage of the ERA was not a foregone conclusion. For some NOW members, the ERA had to be the Columbus NOW's top priority. Within the chapter, some suggested that perhaps NOW members were not doing enough to support the ERA. Just before a major election in October 1972, for example, newsletter editor Betty Carroll asked,

> How many people have REALLY written to their state representatives and senators to encourage passage of the Equal Rights Amendment? If we don't take our equality under the law seriously enough to communicate with these representatives, we don't take our ultimate liberation seriously! ARE YOU A SERIOUS FEMINIST? What have you done lately to ensure passage of the ERA? The time is NOW and we need all the support and LETTERS we can write.[60]

In April of the following year, Nancy Trux asked of her NOW sisters, "are you bored with ERA? Are you biding your time until we can manage to get around to YOUR pet project?"[61] Rather than encourage chapter members to engage in a variety of issues and actions, Trux invoked yet more "rumor" about the ERA: "Sorry sisters … but rumor has it that if we don't get the ERA ratified in Ohio THIS YEAR RIGHT NOW we'll have this albatross around our necks for another SIX!!!"[62] With the 1979 national deadline for ratification looming on the horizon, Trux reminded her NOW sisters that they would be fighting each year, even implying that other "pet projects" would go by the wayside until ratification was secured. She tried to temper her anger by suggesting that she "cares enough to keep pushing because you know that the ERA is the only hope for full personhood for all American women." Her solution: "why don't you do everyone a favor? Why not get us off *your* backs right NOW … get out your ancient typewriter and pound out a few more lines for the ERA?"[63]

A "few more lines" did not help; the Ohio Senate rejected the Amendment in late 1973—a success for the STOP ERA campaign and the resistance of organized labor. However, the Coalition network sustained activism and, when the General Assembly met in January 1974, more than 1,000 pro-ERA activists rallied on the statehouse lawn.[64] NOW member Nancy Mackenzie reminded her sisters in NOW that "we must not be over-confident! Passage of the Equal Rights Amendment in Ohio is NOT a sure thing!"[65] Although her solution was, again, to write letters in support of the ERA, she acknowledged that STOP ERA forces had been powerful in mobilizing in Ohio. However, she did not discuss the powerful anti-ERA strategy of bringing Ohio legislators loaves of bread tied with pink ribbons—symbols of the femininity that the ERA threatened to demolish, according to its opponents.[66] In spite of STOP ERA's intensive lobbying effort, however, Ohio became the thirty-third state to ratify the ERA the following year, in 1974.[67] The STOP ERA forces had been defeated—one of the only times that happened—and organized labor shifted its public position on the amendment.[68] But also, the Coalition maintained its activism in the face of potential defeat.

To be sure, some NOW members had been instrumental in the Coalition; however, the amendment was not the only focus of this chapter. The numerous pleas to chapter members suggest that leaders often badgered members into letter writing and advocacy. Unlike the national organization, this NOW chapter did not give its full weight to the ERA. In large measure, many chapter members turned the work of the ERA over to the Coalition and the NOW members such as Burnside and Trux, who were active in it. Some who were not particularly active on the issue recognized its importance and embraced its potential for change: "NOW attacked the constitution of the United States. That is as to the root as you can get. That is the document that holds this country together."[69] But on the whole, this chapter did not focus its energies on the ERA—even in spite of strenuous opposition. Instead, they undertook their "pet projects," all of which revolved around local women's material rights.

"Cackling Hens" and "Our Sisters in Blue": Bringing Equality to Columbus

Although Columbus NOW chapter members needed to be reminded to work on the ERA, they needed no prodding to pursue local causes that had direct meaning and outcomes for women in the city. The ERA certainly would guarantee equality under the law, but while they waited to see if it would be ratified in the state and across the nation, Columbus NOW women addressed tangible discrimination against women. They worked both within the legal system and in the streets to protest women's unequal status in local establishments and in employment, indicating a firm commitment to securing feminist equality in both the letter and the spirit of the law for Columbus women.

In June 1972, the young NOW chapter in Columbus undertook one of its first public demonstrations against the Red Door Tavern, a popular lunchtime dining spot for a variety of business people in the city. As Janet Burnside recalled, "they had a businessmen-only room in the restaurant. You could be a woman and sit in the front of the restaurant, but the back room was for businessmen only."[70] Segregation in public facilities nationwide had been overturned under Title II of the 1964 Civil Rights Act and was never amended to include sex discrimination. Public facilities in Columbus were desegregated racially under the law since 1959, but sexual segregation persisted, at least at the Red Door Tavern, which boasted a sign designating one section of the restaurant "For Businessmen Only" from 11:00 a.m. until 2:00 p.m. each day.[71] Susan Meates, an increasingly prominent businesswoman who worked near the restaurant, sought to have lunch at the Red Door Tavern on June 8; two of the dining rooms were completely full and Meates went toward the back of the restaurant to be seated. When she was turned away from the men-only dining area, Meates contacted Columbus NOW. When the chapter contacted owner Jack Youngquist about the incident and the "stag room," he replied that he planned to keep the area sex-segregated because "businessmen don't like to eat with a bunch of cackling hens beside them."[72] According to Judy Bell, "we had pickets on duty during the lunch hours for the entire next week."[73] Janet Burnside recalled that they "went over there at noon and demanded that they be seated there. They were turned away, so they went outside and did a demonstration with pickets in front of the Red Door Tavern. And they got press for it."[74] Although the local newspapers did not report the demonstrations (local television news carried the story on the first day of the action), the Columbus *Dispatch* did publish a story when NOW moved from the picket line to the courthouse.

On July 30, 1972, Meates filed charges under the city's ordinance, which forbade discrimination in public accommodations. The city had passed a local ordinance (City of Columbus Ordinance No. 1524-71) banning such discriminatory actions in 1964, but it was not until 1971 that the city government amended the ordinance to include a ban on sex discrimination. When the demonstrations lasted for more than a day or two—and with the threat of legal action—Youngquist posted a smaller note on the original sign that read "Women Served on Request," but Meates and NOW members found his solution to be insulting: "It would be sort of like marking a bar 'For Whites Only—Blacks Served on Request.'"[75] City Community Relations Director Clifford Tyree indicated that the amended city ordinance had never been tested and agreed with the NOW women that "Tavern policy would appear to be in violation of the law." But rather than focus on the issue of discrimination itself, Tyree pointed out that the case might have broader ramifications: "For example, race tracks, ball parks, and bars which schedule 'Ladies Night' could be guilty of discrimination in reverse."[76] If Tyree obscured the realities of sex discrimination and the point that the protesters were making as they picketed the restaurant and then filed a lawsuit, the courts did not: Youngquist was charged with sex discrimination and the NOW members won the case.

Through such an action, the NOW chapter "acquired a lot of respectability" as an action group.[77] In the process, it became a group that women in the city recognized as one that would picket and protest, if need be. According to Barbara Wood, an early member of NOW in the 1970s (and still active in the 2000s), "it was the only publicized organization. There was WAC in town, but NOW had leaflets and forms and stuff," a reference to what she saw as a more visible presence.[78] Coupled with national NOW's growing visibility, some women immediately called the NOW chapter when faced with a discriminatory situation because "we did do actions—not only lawsuits but picketing unfair labor practices."[79] In 1974, for example, NOW member Grace Murakami (who ran the NOW telephone line through her home that year) received a phone call from a woman who owned with her husband a Union 76 gas station. According to one member, "Her husband had just died and Union 76 headquarters sent her notification that because her husband was no longer alive, the company would be selling the station."[80] She called the NOW chapter in an attempt to find any sort of legal recourse to the company's actions; within twenty-four hours, NOW members were demonstrating outside of the gas station, encouraging passersby to honk in support of the woman whose livelihood was threatened. In this particular situation, "you can imagine to the average person having attention called to the fact that a woman is being kicked out of her employment because her husband died, I mean, 99.9% of the people would say that's outrageous."[81] The chapter also brought the matter to the attention of Senator Howard Metzenbaum, the then-junior senator from Ohio. Within two weeks, Metzenbaum intervened publicly on behalf of the woman, who ultimately was able to retain ownership and management of the gas station. "She of course was not a women's libber type," former member Janet Burnside recalled, but "she knew injustice when she saw it."[82] She called NOW, which by this point had gained publicity locally for bringing attention to injustices women faced.

According to Burnside, "that's what was exciting about NOW. You'd find a problem and leap on it and try to solve it. And you'd be noisy. You'd solve it in a noisy way. You were always calling people and having a demonstration."[83] And it was effective: in the early 1970s, Sanese Services, a local company that packaged sandwiches for vending machines, maintained different dress codes for male and female employees. One former Columbus NOW member recalled that "women wore these short skirts in the factory while men wore pants. Women were being hurt on the job, cut and bruised, and complained to Sanese but the company didn't listen to them." Some women workers came to a NOW meeting and Barbara Wood recalled that NOW contacted the company: "We told them, 'I don't know how you feel about pickets at your front door but we sure could be there unless we see some changes.'"[84] Reflecting on her activist days in NOW during the 1970s, Wood maintains that Sanese, and other companies, capitulated and changed their policies because of the threat of pickets: "They knew we might actually do it!"[85] June Sahara concurred that NOW would often demonstrate and that people contacted them because they had heard of NOW, but indicates that NOW was relatively "respectable," which mattered less to WAC.[86]

Over the next several years, the chapter did work to maintain a public sense of "respectability" by undertaking legal action on a variety of issues, although that certainly was not its only, if even significant concern for most members. Instead, it was a way to maintain a public presence. In coalition with the Ohio Civil Liberties Union, for example, Columbus NOW filed a lawsuit on behalf of an unnamed 17-year-old welfare recipient who wanted an abortion but could not afford to have one. This lawsuit presented the chapter with a unique opportunity to raise the issue of reproductive rights in the light of welfare and class in the city. The suit charged that while welfare regulations stipulate that "physicians' services and related hospital costs will be payable for elective abortions for all eligible recipients," State Auditor Joseph Ferguson had refused to permit state and federal funds to be used to pay for such abortions. The lawsuit stalled in the system, ultimately becoming a sidebar to the history of reproductive rights, abortion, and welfare: in September 1976, Congress enacted a labor-HEW (Health, Education, and Welfare) appropriations bill that, with what has become known as the Hyde amendment named for

Representative Henry Hyde from Illinois, stated: "None of the funds contained in this act shall be used to perform abortions except where the life of the mother would be endangered if the fetus were carried to term."[87] The amendment effectively denied any welfare funding for elective abortions and represented the first of a growing list of measures to deny women access to abortions in the United States.

The chapter's lawsuit against the Columbus police department was more successful. In June 1975, two women applicants to the Columbus police department and the local NOW chapter filed a sex discrimination suit in the U.S. District Court, charging that the physical agility part of the qualifying exam was sex discriminatory.[88] At the time of the lawsuit, the physical agility examination consisted of eight components: a 440-yard run, fence climb, under-wire scramble, stair climb, trigger pull, driving test, car push, and sandbag drag. However, in May 1975, 40 of 41 women failed the physical agility part of the exam, while only 27 of 103 men failed; in the next month, 37 of 38 women failed the physical agility test.[89] Columbus NOW member (and later chapter president) Anne Saunier suggested that "the fact that women failed the agility test demonstrates an obvious adverse impact on women applicants as a class ... [I]f the test accurately reflected the duties of police officers, many women would be able to pass the tests."[90]

Youla Brant and Myra Carney, the two aggrieved women applicants, and the NOW chapter filed suit against the city and the police department, and immediately sought class action status to extend the lawsuit to all "women who applied to become officers on or after Jan. 13, 1969 ... who were deterred from pursuing their applications or were rejected for failing to pass the physical agility examination."[91] NOW also charged that the police department restricted women's opportunities for advancement in the department. At the same time that NOW filed the lawsuit, it also filed for a temporary injunction on the physical agility test, indicating that the test had not been given routinely to male applicants and that male officers had no physical requirements in order to keep or advance in their jobs.[92] According to the "Findings of Fact" in the final court decision, male and female officers had the same entry-level pay scales. However, duties assigned to women and men were unequal: women were assigned duties in the juvenile bureau, the jail, and specialized work in the detective and vice bureaus. Women mainly worked cases involving women, children, and the elderly; in vice, women occasionally worked as decoys in narcotics investigations. Patrol and traffic duty as well as supervisory duties were reserved exclusively for men; no woman had ever been a police department supervisor.[93] At the time of the lawsuit, only 20 positions were authorized for women on the force; however, over 1,000 policeman positions were allocated. Actually, there were 14 women on duty in every year from 1963 through 1969; 11 in 1970, 14 in 1971, 19 in 1972, and 20 in 1973 and 1974. In the same time span from 1967 to 1975, the number of men on the city police force increased from 573 to 1,044.[94]

Having established a pattern of discrimination, the chapter pursued the lawsuit, which continued in the courts from June 1975 to October 1978. The city initially appealed to the Circuit Court of Appeals to have the case dropped for lack of evidence, but to no avail; by March 1976, the case was underway in the U.S. District Court, with Judge Robert M. Duncan presiding. However, the legal fees associated with the appeals, as well as the depositions and NOW's appeal for summary judgment rather than jury trial (which was denied), were quite high; according to one former NOW member, "when NOW sued the police department, it broke the chapter. I mean, we didn't have any deep pockets around us."[95] However, the chapter managed to keep up with the legal expenses through pleas for monetary donations and through some pro bono work by the lawyers. Duncan ruled in favor of the plaintiffs and the class represented in the suit in 1978: "The Court concludes that the city of Columbus and the other defendants clearly manifested a purpose to discriminate on the basis of sex by treating males and females differently."[96] With the victory for the plaintiffs, Duncan awarded the chapter a financial sigh of relief because the city had to pay not only damages but also all legal fees.

Whether addressing sex discrimination in public accommodations or on the job, the Columbus chapter of NOW sought to remedy the wrongs that local women experienced and brought to their attention. They preferred to pursue local and immediate change to the longer-term goal of the ERA. Many members did not have to be shamed or have their commitments to feminism challenged when it came to ensuring that Susan Meates could sit down and have lunch with her peers and colleagues or that Youla Brant could earn a living in what was traditionally a man's job. Moreover, they merged the threat and reality of public demonstrations with the legal system to advance equal opportunities for women in Columbus. On the surface, it is not uncommon to see protest strategies coupled with legal strategies. However, at least for some in NOW, their strategies reflected a more radical perspective on so-called liberal feminism—Wood, for example, indicated that "going to the root" by attacking the Constitution was as "radical" as activism could get.[97] She also acknowledged differences between NOW and WAC, indicating that WAC did more of their work by consensus while NOW "continued to operate by a formal system of consensus, regularly rotating coordinators and meeting facilitators."[98] When NOW tried it, however, some members balked: "when it came to getting the work done, you can't do it by consensus. You have to have someone get the bus and organize the time, or make the signs and get to the demonstration on time, and so on."[99]

So, while Columbus NOW officially maintained a formal structure (and, by 1974, implemented parliamentary procedure for chapter meetings), members did identify a radical element to their activism. NOW appeared to some to be "a bunch of liberal feminists, white-gloved and middle class,"[100] but looking at this organization from the inside reveals the myriad and complex theoretical perspectives motivating their actions. These same women who worked to secure equal employment opportunities for Columbus women also grappled with and analyzed society, culture, and their lives as individuals and as women in very radical ways. Indeed, through their record of and reputation for successful demonstrations, NOW was the organization that people knew to contact in order to draw immediate feminist attention to local problems.

The chapter's radicalism in the street is reflected in its newsletters. For Columbus NOW, the newsletter was not just a record of past and upcoming events; it was a place where women shared ideas, issued manifestos, and analyzed society through experience. Turning to this chapter's newsletter reveals a complex mixture of various theoretical perspectives that drove their actions.

"It's Time for Women ... to Throw off Male Domination": Feminist Analyses in Columbus NOW

No matter the organization, chapter newsletters serve a number of functions. Whether informing members about upcoming regional and national NOW conferences, apprising women of the formal process by which a bill becomes law, or providing names and addresses of current legislators, the newsletter was an important venue through which members knew about formal political action and how to undertake it individually. In the first newsletter, chapter president Judy Bell hoped that this new vehicle would allow "everyone who has been looking for us ... [to] be able to find us." Moreover, she noted that "It is all so gratifying [the work NOW members had been doing thus far]. Women are becoming aware. Men are becoming aware, too. At last, it seems, Columbus, Ohio, might be able to contribute its 'fair share' (pun intended) to the national effort."[101] Bell and many other feminists in Columbus NOW did not eschew working with men and always believed that feminism represented a human revolution. They criticized and analyzed women's inferior status through broader social and cultural lenses, reflecting upon the complexities of lived experiences and various feminist solutions to problems women faced.

In March 1972, in the third issue of the newsletter, Bell extended an invitation and suggested the function of the newsletter: "We have a newsletter to get out each month which could benefit from YOUR life's experiences, if you would be willing to share them with us. How much better we all feel when others share with us and help us realize that we are not alone with our thoughts and feelings, our needs and concerns."[102] Bell initiated the use of the newsletter as a venue for personal reflection and analysis by discussing her first public speaking experience, indicating that she was "scared" and "I asked someone else to do it for me. She suggested that we do it together. (What's that line about catty women? Competing for what? Outdoing who? What about the limelight?)" Rejecting the popular idea that some women in the movement were competing to be its "stars," Bell encouraged her sisters to share their experiences, thoughts, and analyses: "we are not alone."[103]

Her fellow NOW members took up the charge and offered their insights on women's place in society. Radical feminists published many newsletters and journals, such as *No More Fun and Games* and *off our backs*, with the goal of offering women alternatives on current events and radical political analyses of gender and women's status in society.[104] Scholars have turned to these publications to chronicle the development of radical feminist thought. In the city of Columbus, WAC publications have been used in part to chronicle radical feminism in the city,[105] but as the NOW newsletters evince, WAC was not the only place where women expressed radical feminist thought and merged radical feminist theory and action.

Writing in the then-new feminist magazine, *Ms.*, in spring 1972, Jane O'Reilly popularized the word "click!" as a way to describe the moment when she experienced a new insight on her life as a housewife. "Those clicks are coming faster and faster," she wrote. "American women are angry. Not redneck-angry from screaming because we are so frustrated and unfulfilled angry, but clicking-things-into-place angry, because we have suddenly and shockingly perceived the basic disorder in what has been believed to be the natural order of things." She went on to list examples of these insightful "clicks":

> In Houston, Texas, a friend of mine stood and watched her husband step over a pile of toys on the stairs, put there to be carried up. "Why can't you get this stuff put away?" he mumbled. Click! "You have two hands," she said, turning away … Last summer I got a letter, from a man who wrote: "I do not agree with your last article, and I am canceling my wife's subscription." The next day I got a letter from his wife saying, "*I* am not canceling *my* subscription." Click![106]

In June 1972, Columbus NOW member and founder Ronnie Rosen identified her "click" moment when she took a Sociology of Women course at Ohio State University. As a result of this class, she challenged "the stereotype female role" and "knew that I was deeply committed to the women's cause and that I had to live this same liberation that I was fighting for."[107] She helped found the NOW chapter in 1971, but "after several months in the organization, I have reached some conclusions." She agreed with NOW's national Eight Point Program, which the national board issued in 1968, and she concurred that "our local chapter is really growing and projects are being organized." However, "I am not content or pleased with any of it. On the contrary, I am angry and impatient because we work so hard and yet it takes so long to move forward just a little," words she likely echoed on June 2 when she spoke at a rally at Ohio State sponsored by WAC, Women's Liberation, and Radicalesbians.[108] She chose to remain a member of NOW "because, as an individual, I know of no other way to help remedy the woman's plight in our society,"[109] but she led a chorus of NOW voices who felt angry about the status of women and girls in U.S. society and chose to put her thoughts on paper and issue them to the chapter as a way to express and rally her NOW sisters.

Rosen's words were followed by those of others decrying sexism and calling for an overhaul of American society rather than just working within the system to create feminist change, an attitude that suggests NOW members were not content working exclusively for the ERA. The chapter initiated woman-only consciousness-raising and "rap" groups, which, according to one member, "was hugely successful as an organizing tool and a grassroots tool."[110] For women who could not or did not attend the consciousness-raising groups, the newsletter functioned in many ways as such, allowing women to address a variety of sexist concerns through printed and circulated manifestos, a medium heretofore claimed by and assigned to radical feminists. In July 1972, member Betty Carroll told the story of how a young man challenged her "women's libber" attitude because she would not purchase products, the profits of which would "help keep *boys* out of juvenile delinquency" but did not help girls and young women in similar situations. She turned this story into a larger analysis of sexist culture: "A trivial incident? Perhaps … but it is the assumption of male prerogatives, rights and privileges by these culturally conditioned male children that I find so infuriating." Moreover, she acknowledged that women could not simply "retreat into one's shell" or act as if these events are isolated or simply do not happen. She reminded her sisters that "chauvinism bangs on your door, invades your privacy, and threatens to poison the minds of your children." Her solution was feminist solidarity: "Advance, not retreat, coupled with an organized plan to combat these chauvinistic assumptions and, most important of all, a strong sense of solidarity and Sisterhood, is the only way to implement change in cultural conditioning."[111]

Of course, "sisterhood" has always been a complicated, even disavowed, term. But in the early 1970s, many feminists used it to invoke a site of solidarity—not singularity—in thought and action. In the name of sisterhood, the chapter announced its pickets of Red Door Tavern, a tangible place to address men, such as Youngquist, who "clearly intends to continue demeaning and degrading, intimidating and harassing women." The chapter ultimately solved the problem through legal channels, but the analysis they brought to bear on the situation, and on the experience Betty Carroll—a self-identified middle-class, married woman and NOW member—shared, was one that could not be addressed through the law alone.

In the following month, three women shared different experiences and analyses of society. Carroll followed up her previous month's story with another "click" moment she had at a local hair salon. While she waited, she leafed through a stack of magazines, coming across "this particular magazine known by the cutesy-poo title of 'Girl Talk' and is dedicated to the proposition that all women have a mental age of 7."[112] Carroll focused her discussion in particular on an article by Arlene Dahl entitled "Don't Let It Throw You," which "says it is far better to live in a world dominated by men than by 'big sisters.'" Carroll was enraged by the article and the magazine, which to her suggested how "it is obviously to their interests to keep the average American woman submissive to the patriarchal system so she has time to shop only for face cream and vaginal spray." And she encouraged her sisters to write to the American Broadcasting Company (ABC), the parent company of the magazine publisher, to "let them know that the American woman will no longer tolerate the media's image of her as a microcephalic creature concerned solely about maintaining her youth, deodorizing her smelly body, and having a whiter-than-white wash."[113] Although Carroll suggested a rather tame solution to her rage, it is telling that she spoke so forcefully about cultural prescriptions for women via magazines. She certainly was not the only one in larger American society to be openly critical of women's magazines—after all, a group of feminists had taken over the offices of *Ladies Home Journal* in 1970 by way of protest and feminists had launched *Ms.* as an alternative to mainstream women's magazines.[114] But in Columbus, and in this particular NOW chapter, Carroll testified locally to the impossibilities of prescribed womanhood and encouraged her sisters in NOW to reject these images and to take action.

For member V. Givens, "action" meant more than letter writing, but, like Carroll, Givens saw the "problems of women" as much larger and more systemic. Taking a long view of women's oppression in society, she noted that "women, after eons of physical evolution, are still relegated to the biological function they commanded in pre-historic time—to womb the sperm, birth it, and nourish it." Suggesting that narratives of evolutionary progress had eluded women, she noted that "we are still regarded as unclean and 'sick' in the normal biological functioning" of childbirth and sold a myth about sex and virginity:

> In this exciting age of cybernetics and space exploration, when science and technology have, for all practical purposes, broken the barriers of every existing frontier, including the creation of life-forms in the laboratory, and overcoming death, women are still expected to be content to remain biological virgins until some earthman-god pierces the sacred hymen and implants his golden semen in her womb while the world still tries to con her into believing that she may be nourishing the next messiah.[115]

After sharing her disgust about the sexual double standard, Givens indicated that women needed to "reject the role assigned to them, throw off male domination, and assert themselves as fully functioning individuals." Her solution: "to invade every sacred male vehicle, regardless of how elaborately it has been constructed, or how well the ramparts are manned." The solution was not in continued struggles for legal rights: "There's no more time to wheedle, ask, demand, connive, or legislate for our rights. We must assert those rights by working where we please, living where we please, and by regulating the biological functioning of our bodies.[116] Furthermore, she wrote, "If this socially castrates the male of the species or traumatizes him into sexual impotency, let us realize at last that it isn't woman who is to blame. The real problem lies in the male's own conceit and self-delusions, and it's a matter he has to come to grips with. State and Church will then give up their supra-dream of male superiority and accept women as the positive, constructive force that we are."[117] This advocacy of separatism and complete rejection of the male and "the penis as the ultimate symbol of superiority and authority" is unheard of in analyses of NOW, but in Columbus, at least some members were advocating what became known as cultural feminism and female separatism, one of the many strands of feminism in this NOW chapter.[118]

Although not all NOW members advocated separatism, they did analyze life from experience and suggest that feminism offered better alternatives for women. Mary Havens, a new member as of May 1972, recalled her coming to feminism in a story that could have been lifted from Betty Friedan's *The Feminine Mystique*: "I was a dissatisfied housewife. I had no life of my own—the days were devoted to being a good wife and a mother of two very young children. And while it is good to be close to another person as I am to my husband, and while young children can be surprisingly enjoyable (sometimes!), neither can be everything." For her, the "click" came when she read Friedan's landmark book—interestingly, Havens is the only NOW member in these three chapters to tie her feminism to *The Feminine Mystique*—and then "found out about the Columbus Chapter of NOW." She writes that "I was very impressed with the enthusiasm of the women working to improve all women's lives … And WOW—all kinds of things are happening!" It was an eye-opening experience for her to see discrimination in the workplace but she was heartened to know that the law and various agencies, such as the Equal Employment Opportunity Commission (EEOC), were working to overcome discrimination for all women. Her feminist activism gave her "a lot to think about besides husband, children, and housework. Working for women's legal rights is a time-consuming and exhausting, complex operation. The housework piles up now because an active involvement in the women's movement is more important, more enriching, and self-directing."[119]

Although Givens suggested female separatism, most members who made the personal analytically salient advocated for liberation alongside men. This idea is congruent with NOW's original statement and philosophy, which always included men as part of the "worldwide revolution for human rights."[120]And women such as Havens and Carroll were not interested in eschewing relationships with men but rather were more interested in pursuing egalitarian relationships with them. Few women in the NOW chapter during the 1970s and early 1980s identified outwardly as lesbians, and most members did not see lesbianism as a political strategy or identity.

Columbus NOW did not have a sexuality and lesbianism task force until 1985 and the newsletters rarely discussed issues related to lesbians' lives or same-sex sexuality, nor was there a public meeting on same-sex sexuality or lesbians' rights until the mid-1980s. Barbara Wood suggested that "that was more of WAC's thing. They [lesbians] went to WAC," a statement that June Sahara corroborated: "WAC was lesbian, NOW was straight. That was just the way it seemed to be."[121] Wood indicated that "NOW didn't do the best job of acknowledging lesbian members" but "it went both ways … I remember one year we went to the Michigan Womyn's Music Festival and … we were trying to raise money and increase membership in NOW. Several lesbians told us that they wouldn't join NOW because we were working on abortion rights and that it was 'our' issue because 'you're the ones sleeping with the enemy. It isn't our problem.'"[122] Janet Burnside suggested that NOW was able to "sidestep that whole issue and never deal with it because the focus was largely on the ERA. Once that struggle was over [in 1982, when the ERA failed to secure the necessary thirty-eight states' ratification], my perception is that NOW [in Columbus] became primarily lesbian and dealt primarily with lesbian issues."[123] She acknowledged that "I may be painting it with too broad a brush, but that was my perception."[124] Still, she may be on to something—in Columbus, many lesbians who identified as feminists pursued membership in WAC in the 1970s. When WAC folded, which was contemporaneous with the defeat of the ERA, NOW remained; many WAC members went on to other progressive and/or gay/lesbian organizations in the city.

"Sidestepping" lesbians' rights and identity in the chapter in the 1970s, members still grappled with the range of female sexuality. For example, under the women's liberation symbol, member Sandra Stout published a poem advocating sexual freedom:

Man, oh Man—I do not need your name
Fame I have in my own name
With my name yours it would be lost
And at such cost:
So I can do your laundry
Your dishes
Your kinky sex wishes.
Man, oh Man—I do not need your name,
Your laundry,
Your dishes—
But once in a while I'll do your kinky sex wishes.[125]

We cannot know what Stout meant by "kinky sex wishes," but it is clear that she sought to reclaim her own sexuality and chose a fun way to address a serious theme in women's lives. Liberation, for her, was eschewing housework and a man's name—these things would overshadow her own life and self. And she certainly did not mince words when it came to male domination as a cultural problem. In another newsletter, the poet Stout published "Topical Disease":

If there's anyone I ever knew
Who will surely contract this new swine flu
For whom inoculation won't do
It's you, male chauvinist pig, it's you.[126]

Liberation was about eradicating sexism; however, liberation for her was not about eschewing sexual pleasure with a man. Unlike separatists, who insisted that women must live completely independently from men—a theoretical perspective Givens promoted—Stout and other members of NOW pursued sexual liberation within heterosexuality. For Stout, at least, it was not problematic to liberate women from male chauvinism while also enjoying and pursuing "kinky sex wishes."

Women's sexual experiences, however, were not always positive, nor did women always discuss openly their "kinky sex wishes." Like feminists across the country and in the city's Women Against Rape, Columbus NOW members discussed rape at chapter meetings and in rap groups; they also read about it in a moving "diary of a rape victim" that "Anonymous" published in the April 1973 newsletter. In this highly detailed chronicle, she outlined the day and time she endured the rape: "November 13, 1972. 12:15 p.m. Chatted five minutes at my apartment door at lunch time with a pleasant black student seeking an apartment. When I attempted to end the conversation to return to work he pulled a small hand gun out of his jacket pocket and told me to let him in. A second man came to the door and was admitted by the first. They both raped me and then took about $35 in cash and some bottles of liquor. I was left tied up on my bed."[127] After she was able to free herself, she called a friend and the police, and went to her doctor (who told her she had "no medical evidence of rape"). The next day, she shared her story with the NOW rap group to which she belonged: "someone said something which made [telling my story] essential. I told my story, shaking ... I'm not alone."

After she recounted her narrative about going to the police department and looking through police photographs of countless men, she contacted Women Against Rape (WAR), although she admittedly did not follow up on this inquiry. She also discussed her ambivalence toward rape in American culture: "March 19. In a letter a friend expressed his anger and referred to the rapists as 'animals.' Felt renewed social guilt. They were born human—did I and my society make them animals?" Another entry:

> November—March. Informed selected personal friends of the incident to get reaction. Men were generally angry ... suggested vicious punishment, castration, death. Hard conservative law-and-order stand. Suspicion grows that this is what they think I want to hear. Women were more gentle and concerned. 'It can't happen' type of horror. Fear, especially in mothers of young daughters.[128]

Betty Carroll, who was then editor of the newsletter, reminded her NOW sisters that "rape is an external manifestation of the internalized contempt in which (some) men hold women ... Obviously there is no single answer but perhaps the elimination of the second-class status of women will work as an impetus to the eradication of rape ... We must NO LONGER accept our conditioning to be 'victims.'"[129] "Anonymous," however, exposed the experience of being raped and then the legal and social aftermath she experienced.

The chapter created a rape task force in October 1973, which WAC and NOW member Karen Jensen chaired, and many members involved in this new task force also joined forces with Women Against Rape (WAR), which was a spin-off of WAC. NOW and WAR member Erica Scurr reported that WAR sought to create a twenty-four-hour rape crisis telephone line, rap sessions for rape victims, self-defense classes in the University area, and other programs to empower women as alternatives to the current legal system that demoralized women, as "Anonymous" had made clear. Much like the Ohio Coalition for the ERA, WAR undertook much (though not all) of the activism in the city on the issue of rape. The chapter addressed these issues, but because coalition forces in the city were strong, members were able to meet other needs for local women. In both coalitions, NOW members were active, indicating the numerous threads of continuity between and among local social movement organizations that creates historically a richer tapestry of community activism.

On at least one occasion, Columbus NOW did take on the issue of rape independently of other organizations. For example, when chapters across the state met in Columbus in December 1976, some members reported that a local department store was selling "mod sox" with the slogan "Help Stamp Out Rape—Say Yes" emblazoned on them. Over 200 delegates to the conference marched downtown to the May Co. department store to confront the store managers.[130] "When efforts to talk to the management of the store failed, the women pulled the "sox" from the display and those who had May Co. credit cards—including Flo Kennedy, keynote speaker for the convention—mutilated their cards."[131] Warren Harris, board chairman of the May Co. Department Stores, reported that the socks were ultimately removed from the stores and reemphasized "standing orders for buyers to avoid controversial merchandise."[132] Although Harris avoided the reality that these socks and, by extension, the companies that sold them, encouraged women to acquiesce to rape, this NOW chapter joined with cohorts across the state and took action at a moment's notice.

In this light, then, and through this elaboration of chapter members' feminist analyses, it is easier to make sense of the "Gahanna Five," whose action opens this chapter. Barbara Wood, one of the women who painted the "Great Wall of Gahanna," reported that the incident, and their feminist philosophy and analysis of rape, came from radical analysis of women's lives and safety; she and her NOW sisters wanted to generate public attention about rape in the city.[133] The law was not working for women, and women were refusing to accept victim status. Exploring chapter members' perspectives through the newsletter, especially about the issue of rape but also general analyses about women's status, makes this action seem less incongruent and in many ways completely normal, even predictable, for this group of white, college-educated women who ranged in age from 25 to 47. As one member stated, "the rap that NOW was a middle-class white-gloved outfit didn't hold in my experience."[134] As their powerful observations and analyses bear, and their actions as, alongside, and on behalf of many working women in the city make clear, Columbus NOW was not just a "white-gloved outfit."

The incident at the "Great Wall of Gahanna" may have been dismissed in the press as "silly 'fun,'" but for the chapter it proved to be quite costly. According to Wood,

> it split the chapter. We had a huge blow up, half of them in the chapter insisting that we had ruined NOW's reputation. We were respectable and they thought we undid it all. I asked, 'Since when are we afraid to say what needs to be said?' 'Since when is "castrate rapists" more destructive than "Nancy is a good lay?"' But it split the chapter, people left in shame that NOW had been ruined because we painted the wall. Some were just ashamed that we'd ruined NOW's reputation, talking about property destruction and vandalism, and others were like 'property destruction?!' But we did it, and we weren't ashamed, because it was about theory and about public signage and getting our message across. It mattered, and it drew attention to the issue of rape in Columbus.[135]

Unlike Memphis NOW, which split over the softball team and the implicit idea that the only true feminist is a lesbian, or San Francisco NOW, which split over chapter leadership, Columbus NOW split over the issue of respectability. Although there was a rift and it is nearly impossible to know from the records who left and for what individual reason, the chapter continued with business as usual.

Navigating the "Sea Change"

In 1979, pro-ERA advocates pushed through a bill in Congress that would grant a two-and-one-half-year extension for the amendment. Like other chapters across the nation, Columbus NOW renewed efforts on behalf of the amendment. However, the fight for the amendment took on a personal tone in the city, one that reflected the national shift to the right. On November 1, 1980, directly before the presidential election, local Republicans hosted a large rally for Ronald Reagan, the party's presidential nominee. About fifty-five women, including many from NOW and Women for Education and Beautification of Society (WEBS), assembled to demonstrate in opposition to Reagan. Carrying signs with such slogans as "ERA Yes—Reagan No" and "Free Nancy Reagan," the women stood at the entrance chanting ERA slogans. After an hour passed, the women entered the building where the rally was being held and marched "peacefully" while chanting "Stop Reagan." According to Patty Squeo (Hughes),

> Reactions were shocking! At one point when we were standing together chanting, people in front of us turned around ready to attack us. They started throwing cans and yelling … Then when a man grabbed a sign from a demonstrator's hand things got real scary. He tore up the sign and started to

go for her. [The crowd] had hatred in their eyes—it seemed like they wanted to kill us![136]

One woman who was present remarked that the incident evinced "a sea change that happened very quickly culturally." Squeo, who had organized the demonstration, "saved us, and I mean truly saved us. These were the Cadillacs and the fur coats … And they started to beat us. The crowd tore our glasses off our faces, they hit us with their purses and briefcases. But she kept us moving so it was harder to pummel one or two of us."[137] The attacks finally stopped when plain-clothes police officers and Secret Service officers intervened and "suddenly it was all quiet again, as if nothing had happened."[138] But, for Squeo and others in the chapter, "it made me think of the type of people we are up against in our struggle to gain equal rights. They are so determined and self-righteous, after all they think they have God on their side! The 1980s are certainly going to be a challenge."[139]

Although the political and cultural seas were changing, and the rights women had secured both locally and nationally were coming under fire, the Columbus chapter maintained a focus on what was happening to women in their city. After this rift, remaining NOW members joined with WAC to expose the desperate and negative plight of women within the legal system, elaborating in particular on the story of Helen Reeves. Reeves had intervened on behalf of a neighbor whose common law husband had pulled a gun and threatened to kill her. When Reeves arrived to help the woman, "Helen was axed in the head and upper part of her body and was shot three times; twice in the abdomen and once in the arm."[140] Reeves spent three months in the hospital; while hospitalized, her house was burglarized. She called Columbus NOW for assistance. NOW and WAC co-hosted a "collection night" so that people could bring clothes and other household items. But what was even more alarming than Reeves' bittersweet tale of survival was the way the defense characterized Reeves in the ensuing trial against the husband. According to the report published in "Right NOW" that NOW and WAC members wrote based on trial testimony, "The Defense intended to show that Helen 'did not fit the traditional role of the submissive female' and that she was 'always sticking her nose' in Basset's [the husband] private business. The Defense intended to show that Helen was the aggressor … and Basset was using self-defense."[141] The report concluded with the now-familiar analysis: "All of the women involved in this case were victims of male abuse, in their private lives and during the public trial. The trial itself was an exemplary exhibition of the details of the oppression of women, but none of these details were addressed in the trial, rather, used against all the women involved." Moreover, they called for "women to support other women who must go through a trial like this one."[142] What they meant by "support" is unclear, but what remains obvious is that, even after the split in the chapter, members remained committed to local women and addressing sexism systemically and not just through the law.

The chapter undertook a few more local efforts for the ERA during the extension period from 1979 to 1982, hosting parades and fundraisers, including a blood drive and a swimathon.[143] But after the chapter divided, it lost any real efficacy in the city. Since members were already affiliated with other organizations, many likely just let their membership in NOW lapse. But for a decade, Columbus NOW embraced change for women at the local level, preferring to see tangible results for women in their hometown. Their strategies and philosophies reflect the city's unrest at the time that the chapter was formed, and NOW was an outlet for some women to express their feminist selves. In spite of, and because of, the fact that this chapter fell between strong pre-existing feminist organizations and coalitions, its members enjoyed great latitude to embrace and redefine feminism and NOW at the local level. Although theirs was more peripheral to historical analysis of the women's movement in many ways when compared to OCSW and WAC, the women of Columbus NOW stayed focused on local women and committed to eradicating sexism in their hometown. They embraced the street activism and political analysis associated with radical feminism, but they did not shy away from working within the formal political system to create change to improve the collective status of women.

This chapter allows a lens into the space of a feminist group that never was "the only game in town," as was the case with Memphis NOW. As such, it never conformed or adhered to any specific agenda or philosophy, but instead responded to the immediate needs and situations of its city, addressing them in the streets, when need be, as well as in compelling theorizing about women's experiences and liberation in the newsletter. Although it aligned with the OCSW and Ohio ERA coalition, the NOW chapter in Columbus never really embraced the ERA as its main issue. And although it also brought radical feminist analysis to bear on women's lived experiences, it maintained a separate organizational presence from WAC. Most of its activism focused on "bread and butter" issues, such as workplace equity and job security and eradicating sexist practices because they were harmful to women. Columbus NOW maintained a focus on local feminist issues and generated tremendous change for women as neither liberals nor radicals but as dedicated feminists committed to activism.

5

A LIBERAL FEMINIST FRONT OF PROGRESSIVE ACTIVISM IN SAN FRANCISCO

"Better than calling yourself a maverick" was the tagline for the 2008 Radical Women Conference, which took place in early October 2008. The slogan is a direct response to then-Republican governor and vice-presidential candidate Sarah Palin, who invoked the label "maverick" to define herself and her running mate; using it here suggested that Radical Women's event and philosophy was better than what Palin and Republicans had to offer with respect to women and working-class people. The weekend event drew over 250 women (and a handful of men) to the Women's Building in the Mission District of San Francisco, a building that since the 1970s has been a symbolic and practical hub of a range of feminist activism and activist organizations.[1] The 2008 Radical Women Conference, sponsored by the organization by the same name, drew participants from around the United States, as well as Australia and Costa Rica, to talk about Marxist feminism, and addressed concrete and longstanding feminist issues such as women's workplace unionizing and on-the-job sex discrimination, homophobic violence and rights for LGBT people, and the spectrum of reproductive rights and justice. It is fascinating that the mobilizing group behind this event is Radical Women, formed in 1967 and dedicated to Marxist feminist analysis and activism. But at the conference, it reinforced that "there is no such thing as a monolithic movement for social and political change."[2]

Although this is true in other case studies here, across NOW chapters generally, and across the women's movement, San Francisco NOW's activism provides a useful inroad into the multiplicity of movement and organizational style and politics. The focus on the material realities of women's lives is a hallmark of feminist activism, and San Francisco's history as a hotbed of radical activism makes it a likely, even obvious, site of this kind of event. But feminist activism in San Francisco did not always evoke explicitly radical identity and calls to action. San Francisco's more nuanced history of feminism longs to be chronicled, but in the 1970s San Francisco NOW served on the feminist front of liberal, progressive social change.

In the early 1970s, NOW Western Regional Director Shirley Bernard reminded her NOW sisters that "The best way to retain members is by getting them involved in a project so that chapter activities become an important part of their lives. Also, as people work together, they experience a growing feeling of concern for each other that leads to the cementing of friendships. Since these friendships evolve from and revolve around feminist activities, gradually a cohesive group of dedicated people emerges that ensures a solid base for feminist activities and chapter growth."[3] She suggested that new members might be interested in a variety of issues, including (but not limited to) education, welfare, child care, study groups, feminist writing groups, legislation, local employment, media images of women, and other services, including divorce and income tax advice and assistance, underscoring the reality that this chapter, or feminism generally, would enforce or adhere to any monolithic ideology or action. What is most telling, perhaps, is that Bernard encouraged her fellow NOW feminists to reach women in their communities where they were, not try to fit them into NOW's pre-existing agenda.[4]

In addition to being a general example of many NOW members' philosophy on chapter growth in terms of members and local influence, Bernard's comments serve as an example of "left coast" feminism.[5] NOW's national offices were never located any further west than Chicago, and then only early on and briefly. Indeed, NOW maintained its national focus by moving its offices to Washington, DC, where it could keep tabs on and influence lawmakers and offer a feminist perspective on legislative issues. This created a vast difference between national NOW and the San Francisco chapter (San Francisco or SF NOW), geographically as well as philosophically. While national NOW turned its attention to the ERA and electing feminist women and men to office—and encouraged its chapters to do the same—San Francisco NOW members turned their attention to issues as they related to women in their communities. Unlike the Memphis and Columbus chapters, the ERA was significant in SF NOW only the extension campaign of the late 1970s. But early in the chapter's history, the focus was on material rights—issues on which national NOW has not had a remarkably strong record. SF NOW members focused on formal politics, but always to advance a larger feminist and liberal, progressive agenda and with a solid recognition that politics could not be divorced from culture. In this way, SF NOW may be the most liberal of the three NOW chapters in this book. But, as one might expect in San Francisco, feminism was rarely seen in opposition or contradiction to other movements for social justice; instead, it was integral to the "world-wide revolution of human rights."

This chapter explores the development of the San Francisco chapter of NOW from 1967, when the Northern California chapter of NOW was formed and from which the San Francisco chapter emerged, to 1982, with the defeat of the ERA. San Francisco has a historical reputation as a "wide-open town"—a place where anything goes.[6] This status shaped the growth of other social movements and communities in the city, most notably the gay and lesbian community; "wide-open" also describes its NOW chapter as members made the organization a place where anything goes. Forming a feminist community in San Francisco was, in some ways, much easier than in Columbus or Memphis. Home to a thriving gay and lesbian community, a student population protesting the war and advocating for free speech, and diverse racial and ethnic populations, San Francisco was a logical place for feminism to emerge. Studying feminism on the West Coast allows for a greater understanding of the ways in which women found their feminist niche in an activist community that had shaped and defined their lives. The growth of feminism, particularly as it was embraced and contested by NOW members, also underscores the challenges of building a feminist community in the Bay Area.

Cultures and communities overlapped in San Francisco, a geographically small community, but shared identities or spaces did not necessarily translate into a cohesive whole.[7] However, in the postwar era, with growing attention to civil rights, especially in the context of gay/lesbian rights but also in the context of racial issues, feminists found common cause in the context of many activisms happening at once. So, when the local NOW chapter formed in 1968, it would never claim to be everything to everyone. The chapter's feminism never merely reflected what the national Board deemed important to feminists. Instead, it highlighted a commitment to a host of local injustices and reflected what mattered to women in San Francisco. The major issues of SF NOW reflect the national agenda but the activism was rooted in local strategies, tactics, and goals. In the work of feminism, NOW women joined forces with activists across the city. As a result, NOW rarely saw itself in competition with other organizations; instead it was part of a local, loose coalition of organizations in pursuit of progressive change. Many of its members came to the chapter from their involvement in other forms of social justice activism. In concert with other groups, the NOW chapter operated within a broad political constituency. Members articulated feminist perspectives on a variety of issues; however, they always did so understanding the impossibility of separating one facet of identity from another. Rooted in coalitions with other groups, the feminism of SF NOW was much more integrated than that of national NOW or other chapters, and this chapter represented a feminist flank of progressive activism in the city.

"Join Us in Common Cause"[8]: Coalition Building in San Francisco

The early history of second-wave feminism in San Francisco is fundamentally a lesson in coalition building. Among NOW members and between NOW and other organizations, feminists early on forged a formal, sustained coalition in the Bay Area Women's Coalition. They also formed less formal coalitions around individual issues and impromptu protest-based coalitions around immediate concerns. Coalition building in general is not a major focus in the historical and sociological literature in the context of NOW, yet it is the only meaningful way to comprehend NOW's feminist history in San Francisco. I turn here first to the Bay Area Women's

Coalition and then to NOW's efforts to build coalitions around child care, abortion, and job discrimination, three major issues around which NOW feminists forged coalitions. This section concludes with a discussion of other impromptu actions that NOW members launched in conjunction with other groups in the city. Through all of these coalition efforts, it is clear that SF NOW was never the only game in town, as was the case in Memphis. Instead, SF NOW members linked with others across the city not only as representatives of NOW but also as activists working to change local politics and culture. For them, it was only in the context of cooperative, coordinated, and broad-based action that progress would and could be made.

In September 1969, at the initiative of the local NOW chapter, women from a wide variety of women's, feminist, and liberation organizations met at Glide Memorial Church in San Francisco for the first women's coalition meeting. Over thirty organizations sent representatives, including (but not only) Women's Liberation, Women for Peace, National Negro Business and Professional Women, Daughters of Bilitis, Delta Sigma Theta Sorority, Society for Humane Abortion, Mexican American Political Association, Young Socialists Alliance, Women's International League for Peace and Freedom, American Association of University Women, and Socialist Workers Party.[9] In the Coalition's first report, organizations were asked to "describe the programs of their groups." NOW represented itself according to its national agenda: "Among the goals of the organization are: extension of state protective laws to men as well as women, expansion of child care centers as a community facility, repeal of laws penalizing abortion, enforcement of Title VII of the Civil Rights Act of 1964, revision in the educational system to open opportunities for women, passage of the Equal Rights Amendment to the U.S. Constitution, revision of divorce and alimony laws, revision of tax laws, full participation of women in political activities, provision of maternity benefits, elimination of discrimination in public accommodations such as restaurants, etc."[10]

NOW advertised that its membership was open to both women and men, as did other groups, including Delta Sigma Theta Sorority, which indicated that it "assists black men in getting educational opportunities previously denied them because of discrimination in the society." Political and labor associations also broadcast the fact that their membership was sex-integrated. Their encouragement of men in the movement stood in direct contrast to other groups, such as Women's Liberation, "a women's organization which grew out of the radical student movement" made up of self-identified "young, white and middle class" women who "aim at individual fulfillment potential of women, rather than limited fulfillment *through* men."[11] Daughters of Bilitis, "part of the homophile movement which includes both male and female homosexuals," by contrast, was aware that "gay organizations that claimed to be co-ed were apt to see women as hostesses or secretary-office workers but not as decision makers" and thus was open only to women. In different ways, then, some groups saw men as integral to feminist advancement while others eschewed their participation or otherwise pursued single-sex organizing and advancement. Still, these groups came together for the purpose of formal coalition building and sought to create change for the whole of women in the Bay Area. Other single-issue groups emerged out of a specific need, such as Women, Inc. Organized in February 1966, "'out of desperation' because of the plight of women in the paper mills in Antioch," Women, Inc. sought to help women who were discriminated against on the job. Women and men formed the Society for Humane Abortion to work toward repealing all laws that penalized abortion and, in the meantime, to help women obtain abortions.[12]

At the first meeting in September 1969, the Coalition agreed upon nine items *by consensus* "to coordinate activities in support of the following programs": developing government-funded child-care centers, continuing communication between women's organizations, compiling a directory of women's groups, establishing coalition of women's groups to protest job discrimination, extending protective legislation to men, promoting women's caucuses in political parties and labor unions, abolishing all penalties for abortion, changing women's self-image in the media, and pledging to cooperate with a local radio station KPFA-FM to promote "relevant programming on women."[13] It is particularly striking that consensus politics, not majority rule, determined the actions and issues of the Coalition. It is also particularly noteworthy that in San Francisco, and among a diverse group of women representing a wide range of organizations, adopting a fundamental right to abortion united rather than divided feminists—unlike what happened a year earlier when national NOW adopted abortion rights as part of its national platform. Moreover, the diversity of this Coalition reveals the broad range of women's and feminist groups in the city. In this context, the local NOW chapter could not possibly afford autonomy or pursuit of issues on its own. Instead, members had to work collectively in order to create feminist political and cultural change. It was through the Coalition, then, that SF NOW made a mark on the city, forcing a reconsideration of second-wave feminism more broadly.

In February 1970, the Bay Area Women's Rights Coalition met again. At this meeting, chaired by Brenda Brush, Vice President of SF NOW, 300 women representing 44 feminist and women's organizations pledged action on a variety of issues. Some of it was rhetorical posturing rather than outright action: "Because his sexist and racist attitudes render him incapable of fulfilling the obligations for the post," the Coalition unanimously opposed the nomination of Judge G. Harold Carswell to the U.S. Supreme Court. But attendees also promised action on a range of local concerns, from bills before the state legislature to union protests at a local university. The Coalition also endorsed a variety of legislative issues, including Assembly Bill 22 (AB 22), which would add "sex" to the state Fair Employment Practices Act and extend state protective labor laws to men. The Coalition also agreed to lend its obviously tremendous support to eight women members of the American Federation of Teachers who recently had been fired for participating in a strike against San Francisco State College. Endorsing "their right to organize and strike as women and their right to political activity without penalty" showed SF

NOW's willingness to side with working women; political protesting and striking became important activities for NOW members on a host of issues. That they embraced such actions here and early on suggests the chapter's allegiance to this tactic and reiterates NOW's commitment in San Francisco to the issues of labor.[14]

The Coalition also proposed a "Bay Area Women's Center" as "'free space' for women, as a meeting place, referral and communication center."[15] This center, finally located off Valencia in the largely Latino Mission District, became a reality in 1979. It became the home to SF NOW and other feminist women's organizations and centers, such as a rape crisis center, a women's health project, and a meeting place for teenage girls in the area. The Coalition also issued a meaningful statement on lesbians' rights in the women's movement. In response both to Betty Friedan's "lavender menace" pronouncement and to the media's insistence that feminists were man-hating bra burners, the Coalition stated,

> as Lesbians, they [are] women concerned with the same issues and wished to participate in the Women's Rights Movement openly and honestly … Although Lesbianism is not a major issue in the Women's Rights Movement, certainly everyone's right to sexual privacy should be respected and that Lesbians represent one among many women's groups which have problems that must be dealt with in our society.[16]

Issuing this statement suggests that lesbians in the Coalition were staving off any possible resistance to their presence in the women's movement, including in NOW.

Through the Bay Area Women's Coalition, NOW members formed alliances and worked with other local feminists and progressives. From its founding until the mid-1970s, the chapter continued Coalition work and initiated three significant, local, coalition-based efforts around the issues of child care, abortion rights, and job discrimination.

"Striving for Women's Greater Liberation": Day Care, Reproductive Rights, and Want Ads

In September 1969, member Mary Morain offered her name and phone number as the chapter's contact person on the issue of child care. However, it was not until May of the following year that the local chapter activated a child-care committee, led by Joanne Ikeda; it held its first meeting on June 1, 1970.[17] As the first course of action, the committee advertised that child care would now be available at all NOW meetings and official functions.[18] All NOW members donated 10 cents each for the child-care provider, irrespective of whether or not they brought children to the meeting, and by October of that year committee members implored their sisters to "help get the ball rolling for free day care centers everywhere."[19]

In April 1971, Marian Ash, who edited "Skirting the Capitol," a statewide newsletter that kept women's organizations up-to-date on legislative issues that affected women, indicated that, at the state level, "tight money will make it difficult to fund day care this year. The only way for people to promote expensive programs is to make it clear that they are willing to pay for such programs. Women must establish their own system of priorities and then try to sell them to economy-minded legislators."[20] In that same month, the NOW chapter advertised for the first time a "day care meeting of representatives of groups interested in the problem. The coalition is out there to get things done."[21] The following August, child care was listed as one of three major goals for the year in the chapter: "How many of our members are working mothers who have trouble finding day care centers for their children?" the newsletter editor asked members. She also indicated that the group would form coalitions with other women's groups to "develop tactics to form a power block. Women must unite in order to achieve their goals, for whatever our differences of approach, we are all striving for women's greater liberation."[22] NOW member Joanne Ikeda joined Letisha Wadsworth, Louise Taub, and Karen Schwalm in linking up with the California Child Care Initiative Committee in August of 1971. One vital issue: fundraising. The Committee sold bumper stickers—"Happiness is Free Child Care"—to raise money to lobby the state for child-care provisions. They also sponsored dinners and movie nights at the YWCA on Sutter Avenue in the Union Square district of the city and hosted "Summer in the City," a two-day festival in late August that provided entertainment, food, and crafts while raising money for the Committee.[23]

At one point, the child-care committee also articulated the concerns of lesbian mothers. The Lesbian Mothers Union (LMU), formed by SF NOW member and lesbian mother Del Martin, formed in July 1971 to address the particular needs of lesbian mothers. "These women have found that neither the homophile nor the women's movement has dealt with their particular needs. They live in constant fear and jeopardy that, on discovery of their identity, their children will be automatically taken away. Custody of children has been consistently awarded by the courts to fathers because they were heterosexual—their only recommendation."[24] Although NOW and LMU worked together, the chapter dedicated itself largely to securing state-funded child-care centers and rarely mentioned issues unique to lesbian mothers.[25]

Child-care centers were becoming part of the national agenda as NOW nationally joined other activists and organizations who sought to make child care a salient political issue. In 1972, the U.S. Congress passed a comprehensive child development bill, which, if signed into law, would provide services for middle-class and poor families. This was not the first time that child care was a national issue; in World War II, the federal government subsidized child-care centers. The bill, which proposed $2.9 billion to set up a nationwide system of child-care centers, passed the Senate, and later the House of Representatives. Nixon vetoed the bill that year, citing, among other things, that it would lead to "communal" child-rearing.[26] This issue, however, did not have meaning only at the national level;

local feminists pursued child care because women in their communities demanded it.[27]

Encouraged by the passage of the 1972 Mondale-Javits child-care bill in the Senate, the chapter was then enraged by Nixon's veto. In May 1973, Linda Festa, who chaired the Child Care Committee, reiterated the chapter's support for "the broadest possible availability of high quality child care for all who wish to use it." Moreover, she wrote that "we [chapter members] declare that what Bay Area parents and children need is a crash program to improve the facilities we have now, rather than shutting down of some 80 percent of the centers women now depend on." In the face of federal threats to childcare, "women are to be deprived of the opportunity to work or to study, and in many cases will be forced onto welfare; children are to be deprived of the right to be cared for in a safe, developmental situation with other children."[28]

Within a month, the Childcare Committee joined forces with other interested groups and individuals and formed CAPA, Children and Parents Action, and initiated a plan to put a child-care initiative on the November 1973 ballot in San Francisco. CAPA members devised a petition that, if passed, would direct the Board of Supervisors (the city's elected government) to maintain existing child-care programs as well as to develop new, more comprehensive ones. According to the wording of the petition, "childcare shall include infant care, pre-school and after-school programs" and "be made available to all San Francisco children."[29] By law, CAPA needed 12,000 valid signatures to introduce the petition onto the ballot; operating on a shoestring budget, it sought donated office space, volunteer time, and funds to run this major effort.[30]

In July 1973, chapter president Lorraine Lahr implored members to help gather signatures. She reminded members that CAPA would not meet its goal of 20,000 signatures (8,000 more than legally required, but they sought solid public support of the issue) "unless every member of NOW backs up their endorsement with action." Reminding the chapter that more was at stake, she wrote, "it is terribly important both for our credibility to the outside world and our internal responsibility that when we endorse, we follow through."[31] CAPA also inserted a two-page informational document into the SF NOW newsletter that month, which offered guidelines for petitioning and reminders to purchase yellow "Childcare—YES!" buttons, which CAPA made to raise funds. By July, San Francisco NOW had joined a broad coalition of organizational and individual endorsers of CAPA, including Assembly members Willie Brown and John Burton, San Francisco Federation of Teachers, Union Women's Alliance to Gain Equality (WAGE), SF National Women's Political Caucus, AFSCME Council 56, and the California Federation of Labor Women's Conference of the AFL-CIO.[32]

On August 6, CAPA organized a press conference to coincide with formally filing signed petitions with the Registrar of Voters. Over 15,000 valid signatures were filed and the petition was introduced as "Proposition M" on the November 1973 ballot. The December 1973 "SF NOW" newsletter reported the good news:

"PROPOSITION M PASSES." Hailed "a great victory for women," Proposition M changed the policy of the City and County of San Francisco, requiring both "to provide low cost quality childcare and that the policy for these centers be made by the parents and faculty of each."[33] The newsletter editor also acknowledged that it was "a coalition of parents, teachers, community organizations, women's groups, and trade unions which grew out of the reaction to the cut-backs in childcare earlier this year. It is important to note that San Francisco NOW has played a leadership role in the group and that most CAPA members are women—many of whom are feminists."[34] This vital coalition was born out of both a local feminist commitment to quality child care for citizens and a response to a potentially threatening situation as a result of federal rollbacks for child-care initiatives. They sought new and better legislation, if not at the federal level then at the local one. Working with literally hundreds of other activists, SF NOW, as a member and leader of CAPA, worked within the system to achieve meaningful feminist change.

The chapter also supported and coalesced with other groups on the issue of abortion. When NOW nationally took a stand in favor of abortion in 1968, it lost many members, including Catholic nuns who had served on NOW's founding board and conservative feminists such as Gene Boyer. By the time that SF NOW was founded that same year, NOW was on record in favor of removing all penalties of law against abortion and securing abortion on demand for all women. Unlike the Memphis chapter, which did not address the issue of abortion whatsoever in the 1970s, the San Francisco chapter embraced abortion rights wholeheartedly in the first five years of its existence.

Society for Humane Abortion (SHA) was one of the groups participating in the first Bay Area Women's Coalition meeting in 1969. At that time, SHA had been writing *amicus curaie* briefs for court cases that challenged contemporary California laws and promoted the idea that "a child has the right to come into the world with love—as 'wanted'" and tied the issue of abortion directly to child abuse and feminism. In direct confrontation with current California law, SHA members also assisted women in obtaining abortions.[35] Prior to affiliating with SHA and other abortion rights' groups in the formal coalition, however, NOW hosted lawyer Wray Morehouse and physician Thomas Hart at the May 1969 meeting to discuss repeal of abortion laws. The unidentified newsletter editor offered what she called a "controversial" editorial on abortion, countering suggestions that abortion equated murder because an embryo is not a human being and "therefore abortion is not truly the murder of a human being." After discussing how animals in nature kill one another for survival, she suggested that "killing of both actual and potential life is one of nature's means of insuring a good life in nature; abortion, the killing of potential physical life, should be one of society's ways of insuring a good life for its citizens."[36] She invited members to respond via letters to the editor, "pro and con," and promised to publish them "as space permits," but either no one took her up on the offer or she declined to publish them after all.

Abortion continued to be a featured topic at chapter meetings. In December of the same year, the speaker was Lawrence Swan, who spoke on the topic "Man's Future in the Hands of Women: The Control of Population." The newsletter editor encouraged a large audience for this "stimulating speaker," although members did not necessarily buy into the notion that controlling population was about men's success and future. NOW members supported the repeal of all abortion laws and offered a public forum for pro-choice speakers, but the chapter chastised Zero Population Growth (ZPG), another group advocating the decriminalization of abortion, for having exclusively male officers and only one woman on a thirty-seven-member board. Karen Jacobs, the newsletter editor, asked, "shouldn't one of ZPG's primary goals be to educate society so that women's function is no longer regarded as that of motherhood? And shouldn't ZPG set an example by appointing women to responsible positions? ... If world population is to decrease, society's attitude toward women must change."[37]

The following month, January 1970, the California Committee to Legalize Abortion (CCLA), another group that participated in the September coalition meeting, spoke at the chapter's meeting. At that time, CCLA was working to put an initiative measure on the ballot to legalize abortion in the state of California, framing their argument specifically in the context of an individual woman's right to choose abortion for herself. Member Cheriel Jensen coordinated the meeting, talking in particular about the mechanics of putting an initiative on the ballot. With a looming deadline for signatures, sixteen members worked to get the initiative before the voters but failed to obtain the necessary number of signatures.[38]

After the failure of the initiative, the chapter's activism on abortion was sporadic, with members largely reporting on various things happening around the area. For example, the April 1970 chapter newsletter alerted members that the Berkeley chapter of NOW would host an "ecology booth" at the Wonder Fair (an Earth Day festival) in Oakland; its purpose was "to demonstrate that the best way to solve the overpopulation problem is to legalize abortion and change society so that women have other roles besides motherhood."[39] At the chapter meeting held the following month, members voted to co-sponsor an "Office Abortion Procedures Symposium" to demystify the medical procedure of abortion at the Jack Tar Hotel in San Francisco.[40] They also promoted a new paper, available to members, entitled "Obstetrics in the Wrong Hands." Anne Treseder of both SHA and SF NOW authored the paper, which addressed "what's wrong with the medical treatment of women."[41]

In June 1970, the newsletter editor (Vicki Selmier, who was at this time also chapter president and editing the newsletter only this one time) included a letter from the California Association to Repeal Abortion Laws (ARAL), which informed sympathizers that Senator Anthony Beilenson had introduced a bill before the State Senate that would repeal the state's 1967 Therapeutic Abortion Bill. By doing so, it "would make abortion, finally, accessible to all women without red tape." Patricia (Pat) Maginnis, president of ARAL, outlined when the Senate Judiciary Committee would be holding hearings about the bill, which senators served on the Committee, how important it was to undertake the "tedious task" of letter writing, and where to go to attend the hearings in person.[42] In this same newsletter, Selmier reminded people that "we do have PRIORITIES," abortion rights among them.

Whether it was Selmier's admonition to focus on chapter priorities, the fact that a feasible bill was before the state senate, or the vibrant personality of Pat Maginnis (who joined NOW in the summer of 1970) that mobilized the chapter into action, by August of that year the chapter moved beyond simply reporting on what was happening in the area of abortion rights and engaged in full-blown activism. At the 1970 Women's Strike for Equality, representatives of the chapter spoke forcefully to a crowd of over 1,000 people, demanding free voluntary abortion for all women and no forced sterilization of any woman.[43]

The December meeting was held at the SHA offices, "provided through the generosity of Pat Maginnis and the wonderful women who work with her there."[44] By the next month, Gina Allen, chapter newsletter editor, reported that the California state legislature was showing no signs of repealing "the restrictive state abortion statutes. Relief, if it is to come at all, must come through the courts and/or collective action of women." She further reported that Rita Hersh, a local law student, sought to file a class action suit on behalf of the women of California, naming the state attorney general and all California county district attorneys as defendants. Her hope was that this suit would result in a ruling that would strike down all California abortion laws, making abortion equal to other medical procedures governed by state health codes.[45] Turning the legal system to women's benefit, Hersh indicated that she needed women as co-plaintiffs—they did not have to be pregnant and seeking an abortion at the time because they were suing for the "*right* to obtain an abortion *if and when it is desired*"—following the pattern set by women in New York, who in 1969 joined a similar class action suit and won.[46] Encouraging women to talk about their abortions was important to ARAL and NOW women—"your stories will keep the record complete—lest we forget what we have suffered. And they may teach male doctors some things that only desperate women have learned. Eventually, the accumulated knowledge might even make doctors superfluous."[47]

By June 1971, Hersh and other NOW members had not filed their lawsuit; however, members were alerted to another lawsuit involving two of their members. On June 10, Pat Maginnis and Rowena Gurner, both NOW members and both chairpersons of ARAL, stood trial on a four-year-old charge of distributing information about abortion in direct violation of California's abortion laws. SF NOW members packed the courtroom with women; Gurner and Maginnis were merely fined and reprimanded.[48] The following week, NOW sponsored the radical feminist practice of a speak-out on abortion at Glide Memorial Church. They protested the fact that current state law prevented women from "exercising the simple human right to control our own bodies. We are speaking out for our right to decide for ourselves whether or not to bear children." The event promised to give opportunities to women to speak about their abortion procedures, legal and illegal, to talk with doctors and nurses about safer abortions, and to talk with counselors. The event also featured NOW member Mynra Lamb's short play "of a man who becomes impregnated and seeks an abortion, 'What Have You Done for Me Lately?'"

Of particular interest is the photograph that accompanied this flyer. In this picture, a group of protesting women is holding signs in favor of abortion. All of them are women of color; the woman in the center holds a sign reading "Legal Abortion Si Yes."[49] ARAL also included an insert on the class action suit, reminding women that the only qualification for joining the suit is U.S. citizenship. They did not have to be pregnant or seeking abortion, but the information sheet that ARAL asked potential plaintiffs to offer statements about whether or not the woman had ever obtained an illegal abortion while a resident of the state and whether or not she would be willing to testify about her experiences.[50] In what had become typical form, in July 1971, SF NOW joined the Women's Ad Hoc Abortion Coalition, which advocated repeal of all abortion laws and opposed forced or coerced sterilization.[51]

By October, SF NOW co-sponsored a "Women's Abortion Action Conference" for women in the western United States. This two-day event, held October 15 and 16 at UC-Berkeley, represented a coordinated effort with "sisters all over the country" who "are getting together to demand control over our own reproductive lives … A major focus of the conference will be to plan the building of massive demonstrations on November 20." The advertising flyer featured two photographs: one was an African American woman with an afro and sunglasses holding a hand-written sign stating "defend women's rights to control their bodies." A second woman, also African American, bore a sign featuring a clothes hanger and words reading, "15,000 women murdered by abortion laws."[52] This chapter used the images of women of color strategically to highlight their commitment to reproductive rights, which was much broader and encompassing than the national board's vow to work on repealing all abortion laws. Even if SF NOW did not attract high numbers of women of color, the chapter did show public common cause and alliance with them. The conference offered participants a "teach-in" on how to repeal abortion laws, workshops on methods of demonstration, building coalitions in unions, on college and high school campuses, and among professional women, an educational session on the then-new book *Our Bodies, Ourselves*, and "constituency workshops" to target "Black women, Asian women, Chicanas, Gay women, Mothers, and Older women."[53] At this point, at least to many NOW members, "the repeal of abortion laws is truly a matter of life and death."[54]

Such action and commitment demonstrates NOW members' commitment to the potentially divisive issue of abortion. Given the racial and ethnic diversity in San Francisco and the history of forced sterilizations of women of color, it was understandable that the local NOW chapter worked across real and perceived differences on the issue of reproductive rights. NOW members and abortion rights' feminists joined the related issues of motherhood, abortion rights, and forced sterilization, creating common ground among women and understanding the issues of reproductive rights and freedom far beyond the decriminalization of abortion. Such was clearly the result of coalition building and working with women across race, class, and sexual orientation.

SF NOW members also built coalitions around the issue of job discrimination. The chapter lamented sweat shop labor conditions in and around San Francisco but did not put much of its energy there. Instead, its main focus was to desegregate— or, in the lingo of the day, "desexegrate"—help-wanted ads in local newspapers, following the national organization's goals. In September 1969, at the same time that NOW was hosting the first Bay Area Women's Coalition meeting, Donna Barnhill of the chapter's newly formed JDC (Job Discrimination Committee) encouraged a rather innocuous letter-writing campaign. Letters would not be addressed to the newspaper editor but instead to members' respective employers, encouraging employers to pressure the newspaper to advertise for employment in alphabetical order rather than "Help Wanted Male" and "Help Wanted Female."[55]

The JDC and NOW members went on to address help-wanted ads, but typically did so outside of any formal coalition with other women's groups. In December 1969, JDC members reported that they joined forces with other "Women's Liberation groups" in the area to assist Women, Inc. with its demonstration against Fibreboard Corporation Paper Mills in Antioch, about 45 miles northeast of San Francisco.[56] Women, Inc. had been active since 1966, fighting for three years against the paper mills. Its members "found themselves discriminated against in employment—progression ladders were blocked; labor pools were segregated; … women were barred from many jobs in the plant." One woman with forty-two years' seniority was laid off while a man with one week's tenure was still employed. After filing cases with the Equal Employment Opportunity Commission, which found and documented discrimination, women did not receive any settlement. In spite of its members' own dilemmas, Women, Inc. had been asked to help other women organize at their plants and in other workplace situations.[57] At the December 1969 demonstration, one of many but the first one that NOW reported in its local newsletter, forty-five protesters picketed the main plant, and the women of Women, Inc. "were pleased, surprised, and grateful for the support of NOW and Women's Liberation. They felt a new sense of camaraderie with other women fighting for their rights. The September Coalition meeting has borne fruit."[58] The following month, in January 1970, JDC held a coalition meeting of women's organizations interested in working to fight job discrimination against women. Among the topics on the agenda were extending protective labor laws to men, eliminating unnecessary protective labor laws for women, getting the EEOC to take up cases of sex discrimination, and demonstrating "against that arch exploiter of women—the Bell Telephone Co."[59]

In May 1970, NOW and allied groups started a "counseling and training service for women wishing to enter the trades and crafts." Coordinated by the JDC, women could take courses with NOW member Margaret Bodfish in carpentry, plumbing, and home repairs. Bodfish specifically encouraged high school girls and young women considering careers in the trades to sign up for the courses. Whether or not the classes were successful or highly attended is unknown, but that such overtures were made belies the notion that NOW was only a middle-class women's organization; instead members sought to provide educational opportunities to working-class women in the chapter and in the city.

JDC also worked with the legislature to fight discrimination against women in higher education. Senator Mervyn M. Dymally, a Democrat from Los Angeles, introduced four bills into the state senate, which NOW and JDC supported, to hire more women faculty and administrators; admit more women into state colleges and universities; offer free, full-time day-care centers for children of male and female students, staff, and faculty; and require elementary schools to adopt textbooks that portrayed women and men in non-stereotypical ways.[60]

By October 1970, JDC proudly boasted about its accomplishments. In the space of just over one year, Barnhill reported that "most every move took on significance and resulted in accomplishment." "Although the results of much work such as personal visits and letter writing are not immediately visible," she iterated what she saw as the major undertakings and successes of the JDC, including over one dozen television programs on women's employment issues, a formalized speaker bureau on job discrimination, and ongoing picketing against Crocker-Citizens and Wells Fargo banks for discriminatory banking practices.[61]

With Barnhill's departure from the chapter (for reasons unknown), the chapter focused less on organizing formal coalition efforts on job discrimination and chan- neled its energies into "desexegrating" help-wanted ads in the local newspapers. This action was not new to the NOW chapter or to NOW nationally; members had been working on the issue since 1968. But this single issue became SF NOW's hallmark contribution to alleviating job discrimination against San Francisco women.

In December 1968, members of the local NOW chapter "had a ball carrying picket signs in front of the Hearst Building in downtown San Francisco."[62] They were protesting the local newspaper, the *San Francisco Chronicle-Examiner*, for having sex-segregated want ads, which advertised "Help Wanted Male" and "Help Wanted Female." Among other activities, the protesters "sang amended Christmas carols rather lustily." Although they did not always picket in front of the newspaper's offices, members devoted themselves to this particular issue for several years. By November of the following year, NOW started picketing the newspaper's offices every Friday afternoon. According to Brenda Brush,

> the picketing started on October 10 when NOW decided to join with a new
> Oakland organization called UNISEX, which is a group of men and women
> who recently became aware of discrimination against women in employment
> and having no knowledge of NOW's work in the field, formed their own

organization and proceeded to become active by picketing the SF newspapers for not desexegrating the want ads. More power to them and to us.[63]

By the next month, however, NOW called off its participation and affiliation with the protest because "we did not have enough pickets, the chief reason being that most of our members work."[64] The members decided to pursue different and less dramatic tactics, specifically meeting with Welles Smith, the president of the San Francisco Printing Company, to urge him to "desex the ads."[65]

The NOW chapter took on the local newspapers in what must have felt like a "David and Goliath" sort of battle, but in their struggle they curried public support and awareness. In January 1970, chapter president Victoria Selmier met with the publisher of the *Oakland Tribune*, a smaller local newspaper, who agreed to publicize more activities of NOW and other women's groups. According to the chapter's newsletter, this particular battle was an important step

> in breaking the newspapers' conspiracy of silence against women. Newspapers fight us by silence, by printing only recipes, fashion needs and beauty hints; they rarely print news about legislation pending on behalf of women or of the activities of women working for their civil rights. Newspapers like to pretend that their readers think that all women are content with housework, low pay, and being some playboy's sex object. It is true that most women are still content with their inferior status, but more and more women are not. It is about time newspapers gave these women a voice.[66]

Moreover, the *Oakland Tribune* integrated its help-wanted ads.[67]

The EEOC, charged under Title VII of the Civil Rights Act of 1964 with handling cases of discrimination, decided early in its formation not to address issues of sex discrimination, spurring the formation of NOW in 1966.[68] Women around the country were angered by this decision, and NOW nationally admonished the EEOC for its refusal to hear sex discrimination cases. In San Francisco, Brenda Brush filed a legal suit against the EEOC and the *San Francisco Chronicle-Examiner* in February 1970. She was not at liberty to discuss her case with her fellow NOW members, but while the suit was pending Selmier held independent meetings between herself and Charles Gould, publisher of the paper. According to the chapter newsletter, "Vicki has a mad hope of getting a voluntary desexification by the National [NOW] meeting in March."

Her hopes would be dashed; the newspaper did not give in to the threat, or reality, of a lawsuit. However, aid came in an appropriate but unexpected form: by April of that year, the EEOC reversed its position, claiming instead that newspapers could be regarded as employment agencies insofar as they published advertisements for jobs. The result of this reversal was that the EEOC finally assumed jurisdiction over newspapers and brought them into compliance with Title VII. The EEOC also submitted an *amicus curaie* brief in support of Brush, who in turn dropped the

Commission from her lawsuit. The chapter continued to cheer Brush's efforts; members also reminded one another to continue calling the newspapers to protest sex-segregated want ads.[69] In February 1971, member Judy Copeland Bratcher began "blitzing advertisers in the Examiner-Chronicle want-ads with letters asking them to get their ads out from under the sexegrated listings and put them in the 'Men and Women' category and also to request the Chronicle desexegrate these ads." Members felt that this practice of pressuring advertisers and the newspaper itself was working; "Many Bay Area newspapers have recently reformed their want-ads practices ... but the Ex-Chron still holds out." Ever optimistic, however, Sharon Rufener, chair of the Job Discrimination Committee, reported that "We may win this one yet!"[70] This feeling was buttressed, no doubt, by new legislation giving the Fair Employment Practices Committee (FEPC) new authority and jurisdiction to reprimand and censure newspapers and other agencies for not complying with Title VII.[71] The Job Discrimination Committee kept members abreast of developments, reminding newsletter readers that it was now illegal under state law to discriminate because of sex in employment and that sex-segregated advertising was evidence of such discrimination.[72]

Until April of the following year, however, such proclamations amounted to preaching to the choir. But on April 11, "Two prominent bulwarks of sexism, the San Francisco Chronicle and the Examiner quietly capitulated to 3½ years of pressure from NOW and removed sex-discriminatory 'Help Wanted Women' and 'Help Wanted Men' headings from their classified ads."[73] On page 22 of the *Chronicle*, in the "Miscellaneous" section of the want ads, between "basement cleaning" and "warehouse liquidations," the newspaper editor printed a notice:

> Times have changed and so has the Want Ads Supermarket—Until very recently engineers were almost invariably male. Telephone operators were female. Today, though, a job title is a description of work that can be (and is) performed equally well by qualified people of either sex. We've combined all listings of job opportunities under one heading, "HELP WANTED". This simplified system will aid both job-seekers and prospective employers.[74]

This was quite a switch: in November 1968, an editorial on "The Unmentionable Help-Wanted Ad" suggested that

> by forcing the most widely-read of all want-ads into a coeducational or homosexual [sic] mold, the [Equal Employment Opportunity] Commission is inevitably fostering confusion, embarrassment, and unimaginable troubles upon advertisers, readers, and innocent female job seekers who, misled by an ad that is sexless, apply for a job that has inalterable male characteristics—like, for example, that of a linebacker, chorus boy, or masseur in a Turkish bath ... The hermaphrodite [sic] Help Wanted ad is impractical in this guys-and-dolls world and any law to compel it must be honored chiefly in the breach.[75]

The newspaper did change its policy, the result of "a lot of dedicated effort," including

> several picketings and leafleting, letters to the editor, over 100 complaints
> phoned into the Fair Employment Practices Commission urging action
> against the papers, a Federal lawsuit filed by NOW member Brenda Brush,
> several cases filed with the FEPC, including ones by NOW members Sue
> Sylvester and Ruth McElhinney, several mass mailings to advertisers, warning
> them that they were breaking the law; 3½ years of pressure from the EEOC,
> 1½ years of pressure from the FEPC, an impending Public Accusation, which
> the FEPC planned to file on April 12 (the paper got in under the wire by
> de-sexegrating on April 11).[76]

That it may well have been the Public Accusation that ultimately forced the hand of the newspaper editors does not deny the fact that NOW feminists worked diligently for the issue of integrating help-wanted ads, even if they already had jobs (indeed, income was vital to women such as Brush, who endured costs of a three-and-a-half-year-long lawsuit). The newsletter editor took great pride in noting that "Help Wanted, Men has now become a historical footnote along with such other cultural oddities as ads which said 'white only, Christian preferred' and 'no Irish need apply.' Good riddance."[77]

Desegregating help-wanted ads in San Francisco represents something that the NOW chapter did in concert with formal coalitions, but in large part their actions took place largely independently of the coalitions. With Brush's 1971 lawsuit, very little information was available about the paper's actions; if other groups joined NOW in letter writing and persuading advertisers to pull their financial support to the paper, it is not documented in the NOW papers, nor do members mention it elsewhere. But this was a NOW action that met with the awareness and approval of the Coalition. It was reported largely in the context of the JDC, but seems to have been an issue NOW tackled largely independently. However, members adopted a variety of tactics, from filing formal lawsuits to street politics, from letter writing and supporting state legislation to staging demonstrations outside of the newspaper's offices, to pressure the newspapers to change their sexist policies.

The chapter, then, from its formation until the end of 1973 was focused on and dedicated to a variety of issues and attuned to them as they affected women from all walks of life. Although the membership may not have been much more diverse than the national averages (and there is no way to ascertain its diversity in terms of race, class, and sexual orientation), it clearly reached out, through coalitions, to understand and work on issues in the context of many women's lives. Motherhood, child care, and abortion, and to a lesser degree job discrimination, were somewhat controversial in their own ways, but SF NOW embraced them and undertook action to seek feminist changes on behalf of all women, reflecting their concern with and activism on behalf of women's material rights and advancement. At the national level, NOW has been accused of offering little more than lip service to material rights, but at both the national and the local levels, NOW feminists undertook meaningful action. In San Francisco, they invoked a variety of strategies and tactics to meet these goals, often turning to legislative ends but not exclusively and never with a focus or eye to meeting political goals exclusively. These issues mattered to women in San Francisco, and the SF NOW chapter took on these issues with force and vigor. It is not to suggest that the chapter did not discuss other issues; instead, it is to point out the various coalitions that the chapter engaged in and pursued. However, by 1973, coalition efforts beyond the chapter gave way to conflict within, and in the following year many people left SF NOW altogether.

A Chapter Divided

Although this chapter built and contributed to a rich feminist community in the city, it also suffered from internal conflict. Seeds of discontent were apparent from its first year or two of existence, but it was not until 1973 and 1974 that the chapter ruptured, creating a split and a second NOW chapter in the city (by the mid-1970s, there were several chapters across the Bay Area). This section traces the divisions, the actual split, and the actions of a new NOW chapter, comprised of members who expressly left SF NOW—the San Francisco chapter itself was left with very little energy in terms of members who were actively engaged and it was threatened with dissolution for about three or four years. Although the chapter was remarkably good at building coalitions, it did not always succeed at keeping internal unity.

Many NOW members were aware of the reality that they could not separate their feminist selves from other aspects of their identity or their activism. From its earliest days, NOW members from San Francisco saw themselves as part of a larger progressive community, reflecting in many ways the experiences of Aileen Hernandez, the first Western Regional Director and second president of NOW—and San Francisco resident. Unable to separate the various movements in which she was involved, Hernandez wrote in 1971, after the membership passed a resolution in opposition to the war in Vietnam, that

> I have been very involved in the peace movement, and I would continue to be whether the Regional Conference had taken a position or not. I am also deeply commited to, and working hard in the black movement for equality. I would find it impossible to decide that *all* my energies had to go to NOW—especially if NOW viewed its own interests so narrowly that it did not see a relevance in the struggle against racism and war ... If women are to be equal in society, there are no issues which should be considered beyond their concern—what women have to do, as feminists, is to develop *feminist* positions on these issues ... It is certainly not *radical* at this time to call for an end to the

conflict in Vietnam; it is almost a postscript to a long, star-studded list of anti-war groups. What would be novel would be for NOW to lead—from a feminist approach—a movement against *all* war.[78]

NOW members, from the chapter level to the top levels of leadership, would never be able to separate themselves into various aspects of their identities—for Hernandez, she would never be simply black, or female, or pacifist; she was all at once. Moreover, the issues she addressed were not at odds with "feminism," and she encouraged her NOW sisters to create and adopt feminist approaches to social, political, and cultural problems.

Hernandez's 1971 correspondence with Eve Norman clearly indicates that there was some objection to merging feminism and other social movement activism, and some, including Norman, suggested that the issues of women might get lost in the many contemporary struggles. Indeed, many feminists struggled with what constituted a feminist issue versus a feminist perspective on an issue. A year prior, SF NOW chapter president Vicki Selmier foreshadowed Norman's complaint, indicating that women's issues mattered the most, at least to her. "Contrary to many of my friends," she wrote, "I do not always believe in dissipating energy on issues other than the status of women. Women are always expected to 'Do Good' and to subjugate their lives to the interests of someone or some issues that are more important. I do not believe anything—WAR, DISEASE, HUNGER, CALAMITY, ETC.—is more important than the Status of Women."[79] There is no record of anyone responding directly to Selmier's statement, but the chapter sought feminist perspectives on and solutions to problems as they affected everyone, incorporating race, class, and sexual orientation into their actions. For example, the chapter joined other feminist and women's groups in the Bay Area for the "Women's Conference for Liberation and Peace," a meeting premised on the notion that "women will be free only in a free and peaceful world," merging the issues of feminism and pacifism. The December 5, 1970 event featured workshops and panels on minority women, education, work, sexuality, family structure, and war—all arguably feminist issues. That the chapter supported this event may or may not be in opposition to Selmier's concerns that women's status mattered most, but it is clear that the members of SF NOW pursued common cause with other groups and pursued a variety of interests, making them feminist issues and eschewing any notion that feminism was not about all aspects of women's and men's lives.

By May 1972, the chapter faced what newsletter editor Adele Meyer called "factionalism needling our chapter at present." The source of this factionalism was "disagreement over the meaning and value of 'sisterhood.'" Some members felt that sisterhood had "too sugary a taste" and that women should advance themselves and their individual goals, even if they were not met with the support of the group majority. Others felt that this perspective was too individualistic; women instead should be working for "the Women's Movement as a whole" and in support of all women, not individual women. Meyer clearly sided with the latter view on sisterhood: "Sisterhood means that our activities have ramifications for all women and for the Movement. It … is a realization that my self interest is inextricably bound to the self interest of other women." At bottom, she suggested that "we must put aside this factionalism and have instead honest personal disagreements."[80]

Although it is not clear how "honest personal disagreements" in the context of "sisterhood" would play out, and it is obvious that Meyer had a specific agenda and chose her words carefully to spotlight her "better perspective," feminists in the chapter were faced with threats of division. In March 1973, chapter president Diane Watson used her resignation (occasioned because she was moving to Seattle) as a moment to address the membership in the newsletter. Feeling "free to pontificate and philosophize about the NOW experience," Watson suggested that members had learned vital skills, including how to raise money, lobby, and develop political muscle. "We seem to find it much easier to criticize the people and systems 'outside' in the culture we're trying to change," she wrote, "than even to suggest to each other that an idea may not be perfect. It has been distressing for me to see members vote in favor of programs or statements with which they fundamentally disagree because to disagree would be 'unpleasant.' We must learn to disagree, to criticize each other's positions or actions, without negating our love and respect for each other." Invoking the sensitive subject of sisterhood, Watson suggested, "if we retain our sense of oneness in our essential sisterhood, we can accomplish everything more happily." However, "one of the things that goes along with sisterhood is sibling rivalry."[81]

Lorraine Lahr assumed the presidency after Watson's departure. By May, she suggested a solution to the potential fragmentation that threatened the chapter: priorities. She wrote in her "President's Column" that "today is not my day for saving the world; I am concerned that the San Francisco chapter fulfill its promise" of being "a major player in the Women's Liberation Movement"; "I believe that is best done by narrowing our goals and activities to what can be actually accomplished now or in the near future." Eschewing the notion that NOW or feminism can "save the world," she indicated that the chapter must have priorities because "we cannot vote to do every worthwhile project and then when the time comes for volunteers, sit on our hands. If we vote yes, we should work yes."[82] As she reminded people in the context of child-care activism, clearly a chapter priority, "It is terribly important both for our credibility to the outside world and our internal responsibility that when we endorse, we follow through."[83] In November of that year, Lahr announced on behalf of the board that the major priority for 1974 would be politics—"'74 is a statewide election year and we should be serving notice on and working for those we think will help women reach their goals."[84]

By the following month, however, it was clear that the looming split in the chapter was immediate. Some people objected to the "priorities" mentality, wishing to work instead on whatever issues were important to them as individuals and on issues that expressed a greater perspective of personhood. But the impetus for the divide came in December 1973, when Lahr expressed great disdain for "members and non-members" who "asked for a vote on the establishment of a second chapter in San Francisco." She reported that "there was a great deal of debate, which was finally resolved by an overwhelming vote against establishing another chapter in the city." Although Lahr thought the situation should have been resolved, she commented that "after asking us to vote we were told that it didn't really matter what we voted as 'they' were going to the national board to get an ok regardless of our decision."[85]

"They" in this case turned out to be Del Martin, Phyllis Lyon, Aileen Hernandez, Patsy Fulcher, and other lesbians, women of color, and their allies, who wanted to leave San Francisco NOW and start another NOW chapter in the city. Their reason for leaving was not about whether or not the chapter had the right priorities: in the words of Martin and Lyon, and echoed by Hernandez, "the leadership in NOW was simply racist and homophobic. We were not going to stand for it anymore."[86] Martin led the charge locally, asking the SF NOW membership in October 1971 for a vote on having a second NOW chapter in the city, a departure from national NOW policy—the national bylaws indicated that there could be only one chapter in each city. At the time, there were five chapters in the Bay Area—Berkeley, Marin, Stanford, Oakland, and San Francisco—and all were active to varying degrees, but the San Francisco chapter was the largest, with over 300 dues-paying members. But in each city proper, there could only be one chapter. When SF NOW members voted down the idea of having a second NOW chapter in the city, Martin sought to change the structure.

Rather than continue to fight at the local level, Martin sought a seat on the national NOW board. After what she recalls as a rather contentious struggle because she ran as an out lesbian (the first to do so), she won the seat. "My first order of business," she recalled, "was to change the bylaws so that there could be more than one chapter in a city. I was tired of the San Francisco NOW chapter and its insistence that we deal only with a few issues. As a Lesbian, I could not just be a feminist. I had to be a full activist and San Francisco NOW was not wanting me [Phyllis: 'us, many of us'] to do this."[87] Martin convinced the national board that there could be more than one chapter in some cities; the board agreed and at the national NOW meeting in St. Louis that year, the membership approved a resolution allowing more than one chapter in a city.

Lahr reported her disapproval of this national resolution to the membership. She felt as though she were "dragged" to the St. Louis meeting in spite of her "heartfelt lack of desire" to attend the national meeting because she knew that Martin and others had already planned to push for the resolution. Feeling swindled and bombarded, she suggested that National NOW needed to be "saved" because the board "does not reflect the mainstream of the movement, but a minority which has the time, money, and interest to go to every meeting." Closer to home, though, Lahr fumed at the recalcitrance of those who sought a second chapter even after the local membership had voted down the proposal: "votes taken mean nothing as you don't live with the outcome if you lose. Of course the minority opinion is important and should be listened to, but not to the extent that you refuse to accept the free decision of the majority. Basically this is the ideological difference that NOW faces."[88]

Despite her paeans to majority rule, some members left San Francisco NOW for the Golden Gate (GG NOW) chapter. Indeed, GG NOW attracted some of the most vibrant and active members (including many who attended meetings but did not necessarily join the organization), and the new chapter of NOW flourished for about three years. By comparison, SF NOW languished. New national NOW board member Martin and former national president Hernandez lent the new chapter an air of legitimacy and commitment to action, and GG NOW set out to address many of the same issues that the SF chapter had undertaken—women and credit, political action, and affirmative action among them.

However, the new chapter also publicly addressed other issues, including sexuality and lesbianism. SF NOW had devoted only one chapter meeting (March 1971) to "the Lesbian in the Women's Movement," which featured representatives from DOB (Daughters of Bilitis) and Gay Women's Liberation.[89] In October 1973, at the same time as the call for a new chapter of NOW, Martin hosted a "rap group with NOW and DOB" in an attempt to "widen the channels of communication," and Martin encouraged DOB members who had not joined SF NOW to consider joining the organization.[90] However, the San Francisco chapter did not institute a task force committee on sexuality and lesbianism until February 1974, after the Golden Gate chapter had already formed. Instead, boasting forty-seven members by June 1974, the Golden Gate chapter worked most diligently to discuss issues of sexuality in the women's movement.

Among issues of sexuality that the task force addressed was the thorny issue of prostitution.[91] Virtue Hathaway, a former SF NOW member and current GG NOW member, penned an "advice column" for the GG NOW Newsletter. In September 1974, "a moral feminist" wrote a letter to Virtue voicing her disapproval that GG NOW co-sponsored the "Hooker's Convention" with COYOTE (Call Off Your Old Tired Ethics) at Glide Memorial Church. "Personally, I don't sympathize with the hookers. I find it degrading that these women should sell their bodies. My friends would rather go on welfare than be street walkers. Just how does NOW justify supporting these loose women?" "Moral" inquired. Virtue responded with the fact that NOW nationally had just supported a resolution in favor of decriminalizing the practice of prostitution. More to the point, however, Virtue suggested that "in the realm of feminist ideology, we have made a fundamental commitment to uphold the right of a woman to do with HER body as SHE chooses. This is the basis of our efforts to repeal the abortion laws." Moreover, "our sexuality has been exploited in many ways for a long time, including within the 'moral' institution of marriage. It is time now for women to break away from the barriers society has imposed upon us." She also encouraged "Moral" to "work toward a society free of exploitation, where female and male sexuality are no longer commodities but at the same time let us begin to understand and support our sisters and brothers who must rent (not sell) their bodies for whatever reason."[92] Linking sexuality, labor, and economy, the GG NOW chapter sought complex solutions and perspectives to complex problems. Moreover, this chapter of NOW was much more willing to address the range of women's sexuality and sexual experiences, something the SF chapter of NOW had not tackled.

Where GG NOW really made its mark, however, was in the Bay Area Women's Coalition (BAWC). Resurrected in July 1974 by members of the Golden Gate chapter of NOW and in concert with members of the National Women's Political Caucus, Black Women Organized for Action, and the Susan B. Anthony Democratic club, the BAWC reunited or otherwise brought together over forty groups, focusing its attention on local political issues as they affected the diverse population of women in San Francisco. In its statement of purpose, BAWC identified itself as "an action-oriented group; our 'motto' is 'Affirmative Action through political clout.' We want to help women become an effective, powerful voice in all areas of local affairs."[93]

Although the BAWC undertook several issues in the mid-1970s, its major focus was the Counter-Commissioners Project, which Martin referred to as the "shadow government."[94] The purpose of this project was "to make our Boards and Commissions more open and accountable to the women of S.F." Because there were no women on any of the city's commissions, the Coalition appointed their own representatives to each commission to attend meetings, read all public materials related to the commission, and analyze commission stands. This project's goal was to "increase our understanding of the issues raised in the City government, to prepare ourselves for city races in 1975, to identify able women with political potential, to be a voice for consumers, and to educate ourselves in the realities of the political process."[95] It was also to put the city's overt yet unacknowledged sexism on display. Mayor Joseph Alioto was responsible for nominating members to serve on the commissions, yet he did not nominate a single woman in 1974. Rather than launch yet another letter-writing campaign, GG NOW members and BAWC shadowed the mayor and the local commissions, creating an obvious female and feminist presence in local political matters.

Each of the city's seven major commissions (Airport, Civil Service, Fire, Health Service System, Parking Authority, Police, and Public Utilities) had either three or five members, all of whom were male. By September 1974, at the start of the new government term, the shadow government "installed" two women commissioners on each governmental board. In January of the following year, when a position came open on the city's Police Commission, the Coalition issued a press release appointing outspoken local feminist and lesbian activist Del Martin as the new Police Commissioner. According to the release, "Ms. Martin informed the mayor [Joseph Alioto] that she was available. Alioto neither interviewed Ms. Martin nor responded to her application. Although he had promised that he would appoint a woman to the police commission—albeit in the heat of his bid for governor—he finally appointed a man."

At the same time, the Coalition pushed the city Board of Supevisors to create a local Commission on the Status of Women in December 1974.[96] Learning about the machinations of city government through the shadow government, the Commission called attention to the need for greater awareness regarding city departments' treatment of women and men as equal in employment opportunities and awards. Moreover, the new commission would also review school textbooks to recommend against those deemed to perpetuate sex stereotyping and it would develop a "Talent Bank of Women" composed of qualified candidates for vacancies on city boards.[97] In January of the following year, amid "muttered sounds of disapproval" that "emanated from some of the men in the audience" the city Board of Supervisors endorsed legislation to create a city Commission on the Status of Women.[98] Although there had been some debate as to the size of the commission (seven members, which supervisors originally proposed, or fifteen, which the Coalition suggested), the final proposal called for eleven members, men and women, to be appointed by the mayor in order to "help women gain equality" in the city.[99] The Coalition further insisted that prospective commissioners must also demonstrate interest in "fostering meaningful equality for both women and men" and have the support of at least fifteen signatories on an application for membership, although the mayor had suggested that the only requirement for appointment was legal residence in San Francisco.[100]

The Coalition was successful; on January 20, 1975, the Board of Supervisors passed the ordinance creating the Commison on the Status of Women with all of the Coalition's demands intact. By May of that year, Alioto had named the commission members, some of whom were affiliated with the Bay Area Women's Coalition. With this success, the Coalition continued work on the "shadow government" or Counter-Commissioners Project, beseeching the Board of Supervisors to increase the number of each commission by two and to appoint women to those slots.[101] For several months they worked diligently to get the local government to make this change, and by January 1976 the new mayor, George Moscone, adopted this idea as his own and increased the size of each commission and appointed women to all of them. The shadow government resulted in significant change on behalf of women. Through the efforts of GG NOW and the BAWC, city government in San Francisco became more representative of its constituency and population in the space of two years.

The Coalition certainly worked on other issues—maintaining support for abortion rights, supporting local labor unions in disputes, and addressing issues of poverty in the city. However, the major point of this departure from SF NOW to the BAWC and GG NOW is twofold. First, many women sought to leave SF NOW but wanted to continue their NOW activism rather than abandon the organization altogether. In the words of Aileen Hernandez, "For all of its faults, NOW had it going on."[102] Martin and Lyon echoed this sentiment: "We were a part of the women's movement and for us that meant being in NOW. We later left NOW altogether, but at the time, it was very important to stay with this organization. It had clout and provided opportunity for lots of other women. We just made NOW our own organization and used it to make important changes for women. We also knew lots of women in the city and we could get things done."[103] Getting things done, then, meant staying with NOW and building on NOW's reputation both locally and nationally. Second, this departure from the San Francisco chapter demonstrates how some women were not ready to abandon the potential and possibilities that coalition building offered. Coalitions were essential to the political landscape of San Francisco, and to NOW chapters in the city. It was only through coalitions that some women felt they could achieve feminist goals. Working only on what some defined as NOW's "priorities" was, to some, political and feminist myopia.

The Bay Area Women's Coalition ultimately dissolved by mid-1976. The reasons for this are not documented anywhere, but by the fall of 1976 Martin was appointed to the Commission on the Status of Women, a position she enjoyed for two years. She was also actively writing, having just published her book *Battered Wives*.[104] Hernandez had founded an urban consulting firm, Hernandez and Associates, in 1967, but in the ten years that had passed, she had been working in cities around the country and spent less and less time in San Francisco. She also had been instrumental in other organizations, including the National Black Feminist Organization and Black Women Organized for Action. Margo St. James and Gayle Gifford, both NOW members and COYOTE members (St. James founded COYOTE), were fighting to decriminalize prostitution. With changes in the political landscape, prostitution-rights organizations were starting to create health centers for streetwalkers and to join in common cause with other groups who had been marginalized by discriminatory laws, such as nonviolent drug users who were starting to face harsh mandatory sentencing. With their major goals obtained, the women of the coalition set about to undertake the work that was a product of the changes they had created.

A Chapter Reinvigorated

By 1977, the Golden Gate Chapter existed only on paper in the National NOW offices. There were no active members, no newsletter, and no reports of activism on behalf of the chapter. Alongside the Bay Area Women's Coalition, members of GG NOW moved into other facets of activism, ceased local activism altogether, or moved out of the city. But the San Francisco chapter, which had been in many ways a "paper" chapter (and at points in time between 1974 and 1977, ceased to publish a newsletter or appear in media sources), was reinvigorated, largely due to the national surge in passing the Equal Rights Amendment (ERA) and to the local shifts in the political landscape. The chapter also revived efforts for abortion rights and issues of sexuality, but in the main it was the ERA that stimulated chapter growth. By 1982, with the defeat of the ERA, the chapter waned again, but for about five years the chapter maintained a solid focus on this priority.

Of course, prior to the splintering of the chapter, the ERA had been an important issue for SF NOW members. In January 1970, prior to passage of a national ERA in Congress, the chapter asked the local Board of Supervisors to pass an ordinance prohibiting sex discrimination throughout the city and county of San Francisco, and the Board voted "yes" in favor of equal rights for women in the city. With this local success, chapter members kept their eyes on what was happening with the national ERA, encouraging members to write letters to get the amendment out of congressional committee and onto the House floor and to vote in the upcoming election for pro-ERA senators and representatives.[105] In July 1971, the chapter listed passage of the ERA as one of its three priorities. Because the local government did not need convincing, members saw their chapter's role as one of "educating members and the public about the necessity of the amendment."[106]

By August 1971, however, union opposition to the ERA was growing in the Bay Area. Reasons for the challenges are familiar and are echoed in histories of union feminism—many labor feminists and women in the unions argued that if the ERA were passed, the labor legislation that protected them on the job would be eliminated. The chapter newsletter reminded readers that "protective laws based on sex have already been knocked down by Title VII." Moreover, "that's why NOW is working with other groups to enlarge protective labor laws to apply both to men and women. We are also working for the [national] equal rights amendment."[107] In this issue, member Virtue Hathaway penned an elaborate cartoon featuring a large man representing "union opposition" next to prison cell labeled "dead end jobs" and "union neglect of women's rights"; in this cell are dozens of women with mournful expressions on their faces. The man tosses away a key bearing the label "equal rights amendment." The point demonstrates the resistance that SF NOW members felt: large labor unions could determine the fate of many working women, ultimately offering them only dead-end jobs, low wages, and sex discrimination if they continued to thwart the ERA.[108]

When the ERA passed Congress in 1972, thirty-eight states were required to ratify the amendment and change the constitution. In the California state legislature, assembly members voted in April 1972 to approve the amendment. In front of "about 1,000 cheering women and several very unhappy women," assembly members approved the ERA. Opposition from Union WAGE (Union Women's Alliance to Gain Equality) was not strong enough to persuade the California Assembly to reject the ERA. One assemblyman, Alister McAlister, felt that, if the ERA became law, "men would be able to swear in front of women"—to which one NOW member quipped, "Goddamn, I never realized there was a law making that illegal." He was also evidently concerned that it would overturn statutory rape laws, in spite of the fact that California did not have one at the time.[109] When the ratification resolution moved to the state Senate, "California came dangerously close to losing the Equal Rights Amendment." As senators debated what one senator called the "Minnie Mouse legislation," they heard testimony from powerful leaders of state-organized labor, including John Henning of the California Labor

Federation, who testified that the ERA would eliminate protective labor legislation for women.[110] The Senate ultimately refused to bring the resolution out of the Judicial Committee.

By October of that year, however, Senator James Mills reversed his position and decided to vote to send the ratification resolution (Assembly Joint Resolution 17) to the floor of the Senate. His reversal was formally attributed to the result of a blue-ribbon panel of experts to assess the legal impact of the ERA, but NOW members speculated that it was likely the result of a recall campaign initiated by a coalition of women in his home county of San Diego and his desire to seek the office of governor in 1974 or 1978.[111] The issue, however, that remained was labor opposition to the ERA. Diane Watson met with Union WAGE leaders, at which time NOW agreed to support AB 1710 in exchange for Union WAGE's support for ERA ratification in California and also in other states where the amendment had not yet been ratified.[112] In the following month, November 1972, the state assembly and senate ratified the ERA, joining twenty-six other states in ratifying the amendment that year.

By 1977, however, when the chapter revived, the ERA was still in need of three more states to ratify the amendment. By 1975, the thirty-five states that were going to ratify the amendment had done so. But the deadline was rapidly approaching, and NOW nationally was mobilizing for an extension of the ERA deadline to June 30, 1982. In November 1977, when the chapter issued its first newsletter in six months, the ERA was literally front and center. On the front of the newsletter was a drawing of "Ms. Claus," obviously a member of NOW, bearing the feminist gifts of affirmative action, child care, reproductive rights, and the ERA. Someone had also altered the lyrics of "Santa Claus is Coming to Town," to suggest instead that "Equal Rights is Coming to Town."[113] On a less playful note, the chapter signed on to NOW's national boycott of states that had not ratified the ERA, encouraging members not to "travel or vacation in unratified states" and to "try to persuade all organizations of which you are a members to join us in boycotting these states."[114] The following month's newsletter recounted the effects of NOW's "economic sanctions" against states that had not ratified, indicating that several professional organizations—including the American Association of University Women, the Modern Languages Association, and the American Psychological Association—agreed not to hold conventions in unratified states.[115] In December, the chapter also co-sponsored a press conference with the SF Commission on the Status of Women, Common Cause, and Bay Area Women's Coalition, asking Governor Jerry Brown to spend no state money on out-of-state expenses in states that have not ratified the ERA. The newsletter indicated that NOW supported this stance on the ERA, which the governor "received enthusiastically," pledging his support for the pro-ERA position and economic boycott.[116]

Beyond working in the legislative arena, members also took to the streets in support of the ERA—this in spite of the fact that the ERA had passed in their state five years before and a local ERA had been enacted seven years prior. For example, on Mother's Day 1979, SF NOW members met at member Val Weston's home and went in teams to shopping areas in San Francisco to distribute ERA buttons, membership information, and pro-ERA petitions. NOW members nationwide were gearing up for the extension campaign, but locally members also wanted to draw attention to issues of equality by giving "mom what she has always needed—a chance for equal rights."[117] By August 1979, members put the ERA on the agenda at every event possible, including a local Walkathon in which a dozen members walked with pro-ERA placards and distributed information about the ERA and NOW's boycott.[118]

Mirroring what was happening among national organizations, any rifts between SF NOW and local labor were repaired by 1980. At the International Women's Day celebration, a range of speakers, including Addie Wyatt and NOW president Ellie Smeal, addressed the broad feminist/labor coalition in support of the ERA. The photograph on the cover of the newsletter featured women who had partici-pated in the previous year's IWD (International Women's Day) demonstration—a racially and ethnically diverse group of women and men under a large banner encouraging people to "Join San Francisco NOW!"[119] In addition to this event, NOW members joined union members in the "Bay Area Labor Salute to the ERA," a rally that drew approximately 250 people. This rally "shows that the coalition of union organizations and women's rights groups has tremendous poten-tial for building the kind of movement that can win ERA ratification."[120] News-letter notes continued to praise the newfound love and coalition building between feminists and union activists, encouraging members to travel with local labor con-tingents to Chicago for the major ERA rally to be held on May 10 in the as-yet-unratified state of Illinois.[121] Back on the local front, the chapter launched a picket that involved NOW women, local labor activists, and university students at the Mormon temple in Oakland. Approximately 200 picketers protested in opposition to the church, which opposed the ERA and donated large sums of money to anti-ERA organizations and candidates for elected office.[122]

This demonstration at the Mormon temple, in particular, offered the moment to reflect on why it was that San Francisco feminists in NOW continued to demon-strate and work on behalf of the ERA. "This kind of event and the attendant press coverage, which was fairly extensive in this case, does a great deal to keep the ERA in the minds of its supporters and to expose its opponents and their questionable activities. Our time for passage is running short. We must not let it run out."[123] And on the point of public demonstration, SF NOW felt that public action was the only way to mobilize people to action on behalf of the ERA. Carole Seligman, newsletter co-editor, opined that

> SF NOW has long been providing more militant action proposals to National NOW both by example and by resolutions at NOW conferences. Now the need to provide an alternative strategy—one of *mobilizing* our members in national visible actions—is more necessary than ever before … If the attacks

that this [Reagan] administration levels against us go unanswered in the field of *action*, more and more deadly attacks will follow. Massive mobilizations keep our issues in the spotlight, inspire our supporters, and put our enemies on notice that the political costs of denying a popular movement will be heavy indeed.

Her forceful words were concluded with a plea to get as many SF NOW members as possible to Washington, DC for the National NOW conference in an attempt to persuade national leaders and membership to pursue more demonstration tactics.[124]

In spite of the rhetoric and paeans to "militant" actions on the part of NOW locally and nationally, the national board rejected militancy in favor of one more march in Florida. Like Memphis NOW, the SF NOW chapter was back in business with the renewed effort of the ERA; also like Memphis NOW, with its defeat, the chapter could not sustain prior levels of activism. Not until the late 1980s did the local chapter reemerge as a local force.

Conclusions

After fourteen years of existence and a major rift in the organization, members continued to pursue their own issues through and with the support of the organization and in concerted effort with other groups in the city. Such activism recalls one of the earliest SF NOW newsletters in which the editor encouraged members to "do your own thing" and reminded activists that they "have many diverse reasons for joining N.O.W. You can find purpose and a sense of accomplishment in working at what interests *you*."[125] Indeed, members of SF NOW (as well as GG NOW and the BAWC) did their own thing, individually and collectively. Their activism was rooted not only in personal interest but also in enhancing and strengthening the community. As the chapter pursued feminist goals, its members rarely divorced them from other contemporary social justice issues.

Most of their battles were fought within the liberal establishment, but their strategies were not simply liberal ones. Instead, their activist repertoire included everything from letter writing to public protests. They publicly shamed local leaders who resisted NOW and/or feminism; they applauded those who supported them (and pledged their support at the polls). They held speak-outs on abortion and demonstrations to "desexegrate" help-wanted ads; at the same time they met with local and state leaders to enact legislation to allow women to obtain legal, safe abortions and with local newspaper editors to change policies. In a city where you could join any number of groups, NOW was able to secure its place as a local political feminist force, but, as was the case in Memphis, would never serve as the only organization or site of feminist activism.

As the core of its activism, SF NOW focused its attention on issues related to women's rights and abilities to work—job discrimination, child care, removing sex categorization from help-wanted ads, and protection on the job. As they tackled issues that reflected material rights, they worked on the ground to create meaningful change for women. Offering much more than rhetoric, SF NOW feminists created significant coalitions on issues of child care and abortion rights and fought to make change in the city and the state so that women would have greater opportunities for economic advancement. They focused on economic issues and pursued ways to enhance women's economic lives, whether through better job opportunities, child care, or reproductive control. When the chapter divided, many energetic members went to the new GG NOW, which maintained a focus on coalition building. Through a solid coalition effort, these women changed the face of city government.

The history of SF NOW illuminates in significant ways how feminists worked across the politics of identity to create feminist change on the ground. Rather than see difference of race, class, or sexual orientation as an obstacle, SF NOW members embraced difference in coalitions. They did not set aside such differences; instead, they worked through them, using them as a source of strength. Members of San Francisco NOW redefined for themselves what feminism was, eschewing the notion that it was simply a white woman's term and that NOW was simply a white women's organization. Much of this likely reflects "left coast" feminism or feminism in a "wide-open town," and SF NOW members' activism, like that of other San Franciscans, reflected the political and cultural space for creating change. San Francisco feminists in NOW did not embrace a regional identity as such, although they were always aware of the geographical (and philosophical) distance between themselves on the West Coast and the national offices on the East Coast. Moreover, they did not enter into conflict with the local government to the same degree as NOW chapter members in Memphis and Columbus. As the feminist front of progressive change, SF NOW would be successful only in coalitions with other organizations, and they were. The context, then, in which their feminism emerged certainly shaped their activism and gives us reason to reconsider the role of location in understanding feminism on the West Coast.

6

LEARNING FROM GRASSROOTS
ACTIVISMS IN THE PAST

In 2002, the Columbus chapter of NOW solicited members and interested parties
to take an online survey on the status of the chapter and of women in the city. A
paperless survey via the web stands in striking contrast to the reams of paper surveys
filed away in archives (as well as people's basements and attics), and that alone serves
as one of *countless* reminders of how much has changed since the heyday of the
movement for women's equality and liberation. And we must attend to change
both in the aftermath and as a result of feminist activism. But what remains the same
from the 1970s to the 2000s is the chapter's motive: allegiance to grassroots politics
and effecting change at the local level. The 2002 survey led with the statement that
"NOW seeks to remain *grassroots* and engage in actions that benefit women, men,
and children in Central Ohio … recogniz[ing] two primary principles: 1) All politics
are local and 2) the personal is political."[1] Thirty years prior, in 1972, chapter
members asked of people in Columbus, "would you like to know what is going on
in the women's movement locally as well as nationally? Many things are happening,
but would you like to MAKE them happen? Really DO something about the
problems that concern you most? Then what are you waiting for? We need you,
your ideas, your help and support. Join our organization as a member—make it
your organization."[2]

That "all politics are local" and NOW "is your organization" suggest that this
chapter, and many sites of grassroots feminist activism, go beyond national directives
and formalities to embrace women's needs in their own day-to-day lives. Far
beyond paeans to feminism as a nationally identified movement, feminists were
responding to local situations—hence the commitment to feminist activism on
the ground, addressing local concerns in locally significant ways. Most of the feminists whose words, actions, and theories are chronicled in this book were part of a

national organization for women, but they constructed, contributed to, and contested feminist communities in their respective cities.

Any historical perspective of a social movement treats it as if activists did not
know what the conclusion would be. In the case of feminism, we have to
remember that there was never a foregone conclusion with respect to how feminist
actions would go. When Memphis NOW members took to Overton Park to protest rape, when Columbus NOW members picketed in front of Red Door Tavern
to protest discrimination in public accommodations, or when San Francisco NOW
members demonstrated in front of the *Chronicle-Examiner* offices to challenge sex-
segregated want ads, they could not anticipate fully how other chapter members,
fellow feminists, city residents, or others would respond. They also could not pre-
dict if their action would translate into success. But what is incredibly meaningful—
and often overlooked in feminist activism since the 1970s—is their willingness to
step into the breach, even if it meant making mistakes. And to be sure, they made
mistakes. Persistent racist, classist, and homophobic actions permeate the histories
of feminism nationally and locally, as do overt challenges to these actions and
perspectives. And, from these missteps, we see the development of deeper
analyses of feminist perspectives that operate from anti-racist, anti-homophobic, and
anti-classist points of view. With reflexivity and political education in the
histories and deep roots of sexism, racism, classism, and homophobia, we are
much more able to address local issues with myriad tactics toward goals of social
justice.

In *Groundswell*, feminists engaged around all of these dynamics in face-to-face
ways. In every place, such engagement led to fracture and divide, particularly
around issues of hetero- and same-sex sexuality. Memphis NOW split over the
softball team, which stood as a thinly veiled euphemism for a sense that the chapter
was starting to appear to be run and populated by lesbians. In San Francisco, some
members just were not willing to stand for what they perceived to be homophobia
and racism; they left SF NOW to form a different chapter of the same organization.
To them, NOW was not the problem; local feminists in the chapter were. It is easy
to see divides as problematic, but many social movement scholars agree that division
and disagreement are often signs of vitality. Indeed, here, they represent feminists'
willingness to engage difficult, interpersonal problems that might have been reflected nationally or between and among visible leaders but really had the most resonance on the ground. They demonstrate how "sisterhood" may have been
employed as a term, especially in San Francisco, but that it would never suffice as an
organizing principle. But what did work was a sense of community, which as
sociologist Nancy Naples suggests, "is created in and through struggles against violence and for social justice and economic security, as well as through casual interactions with people who share some aspect of our daily lives."[3] *Groundswell*
illustrates not only that feminists in the 1970s created and contributed to their
communities but also how such community building and shaping took place.
Moreover, it highlights the local context in which feminists were able to create and

sustain their identities, organizational ties, and community dynamics. Whether in a sleepy little river town in the mid-South, a Midwestern capital city, or the wide-open town on the West Coast, women developed feminist consciousness not only through a national feminist "imagined community" but also through day-to-day experiences in their own cities.

Groundswell offers insights into the different ways feminists acted with respect to the same or similar issues. In the ten years between 1972 and 1982, the National Organization for Women focused on passage of the ERA and beseeched its chapters to continue work for the amendment, and chapters responded—it was the only way that all chapters toed the national line, even if with different means and relevance. Once the amendment passed both houses of Congress, the ERA became a *local* issue for feminists. National NOW issued many statements on the amendment and its leaders and members throughout this ten-year period believed that the amendment would become the twenty-sixth amendment to the Constitution.[4] And they had reason to be optimistic: by the end of 1972, twenty-two states had ratified the amendment, and five years later, thirty-five states were on board. When NOW and other feminist groups lobbied Congress in 1979 for an extension to the ratification deadline, the organization redoubled efforts, organizing marches in Washington, DC and in Chicago and Tallahassee, capitals or major cities in states that still offered a chance to ratify.

The case of Memphis NOW makes abundantly clear that feminists did not anticipate how opponents to the amendment would organize, and with such success that the state legislature rescinded its support of the ERA. In Columbus, likewise, the chapter faced entrenched organized resistance, not only from STOP ERA and Phyllis Schlafly but also from labor unions who had a home in the city and the region. In both chapters, and unlike San Francisco NOW, when Congress breathed new life into the ERA, chapter members responded to national NOW's call to push the amendment through three more state legislatures. Members of Memphis NOW traveled to Chicago and Tallahassee, promising to "bury the image of the helpless, stay-in-your-own-backyard Southern belle."[5] Columbus NOW feminists preferred to stay in their own hometown, drawing attention to the ERA in what became a bloody standoff between pro-ERA activists and pro-Ronald Reagan (who was anti-ERA) supporters.[6]

Members in all three chapters shared a sense that the amendment would not be defeated—as one feminist shared with me conversationally, "we were ... so optimistic about the future of humanity."[7] Optimism, however, was insufficient in the face of the well-mobilized opposition—Eagle Forum, STOP ERA, Concerned Women of America, and other organized, conservative religious and political forces, all of whom worked to bring together masses of people to oppose not only the amendment but also welfare, affirmative action, and other progressive legislative measures.[8] For those opposed to the ERA, the amendment tapped into their worst fears. As one Oklahoma woman suggested, the ERA "would affect my life more than anything else—it would affect my religion—it would affect my own financial situation in that it would change Social Security Laws. It would affect my home life in that my daughter would have to go to war. It would affect everything in my life—if this Equal Rights Amendment were passed!"[9]

Defeat was difficult, as NOW members in each chapter, and feminists across the nation, watched as June 30, 1982 came and went. The tides had shifted, to be sure, and the defeat of the ERA was a significant turning point for many women in NOW. One Memphis NOW member poignantly recalled how defeat affected her personally: "My husband and I were watching television all night, switching back and forth between channels to hear any of the latest updates. I knew it was inevitable and fruitless to torture myself like this, but I just had to know. They finally announced that the ERA had failed. And I just sat there on my bed and cried. He kept … telling me it would be ok. But I knew it wouldn't, saying it wouldn't be ok."[10] Saddened, angry, and in the case of some in Columbus NOW, literally beaten and bloodied, feminists in NOW struggled with how to cope. In San Francisco, one NOW member promised revenge at the polls through these revised lyrics to the song "Hey Look Me Over":

> You screwed us over, you voted nay
> We're going to get you come election day
> Don't count your votes, boys, don't feel secure
> We're going to get you in the end of that you can be sure
> We'll be back by the millions, you know this is true
> Hang on to your ass boys, we're coming after you
> So here's the lesson we learned that year, on this you can rely
> When we are screwed, we multiply.[11]

Whether or not they made good on the promise to unseat them in subsequent elections, it is clear that the defeat resonated with NOW members in their chapters, communities, even their own homes. But anger, however righteous, was not enough to rally after the amendment's defeat. And in the face of successful opposition to the amendment, and to so-called women's rights, feminism, and progressive activism in general, the women's movement abated.

Although NOW chapters suffered a decline in membership nationwide and in each chapter studied here, the chapters themselves never disappeared. Part of this reason, as this project demonstrates, is that, at the local level, NOW never was a single-issue organization. Whether or not the ERA passed or failed was important, to be sure, but it never was the only issue chapter members addressed. In Memphis, San Francisco, and Columbus, NOW members and activists had faced and sought to solve a variety of issues—rape, domestic violence, child care, equal employment, sexual harassment on the job, sex-segregated want ads, the cultural perpetuation of sexism, the "second shift," and more. As Janet Burnside, former Columbus NOW member, noted, "that's what was exciting about NOW. You'd find a problem and leap on it and try to solve it."[12] The issues they addressed depended not just on a national feminist agenda and a singular "wave" of feminism, but also on their day-to-day experiences and observations. As Aileen Hernandez explained, NOW chapters (and perhaps, by extension, feminists) would never "look like cookie cutters of each other because the local issues differed dramatically from place to place."[13] Exploring their divergent strategies and goals—the dynamics of feminism in action—reveals the importance of understanding how local context shapes and is shaped by feminist activism.

Addressing such a wide range of issues meant employing a wide variety of strategies. In some situations, "you'd be noisy. You'd solve [problems] in a noisy way. You were always calling people and having a demonstration."[14] Each chapter used street politics, direct actions, and other forms of demonstrations for different issues. In Memphis, for example, chapter members "took back the night" in a march around Overton Square to protest rape and the commodification of women, while Columbus feminists in NOW drew both public and legal attention to the overt sexism of a businessmen-only dining area and a local business's sign promoting violence against women. In San Francisco, chapter members marched for reproductive rights and targeted the local newspaper's offices in protest of sex-segregated want ads. In other situations, NOW chapters employed less dramatic means to meet goals, often seeking to force businesses and employers to comply with equal employment legislation. Whether suing the police department, as Columbus NOW did, or suing the *San Francisco Chronicle-Examiner*, as San Francisco NOW did, chapter members were not afraid to use the courts to their advantage and force the letter, if not the spirit, of new laws.

Merging planned and spontaneous demonstrations with legal actions becomes, then, a historical hallmark of NOW feminists. San Francisco NOW demonstrated outside of the newspaper's main offices while it simultaneously filed a lawsuit; likewise, Columbus NOW picketed the Red Door Tavern and sued its owner at the same time. Memphis NOW members never officially filed any lawsuits, preferring instead to draw public attention to rape, for example, and forcing the city to respond efficiently and effectively. Moreover, in Memphis, the NOW chapter did not have the resources to pursue lawsuits (although one Columbus NOW member recalled that her chapter did not have "deep pockets" and suing the police department "nearly broke the chapter").[15] But the chapter and feminists in the city, perhaps even throughout the South, never were as successful pursuing legal equality. In Memphis, gender difference was more pronounced culturally and feminists successfully employed difference from men to make concrete gains. Whether drawing attention to rape—a crime perpetuated by law only against women—or insisting that the "Southern belle" would help the South "rise and ratify" the ERA, Memphis NOW members reluctantly invoked women's equality to men. But in Columbus and San Francisco, women in the respective NOW chapters were able to employ rhetoric of sameness with men and force legal equality because the cultural contexts mandated it. Rhetoric of difference shaped the actions of the chapter members less in these two cities.

These three chapters are still in existence, albeit with fewer members than they enjoyed during the heyday of feminist activism in the 1970s. Each is also confronting remarkably similar issues, from lesbians' rights to reproductive justice, from media and educational representations of women to realities of sexual violence. That the issues of the past remain the issues of the present should give us pause—we may have come a long way, but we still have a long way to go, and the histories of these chapters, and of feminism more generally, should inform our current activisms.

Through a grassroots lens on these three NOW chapters, *Groundswell* reveals the limitations of the liberal/radical divide as a historical framework for understanding second-wave feminism in the United States. None of these chapters can be forced under the rubric of liberal feminism, often equated with NOW in academic scholarship. As this project makes clear, local contexts mandated a variety of strategies, both in the courts and in the streets. Moreover, women who joined NOW were not particularly moved by national calls to feminist actions. Although much is made of the importance of Friedan's *The Feminine Mystique* as a milestone in the movement of feminism from abeyance to "white-hot mobilization,"[16] only one member, Columbus NOW's Mary Havens, mentioned that this book was instrumental to her becoming a feminist and joining the NOW chapter. For many others, motivations to join the NOW chapter ranged from moving to a new city and looking for other feminists and women's community to a personal "click" moment on the job, from a personal experience of violence at the hand of a husband or boyfriend to a general desire to alleviate frustration with sexism through activism. Various actions also drew attention to the respective chapters, which then drew new members. For example, within six months of Columbus NOW winning its lawsuit against the police department, membership, at least on paper, doubled.[17] In Memphis, the successful city-league softball team "grew the chapter for years."[18]

Moving beyond the liberal/radical divide, then, allows us to examine similarities and differences between and among these three chapters of NOW. Local context also shaped the place of the NOW chapter within the city's political history and contemporary activism. In Memphis, NOW was the only game in town; as such, it was everything to everybody. By contrast, San Francisco NOW was a part of a force for progressive and feminist change. It never would be the only place where feminists converged, but it was where people went if they wanted to be on the forefront of progressive coalition building while providing a feminist framework for change in the city. Columbus NOW, however, was occupied space between the two networks of feminist activists already in operation in the city; indeed, Columbus is the only city of the three under study here that has classic and separate liberal (or self-defined as "moderate") and radical feminists. NOW in this city fell somewhere in between and oftentimes beyond this divide.

Of the three chapters, only members in Columbus NOW outwardly expressed a self-defined radical feminist politics, although members in all three chapters identified with the movement for "women's liberation." None embraced what scholars have called "liberal feminism" or identified as "liberal feminists." By minimizing preconceived notions about this organization and the women's movement and exploring instead how feminists identified themselves and what they did to create feminist change in their communities, this project advances a historical analysis of NOW. As such, it reshifts epistemological foundations of second-wave feminism, challenging how we know what we know about this organization and the movement by taking a grassroots perspective to explore this organization and this movement historically. Each chapter, in its own way, is an outlier when compared to the other two, which further illustrates the impossibility of thinking about NOW, and by extension second-wave feminism, as exclusively liberal or radical.

As each chapter sought to represent feminist action in its respective city, chapters did not always handle change and difference easily, and, as noted, each chapter divided. SF NOW was the first chapter to split, which it did in 1973; many of those who left formed a second chapter of NOW in the city to continue feminist work under the auspices of NOW but with a different local leadership and mission. The Columbus chapter split six years later over what one called "respectability." After the Gahanna Five painted the "Great Wall of Gahanna," some members protested that the hard work of the chapter in building respectability through its successful lawsuits and demonstrations ruined the chapter's reputation. Whether or not the chapter seemed to be a "lesbian" organization divided the Memphis chapter. The successful softball team "grew the chapter" but, for some, the increase in lesbian membership and visibility of lesbians affiliated with NOW was too much, prompting some members to leave the organization altogether.

These rifts, apparent only when we study NOW chapters and the development of feminism in various communities, suggest that social movement organizations do not always agree on who the organization and the movement represents.[19] As the chapters sought to implement inclusivity, indeed, be an organization "for women," members struggled over which women that meant. As they did so, they did not address difference outwardly to much success. It is of no surprise that NOW, either nationally or among its chapters, never boasted a large membership of women of color. However, viewing this organization's failure to attract a large number of women of color obscures the agency of Black, Latina, Asian, and Native American women to pursue their own "separate roads to feminism" and their own organizations. Moreover, it obscures what NOW feminists did in concert and coalition with various other feminist and women's groups across racial and class divides, especially in local communities. SF NOW's child-care coalition, Columbus NOW's lawsuit against the police department, or Memphis NOW's comprehensive rape crisis center did not address white women exclusively; nor were members motivated to work only on behalf of or with other white women. Instead, they worked together from the venues and organizational presences with which they were comfortable and built coalitions on the ground. Rather than reiterate the already-established fact that most white women's organizations failed when they sought to do "outreach," I explore instead how and when NOW chapters engaged in various coalitions and projects to effect change in the lives of all women. Many NOW members on the ground did not want to undertake "outreach"; instead they sought to work with other women and feminists to create meaningful change.[20]

The dawn of the twenty-first century is a fortuitous time to examine and analyze social movements of the 1960s and 1970s, and the women's movement is no exception. Forty-plus years allow for historical distance, and we are able to see shifts in social movements generally without waxing nostalgic for days gone by. As feminists, we struggle with tropes of the passing of feminism, either into obscurity and irrelevance today or into death altogether. We are inundated with insistences that our movements of the past are dead or hardly recognizable today, and pundits from all points on the political spectrum query whether feminism is dead and insist upon the end of the women's movement, as feminist Courtney Martin did in 2009.[21] Of course, the "premature burials" of feminism are nothing new.[22] Generational divides seem to precipitate these death knells as older and younger activists insist on their differences in style, strategy, and substance. Martin, for example, imagines a movement of the past that was about "marching in the streets, about taking over offices, about riding around the country in vans, falling in love." She notes that it "sounds like they had a whole lot of fun, but also managed to make some profound political change" but insists that "the era of a singular feminist agenda is over." Even as there is continued gender-based activism, feminism as it must have been "during the heyday of direct action" is the past, not the present or future. She insists finally that there will never be a "global, or even national uprising of women focused on one singular goal ... And that's not a bad thing" because there will always be many women who continue the work of feminism. She confesses that her feminism is "a little less romantic" but what is most romanticized is her image of feminism gone by. I draw on Martin's short piece here because she underscores even further the need to understand our feminist history. She expects that hers is a "million little grassroots movements" versus a monolithic feminist agenda of the second-wave era. But the generation before her—us, since she and I are close in age—never had a singular agenda.

Older activists pen letters to younger activists, as Phyllis Chesler did in 1997, to instruct them, rather dismissively, on how to get it right; many others have lamented that they cannot find young feminists in the movement.[23] Mimeographed and mailed newsletters have been replaced, by and large, with "in real time" media hits, and the eruption of social media allows many groups and individuals to organize and mobilize through Facebook, YouTube videos, Twitter, blogs, and other virtual networks. Martin is right: feminists are online, even as they still move into the streets, as they did in the 2004 March for Women's Lives and did in cities around the world in 2011 SlutWalks. The "picket lines and in-person consciousness raising groups"[24] may be a thing of the past, but I am not so sure. What I do know is we may not be looking at the end of a movement as much as we have to confront the reality that times have changed. Since September 11, 2001, or even before, with the WTO demonstrations in Seattle in 2000, the streets no longer belong to activists as they did once before.

Means of mobilization and activism may be different, but many issues remain the same. Scholars and activists alike may continue to debate the efficacy and impact of new social media outlets as tools of social movement organization and the shifts in political communication and strategies for organization. But we cannot lose sight of the reality that what gets lost in the continued popular insistences that feminism is dead, or so radically transformed that "girl power" is actually feminist, is that we are losing historical ground. When activists' papers are not archived, oral histories are not recorded, and assumptions about our shared and different pasts as feminists (and paths to feminism) prevail, students, scholars, and activists of the current and next generations are left to assume that feminism simply happened and operates around us.[25] Contemporary feminism is both "everywhere and nowhere," as Jo Reger brilliantly suggests,[26] but we as scholars and activists are obliged to push back against the dominant idea that feminism is something that happened in the past and is now over, whether it is still necessary or not. In this political and cultural moment, calling for or suggesting the end of feminism is not only inaccurate but also is incredibly detrimental.

To counter these voluminous and, at times, seductive calls of feminism's demise, scholars have an important role to play. Scholars of social movements—general theoreticians as well as social scientists and historians of activism—have been developing analytical frameworks as well as nuanced studies of this era to move beyond the familiar, often biographical observations of this time as romanticized heady days of activism.

More and more scholarship refutes the labeling of feminism as liberal or radical (or, to a lesser extent, socialist or lesbian), and with the production of historical scholarship it becomes clear that feminists have always had complex points of view, embraced a number of strategies and goals, and sought alliances with numerous organizations and networks. As Nancy Hewitt aptly noted, there are no permanent waves, but there are also not stable categories of categorization. Yet these labels have tremendous staying power, undergirding persistent and broad narratives about feminism, especially in the 1970s. *Groundswell* will not be the final book to address this problem, but we have to consider moving away from these overly simplistic narratives. And it matters, whether we seek to desist with the continued premature burials, insistence that feminists suffer from "ritualistic matricide," undo false myths about feminists, or tell more accurate histories of our past so as to enrich our future; as feminist theorist Clare Hemmings keenly reminds us in her work on telling feminist stories, "we know better."[27]

By understanding activists in their own milieu and communities, and by exploring how they sought to address change in their own communities, we can push back against dominant narratives about feminism. When feminists today put forth ideas that their movement is multifaceted and can no longer push toward a singular feminist agenda, I scratch my head wondering where they got the idea that any feminist movement *ever* had a singular agenda. In *Groundswell* alone, feminists took on the ERA (which was a state-based issue for the decade in which it passed

Congress to its defeat), rape, reproductive justice, economic inequality, sex-segregated want ads, child care, on-the-job discrimination, and more. Furthermore, they pursued goals on all of these issues through various strategies, from letter-writing campaigns and political elections to speak-outs and "zap" actions—all while in deep conversation with one another. Sometimes conversation gave way to conflict, but feminists continued to fight from a multifaceted agenda.

So we have much work to do to keep our feminist histories vibrant and alive. To do so, we must embrace Clare Hemming's reminder to tell stories differently. If we are to break out of narratives of progress or loss for feminism—the idea that we have advanced feminist goals and agendas or lost them—we must turn our attention back to historical research. Beyond that, we must incorporate history—and the importance of history—into our current conversations and activisms, to provide a foundation on which we build our present and future activisms. So perhaps part of telling stories differently involves telling different stories. As Gerda Lerner poignantly observed, "We live our lives; we tell our stories. The past becomes part of our present and thereby part of our future. We experience; we give voice to that experience; others reflect on it and give it new form. That new form, in turn, influences and shapes the way next generations experience their lives. That is why history matters."[28]

But we also need to understand that which makes obvious sense to us as activists but continues to elude us in our activism and narrativizing about it: work is often global and local at the same time. In 2011, SlutWalks burst onto the public scene, and met immediately with internal and external criticism. Although they were nationally and internationally recognizable by the name, nearly every walk took on local dimensions. As I wrote in *On the Issues*, the first SlutWalk emerged in Toronto when a local constable advised women that if they did not want to be raped, they should avoid "dressing like sluts."[29] Women took to the street there, and the idea of SlutWalk took off—not because of what happened in Toronto, but because that kind of victim-blaming and justification for sexual violence against women happens everywhere. In different cities around the world, local issues drew women and men to protest under the name "SlutWalk." It is more than a global movement and more than a series of local, unrelated actions. The depth and complexity is in between. When we look back historically, we see this is the case in nearly every social movement—there are always local dimensions that compel people to act, and such dimensions never fit neatly into any one dominant narrative of a social movement. And chronicling these voices is significant, not only because it introduces different voices but also because it creates depth and dynamism to a movement that a singular narrative cannot possibly capture. Through a historical lens, SlutWalks of 2011 may be the Take Back the Night marches of the 1970s and 1980s (and which still exist today). But even more, that they have national and global significance *as well as* local dimension allows for a more complex dynamic in feminism, one that moves way beyond the overly simplistic ways we continue to talk about, teach, and understand our movement.

NOW, and the women's movement for liberation, are coming into fifty years of existence. Feminism is not dead, even as the internal and external parameters are shifting. Tensions over this last half-century are signs of vitality and growth, which also invites pain and struggle. Through success and defeat, NOW and this movement has survived. Much of this success is attributable to its members' dynamic feminism—a willingness to employ necessary strategies, moving beyond the liberal/radical divide, eschewing debate over which of the "waves" we're in and pursuing instead hard work. The histories told here bear out the dynamics of feminism in the 1970s, during the heyday of so-called second-wave feminism. Such a perspective builds upon the histories of feminisms across time and space, echoing sociologist Raka Ray, who reminds us in her work on local feminist activism in India that "if we do not closely understand the dynamics of the local, we fall once again into the trap of universalizing and homogenizing" women's experiences and movements for social change.[30] Chapter members were never just part of a *national* organization; instead, they were grassroots activists "ordinary women attempting to accomplish necessary tasks, providing services."[31] They were not movement "stars," nor did they seek to be; instead, they were, in the words of former Memphis NOW member Linda Raiteri, "individual women … ones, and lots of ones make millions."[32]

NOW has maintained a feminist presence both nationally and in all fifty states across the years—in the three cities I have studied, NOW members still operate chapters, and they still seek to bring a feminist presence to a host of other social movement organizations and issues, including anti-war and anti-globalization efforts; GLBT community activism; discrimination on the basis of race, religion, or ability; and environmental issues. Into the twenty-first century, feminists are revitalizing local NOW chapters in cities across the United States, including Toledo (Ohio), Jefferson County (Colorado), and Portland (Oregon); and on college campuses, including Central Connecticut State University, Georgia Southern University, and Florida International University.[33]

After almost fifty years—or perhaps because of it—NOW remains at the forefront of people's minds when it comes to feminist direct action. For example, when the Harvard Alumni Association and the Harvard Club of New York City announced that university president Larry Summers would be feted at a reception on March 31, 2005, feminist activists (many of whom were active in the second wave as self-defined radical feminists, both in and beyond NOW) on a particular listserv called for a demonstration to protest the event. When one suggested "how about a picket?" others chimed in that a "ladies against women" type of demonstration would be most appropriate.[34] They started to suggest potential slogans to protest Summers' recent sexist remarks about how women were biologically ill-equipped for research in math and the sciences—"59¢ is too much—real women do it for free!" (a nod to the point that in the 1970s, a woman made, on average, 59¢ to a man's dollar) and "I want love, not logarithms" were two of several particularly amusing slogans. As is often the case on listservs where email travels in real time—

and far different from the days when NOW chapters were trying to stay in touch with one another via postal mail and WATTS lines—feminists fired messages back and forth encouraging protest. The first organization mentioned to coordinate the demonstration—NOW. Why these individual women, many of whom identified as radical feminists in the 1970s, suggested NOW, I do not know. However, as this project has made clear, a local NOW chapter *would* coordinate such a demonstration because it always has.

NOTES

1 Beyond the Friedan Mystique: The Importance of Grassroots Feminism

1 Interview with Aileen Hernandez, August 12, 2002.
2 "August 26 is 'Do your thing' day for equality for women!" Flyer from NOW national board to chapters, n.d., personal correspondence of Aileen Hernandez, copy in author's possession.
3 *Documenting the Midwestern Origins of the 20th Century Women's Movement.* Oral History Project, dir. Gerda Lerner, Wisconsin Historical Society, Madison, WI; Gerda Lerner, "Midwestern Leaders of the Modern Women's Movement: An Oral History Project," *Wisconsin Academy Review* 41, no. 1 (1994–95): 11–15; *Step by Step: Building a Feminist Movement, 1941–77,* dir. Joyce Follet (Women Make Movies, 1998).
4 Interview with Heather Booth, April 7, 2004.
5 Stephanie Coontz, *A Strange Stirring: The Feminine Mystique and American Women at the Dawn of the 1960s* (New York: Basic Books, 2011), xv.
6 Betty Friedan, *The Feminine Mystique* (New York: W.W. Norton, 1963); Daniel Horowitz, *Betty Friedan and the Making of the Feminine Mystique: The American Left, The Cold War, and Modern Feminism* (Amherst: University of Massachusetts Press, 2000).
7 Horowitz, *Betty Friedan and the Making of the Feminine Mystique,* 4.
8 Email correspondence, Cynthia Harrison to Stephanie Gilmore, January 25, 2002.
9 Flora Davis, *Moving the Mountain* (Urbana: University of Illinois Press, 1999); Sara Evans, *Tidal Wave: How Women Changed America at Century's End* (New York: Free Press, 2003); and Ruth Rosen, *The World Split Open: How the Modern Women's Movement Changed America* (New York: Viking Press, 2000).
10 Susan Faludi, *Backlash: The Undeclared War against American Women* (New York: Anchor, 1992); Estelle Freedman, *No Turning Back: The History of Feminism and the Future of Women* (New York: Ballantine, 2002); Susan J. Douglas, *Enlightened Sexism: The Seductive Message that Feminism's Work is Done* (New York: Times Books, 2010).
11 Judith Ezekiel, *Feminism in the Heartland* (Columbus: Ohio State University Press, 2003); Anne Valk, *Radical Sisters: Second-Wave Feminism and Black Liberation in Washington, DC* (Urbana: University of Illinois Press, 2010); and Anne Enke, *Finding*

the Movement: Sexuality, Contested Space, and Feminist Activism (Durham, NC: Duke University Press, 2007).

12 U. Kalpagam, "Perspectives for a Grassroots Feminist Theory," *EPW Perspectives* 37 (November 2002): 4686–93.

13 On ethnicity and nationalism, see Robert Reid-Pharr, "Extending Queer Theory to Race and Ethnicity," *Chronicle of Higher Education* 48, no. 49 (2002): B7–B9; see also Zoe Anderson, "Queer(ing) History: Queer Methodologies, Pedagogies, and Interventions in the Discipline of History," *Student Engagement* (2007). Danielle Clarke, "Finding the Subject: Queering the Archive," *Feminist Theory* 5, no. 1 (2004): 79–83, quotation on 80.

14 Raka Ray, *Fields of Protest: Women's Movement in India* (Minneapolis: University of Minnesota Press, 1999), 6.

15 Kalpagam, "Perspectives for a Grassroots Feminist Theory."

16 Temma Kaplan, *Crazy for Democracy: Women in Grassroots Movements* (New York: Routledge, 1996), 6.

17 Jocelyn Olcott, *Revolutionary Women in Postrevolutionary Mexico* (Durham, NC: Duke University Press, 2005), 24.

18 Ray, *Fields of Protest*, 3.

19 Ibid.

20 Kalpagam, "Perspectives for a Grassroots Feminist Theory."

21 Rosen, *The World Split Open*, xiv.

22 Jennifer Baumgardner and Amy Richards, *Manifesta: Young Women, Feminism, and the Future* (New York: Farrar, Straus, and Giroux, 2000), 17.

23 Nancy Hewitt, "Introduction," in *No Permanent Waves: Recasting Histories of U.S. Feminism* (New Brunswick, NJ: Rutgers University Press, 2010), 1–14.

24 Vicki Ruiz, "Shaping Public Space/Enunciating Gender: A Multiracial Historiography of the Women's West, 1995–2000," *Frontiers: A Journal of Women's Studies* 22, no. 3 (2001): 22–25, quotation on 23.

25 Premilla Nadasen, "Black Feminism: Waves, Rivers, and Still Waters," *Feminist Formations* 22, no. 1 (2010): 98–105.

26 Adrienne Rich, "Notes on a Politics of Location," *Blood, Bread, and Poetry* (New York: Norton, 1989), 210–31); Susan K. Freeman, "From the Lesbian Nation to the Cincinnati Lesbian Community: Moving toward a Politics of Location," *Journal of the History of Sexuality* 9, no. 1–2 (2000): 137–74; Caren Kaplan and Inderpal Grewal, eds., *Scattered Hegemonies: Postmodernity and Transnational Feminist Practice* (Minneapolis: University of Minnesota, 1996).

27 Amrita Basu, ed., *Women's Movements in the Global Era: The Power of Local Feminisms* (Boulder, CO: Westview Press, 2010); Kaplan and Grewal, eds., *Scattered Hegemonies.*

28 Rich, "Notes on a Politics of Location"; Donna Haraway, "Situated Knowledges: The Science Question in Feminism and the Privilege of Partial Perspective," in *Simians, Cyborgs, and Women: The Reinvention of Nature* (London: Free Association Books, 1991), 183–201; Kaplan and Grewal, eds., *Scattered Hegemonies.*

29 Byron Miller, *Geography and Social Movements: Comparing Antinuclear Activism in the Boston Area* (Minneapolis: University of Minnesota Press, 2000), 3.

30 Verta Taylor and Nancy Whittier, "Collective Identity in Social Movement Communities: Lesbian Feminist Mobilization," in *Frontiers in Social Movement Theory,* ed. Aldon D. Morris and Carol. McClurg Mueller (New Haven, CT: Yale University Press. 1992), 104–32.

31 Albert Hurtado, "Settler Women and Frontier Women: The Unsettling Past of Western Women's History," *Frontiers* 22, no. 3 (2001): 1–5, quotation on 5.

32 Leila J. Rupp, *Worlds of Women: The Making of an International Women's Movement* (Princeton, NJ: Princeton University Press, 1997), 6.

33 Victoria Wolcott, *Remaking Respectability: African American Women in Interwar Detroit* (Chapel Hill: University of North Carolina Press, 1996), 4.

34 Marisa Chappell, "Demanding a New Family Wage: Feminist Consensus in the 1970s Full Employment Campaign," in *Feminist Coalitions: Historical Perspectives on Second-Wave Feminism in the United States*, ed. Stephanie Gilmore (Urbana: University of Illinois Press, 1998), 252–81.

35 Jo Reger, "Social Movement Culture and Organizational Survival in the National Organization for Women," Ph.D. dissertation, The Ohio State University, 1997; Jo Reger and Suzanne Staggenborg, "Patterns of Mobilization in Local Movement Organizations: Leadership and Strategy in Four National Organization for Women Chapters," *Sociological Perspectives* 49 (2006): 297–323; Maryann Barakso, *Governing NOW: Grassroots Activism in the National Organization for Women* (Ithaca, NY: Cornell University Press, 2004).

36 Verta Taylor, "Social Movement Continuity: The Women's Movement in Abeyance," *American Sociological Review* 54 (1989): 761–75; Cynthia Harrison, *On Account of Sex: The Politics of Women's Issues, 1945–1968* (Berkeley: University of California Press, 1989); Sonia Pressman Fuentes, *Eat First——You Don't Know What They'll Give You: The Adventures of an Immigrant Family and Their Feminist Daughter* (New York: Xlibris, 1999).

37 Hewitt, *No Permanent Waves*; Gilmore, *Feminist Coalitions*.

38 Jo Freeman, *The Politics of Women's Liberation* (New York: Longman, 1975).

39 See also Alice Echols, *Daring to Be Bad: Radical Feminism in America, 1968–1975* (Minneapolis: University of Minnesota Press, 1989); Nancy Whittier, *Feminist Generations: The Persistence of Radical Feminism* (Philadelphia: Temple University Press, 1995); Rachel DuPlessis and Ann Snitow, eds., *The Feminist Memoir Project: Voices from Women's Liberation* (New Brunswick, NJ: Rutgers University Press, 2007); Barbara Crow, ed., *Radical Feminism: A Documentary Reader* (New York: Routledge, 2005); and Linda Gordon and Rosalyn Baxandall, eds. *Dear Sisters: Dispatches from Radical Feminism* (New York: Basic Books, 2001).

40 Barbara Ryan, *Feminism and the Women's Movement: Dynamics of Change in Social Movement Ideology and Action* (New York: Routledge, 1992); Myra Marx Ferree and Beth Hess, *Controversy and Coalition: The New Feminist Movement Across Four Decades of Change* (New York: Routledge, 2000); Freeman, *The Politics of Women's Liberation*; Sara Evans, *Personal Politics: The Roots of the Women's Liberation in the Civil Rights Movement and the New Left* (New York: Vintage, 1980); Echols, *Daring to Be Bad*.

41 Benita Roth, *Separate Roads to Feminism: Black, Chicana, and White Feminist Movements in America's Second Wave* (New York: Cambridge University Press, 2003).

42 Freeman, *The Politics of Women's Liberation*; Evans, *Personal Politics*; Echols, *Daring to Be Bad*.

43 Taylor and Whittier, "Collective Identity in Social Movement Communities."

44 Roth, *Separate Roads to Feminism*. See also Evelyn Brooks Higginbotham, "African American Women's History and the Metalanguage of Race," *Signs* 17, no. 4 (1992): 251–74.

45 See Marjorie Spruill Wheeler, ed., *One Woman, One Vote: Rediscovering the Woman Suffrage Movement* (Troutdale, OR: NewSage Press, 1995); Jean H. Baker, ed. *Votes for Women: The Struggle for Suffrage Revisited* (New York: Oxford University Press, 2002).

46 Jane Sherron DeHart, "Second Wave Feminism(s) and the South: The Difference that Difference Makes," in *Women of the American South: A Multicultural Reader*, ed. Christie Anne Farnham (New York: NYU Press, 1997).

47 Lucy Eldersveld Murphy and Wendy Hamand Vanet, eds., *Midwestern Women: Work, Community, and Leadership at the Crossroads* (Bloomington: Indiana University Press, 1997); Genevieve McBride, ed., *Women's Wisconsin: From Native Matriarchies to the New Millennium* (Madison: Wisconsin Historical Society, 2005).

48 Glenda Riley, foreword to Murphy and Vanet, *Midwestern Women*, ix–xi, quotation on ix.
49 See McBride, ed., *Women's Wisconsin*; and Lerner, "Midwestern Leaders of the Modern Women's Movement."
50 Murphy and Vanet, *Midwestern Women,* 1–14, quotation on 11.
51 Vicki Ruiz, "Shaping Public Space/Enunciating Gender"; Judy Yung, *Unbound Feet: A Social History of Chinese Women in San Francisco* (Berkeley: University of California Press, 1995); Nancy Shoemaker, *Negotiators of Change: Historical Perspectives on Native American Women* (New York: Routledge, 1994); Andrea Smith, *Conquest: Sexual Violence and Native American Genocide* (Boston: South End Press, 2005); Judy Wu, *Doctor Mom Chung of the Fair-Haired Bastards: The Life of a Wartime Celebrity* (Berkeley: University of California Press, 2005).
52 Mary Bernstein, "Celebration and Suppression: The Strategic Uses of Identity by the Lesbian and Gay Movement," *American Journal of Sociology* 103 (1997): 531–65; Mary Bernstein, "Identities and Politics: Toward a Historical Understanding of the Lesbian and Gay Movement," *Social Science History* 26 (2002): 531–81; Leila J. Rupp and Verta Taylor, *Drag Queens at the 801 Cabaret* (Chicago: University of Chicago Press, 2003).
53 Maxine Molyneux, *Women's Movements in International Perspective* (New York: Palgrave, 2001).
54 Verta Taylor and Leila J. Rupp, "Researching the Women's Movement: We Make Our Own History, But Not Just As We Please," in *Beyond Methodology: Feminist Scholarship as Lived Research*, ed. Mary Margaret Fonow and Judith Cook (Bloomington: Indiana University Press, 1991), 121. See also Joey Sprague, *Feminist Methodologies for Critical Researchers: Bridging Differences* (Thousand Oaks, CA: Sage, 2002), and Sharlene Hesse-Biber and Patricia Leavy, *The Practice of Qualitative Research* (Thousand Oaks, CA: Sage, 2010).

2 In the Midst of the "World-wide Revolution of Human Rights": Creating the National Organization for Women

1 Material in chapter 2 was gleaned, in part, from Stephanie Gilmore and Elizabeth Kaminski, "A Part and Apart: Lesbian and Straight Feminists Negotiate Identity in a Second-Wave Organization." *Journal of the History of Sexuality* 16, no. 1 (2007): 95–113.
2 NOW Statement of Purpose, in *Feminism in Our Time: The Essential Writings, World War II to the Present*, ed. Miriam Schneir (New York: Vintage, 1994): 95–102, quotation on 96. All references to the NOW Statement of Purpose will refer to this reprint.
3 Mary Weigers, "Beneath those Charred Bras Revolution Smolders," *Washington Post*, March 8, 1970, G1, G3.
4 Godfrey Hodgson, *The World Turned Right Side up: A History of the Conservative Ascendancy in America* (New York: Mariner Books, 1996). See also Lisa McGirr, *Suburban Warriors: The Origins of the New American Right* (Princeton, NJ: Princeton University Press, 2002); Donald Critchlow and Nancy Maclean, *Debating the American Conservative Movement* (Lanham, MD: Rowman and Littlefield, 2009); Daniel Williams, *God's Own Party: The Making of the Christian Right* (New York: Oxford University Press, 2010).
5 Rosemarie Putnam Tong, *Feminist Thought: A More Comprehensive Introduction*, 2nd edition (Boulder, CO: Westview Press, 1998), esp. chaps. 1 and 2.
6 While they do not necessarily call it the "long decade," Maurice Isserman and Michael Kazin discuss the decade of the 1960s not as numerical but as cultural,

"defined by movements and issues that arose soon after the end of World War II and were only partially resolved by the time Richard Nixon resigned from the presidency" in 1974; Maurice Isserman and Michael Kazin, *America Divided: The Civil War of the 1960s* (New York: Oxford University Press, 2000), ix. More and more scholars are troubling historical periodization by decades, referring to movements in much longer spans than a single decade or two can represent. Jacquelyn Dowd Hall, "The Long Civil Rights Movement and the Political Uses of the Past," *Journal of American History* 91, no. 4 (2005): 1233–63.

7 Susan M. Hartmann, *The Other Feminists: Activists in the Liberal Establishment* (New Haven, CT: Yale University Press, 1998).
8 Benita Roth, *Separate Roads to Feminism*.
9 Isserman and Kazin, *America Divided*, 4–5.
10 Dan Berger, ed., *The Hidden 1970s* (New Brunswick, NJ: Rutgers University Press, 2010).
11 Isserman and Kazin, *America Divided*, 11.
12 Roth, *Separate Roads to Feminism*; Isserman and Kazin, *America Divided*; Ruth Rosen, *The World Split Open,* and Sara Evans, *Tidal Wave: How Women Changed America at Century's End* (New York: Free Press, 2003).
13 Roth, *Separate Roads to Feminism*, 5.
14 Harrison, *On Account of Sex*; Hartmann, *From Margin to Mainstream: American Women and Politics since 1960* (New York: Knopf, 1980); Hartmann, *The Other Feminists*; Joanne Meyerowitz, ed., *Not June Cleaver: Women and Gender in Postwar America, 1945–1960* (Philadelphia: Temple University Press, 1994); and Rupp and Taylor, *Survival in the Doldrums: The American Women's Movement, 1945 to the 1960s* (New York: Oxford University Press, 1987).
15 The definitive study of the PCSW is Harrison, *On Account of Sex*. See also Hartmann, *From Margin to Mainstream*; Ferree and Hess, *Controversy and Coalition*; and Rupp and Taylor, *Survival in the Doldrums*.
16 Ferree and Hess, *Controversy and Coalition*, 63. See also Dorothy Sue Cobble, *The Other Women's Movement: Workplace Justice and Social Rights in Modern America* (Princeton, NJ: Princeton University Press, 2005); Margaret Margaret Fonow, *Union Women: Forging Feminism in the United Steelworkers of America* (Minneapolis: University of Minnesota Press, 2003); Nancy Maclean, *Freedom is Not Enough: The Opening of the American Workplace* (Cambridge, MA: Harvard University Press, 2008); and Katherine Turk, "Out of the Revolution, Into the Mainstream: Employment Activism in NOW's Sears Campaign and the Growing Pains of Liberal Feminism," *Journal of American History* 97, no. 2 (2010): 399–423.
17 Robinson, "Two Movements in Pursuit of Equal Opportunities," *Signs* 4, no. 3 (spring 1979): 413–33.
18 Ferree and Hess, *Controversy and Coalition*, 63–64.
19 Jo Freeman, "The Origins of the Women's Liberation Movement," *American Journal of Sociology* 78 (1973): 792–811, quotation on 798.
20 Rupp and Taylor, *Survival in the Doldrums*; Harrison, *On Account of Sex*; Hartmann, *The Other Feminists*; and Maryann Barakso, *Governing NOW*.
21 Verta Taylor, "Social Movement Continuity," and Rupp and Taylor, *Survival in the Doldrums*. In *Worlds of Women*, Rupp traces the history of the international women's movement during this era of abeyance in U.S. feminism, which also involved many U.S. feminists.
22 Friedan, *The Feminine Mystique,* 1.
23 Coontz, *A Strange Stirring*, xix.
24 McBride, ed., *Women's Wisconsin*.
25 Toni Carabillo, Judith Mueli, and June Bundy Cisca, *Feminist Chronicles, 1953–1993* (Los Angeles: Women's Graphics, 1993), 47. For more on Pauli Murray, see "Pauli

Murray's Notable Connections," *Journal of Women's History* 14 (summer 2002): 54–87. In this symposium, scholars traced different aspects of Murray's political and personal life. See especially Susan M. Hartmann, "Pauli Murray and the 'Juncture of Women's Liberation and Black Liberation,'" *Journal of Women's History* 14, no. 2 (2002): 74–77.

26 Daniel Horowitz, *Betty Friedan and the Making of the Feminine Mystique*.

27 Betty Friedan, *Life So Far* (New York: Simon and Schuster, 2000), 171–72.

28 Ibid., 169.

29 Barakso, *Governing NOW*.

30 Minutes of the Organizing Conference, National Organization for Women (NOW), Saturday, October 29, 1966, National Organization for Women Collection, Schlesinger Library, Harvard University (hereafter NOW Papers).

31 McBride, ed., *Women's Wisconsin*.

32 NOW, "Statement of Purpose," in Schneir, *Feminism in our Time*, 95–102.

33 Ibid., 97.

34 Ibid.

35 Ibid., 102.

36 Friedan, *Life so Far*, 171. Emphasis in original.

37 NOW, "Statement of Purpose," 97.

38 Ibid., 100. On the feminist childcare battle, see Natalie Fousekis, *Demanding Child Care: Women's Activism and the Politics of Welfare, 1940–1971* (Urbana: University of Illinois Press, 2011).

39 See, for example, Valerie Solanis, "SCUM Manifesto," in Crow, *Radical Feminism*, 201–22; Redstockings, "Redstockings Manifesto," in *Radical Feminism*, 223–25; Joreen Freeman, "The Bitch Manifesto," in *Radical Feminism*, 226–32; and Radicalesbians, "The Woman-Identified Woman," in *Radical Feminism*, 233–37.

40 Nancy Gabin, *Feminism in the Labor Movement: Women and the United Auto Workers, 1935–1975* (Ithaca, NY: Cornell University Press, 1990); Dennis Deslippe, *Rights, Not Roses: Unions and the Rise of Working-Class Feminism, 1945–1980* (Urbana: University of Illinois Press, 2000); and Cobble, *The Other Women's Movement*.

41 Kathleen C. Berkeley, *The Women's Liberation Movement in America* (New York: Greenwood Press, 1999), 35.

42 On abortion, see Kristin Luker, *Abortion and the Politics of Motherhood* (Berkeley: University of California Press, 1988); and Fay Ginsburg, *Contested Lives: The Abortion Debate in an American Community* (Berkeley: University of California Press, 1989). On polarized language used in the abortion debate, see Dawn McCaffrey and Jennifer Keys, "Competitive Framing Process in the Abortion Debate: Polarization-Vilification, Frame Saving, and Frame Debunking," *Sociological Quarterly* 41, no. 1 (2000): 41–61. On the ERA, see Jane Mansbridge, *Why We Lost the ERA* (Chicago: University of Chicago Press, 1986); Mary Frances Berry, *Why ERA Failed: Politics, Women's Rights, and the Amending Process of the Constitution* (Bloomington: Indiana University Press, 1986); and Donald Mathews and Jane Sherron DeHart, *Sex, Gender, and the Politics of ERA: A State and a Nation* (New York: Oxford University Press, 1990). Ruth Murray Brown, *For a "Christian America": A History of the Religious Right* (Amherst, NY: Prometheus Books, 2002) and Williams, *God's Own Party*, discuss both issues in the context of the religious right and conservative ascendancy in postwar United States.

43 Brown, *For a "Christian America"*; Williams, *God's Own Party*.

44 Mansbridge, *Why We Lost the ERA*; Berry, *Why ERA Failed*; and Mathews and DeHart, *Sex, Gender, and the Politics of ERA*.

45 Luker, *Abortion and the Politics of Motherhood*; and Suzanne Staggenborg, *The Pro-Choice Movement: Organization and Activism in the Abortion Conflict* (New York: Oxford University Press, 1991).

46 "Lady Objects to 'Maude' Episode," *Los Angeles Times*, November 21, 1972, part 4, 16.

47 "Notes on People," *New York Times*, November 25, 1972, 13.
48 "NOW Suit over Maude Abortion Show Denied," *New York Times*, November 25, 1972, part 2, 3.
49 "Virginia Slims American Women's Opinion Poll," March 24, 1972, Carabillo/Mueli Files.
50 NOW, "An Invitation to Join," September 1966, in *Feminist Chronicles, 1953–1993*, 164. Available online at http://feminist.org/research/chronicles/chronicl.html.
51 Ibid.
52 Barakso, *Governing NOW*, 60.
53 Letter, Alice Rossi to Betty Friedan, August 23, 1966, quoted in Barakso, *Governing NOW*, 30.
54 Letter, Betty Friedan to Alice Rossi, October 12, 1966, quoted in Barakso, *Governing NOW*, 30.
55 Some scholars posit that NOW did a poor job of addressing poverty in women's lives, offering little more than lip service. See, for example, Marisa Chappell, "Rethinking Women's Politics in the 1970s: The National Organization for Women and the League of Women Voters Confront Poverty," *Journal of Women's History* 13, no. 4 (2002): 155–79; Chappell, The War on Welfare: Family, Poverty, and Politics in Modern America (Philadelphia: University of Pennsylvania Press, 2009), and Lisa Levenstein, *A Movement without Marches: African American Women and the Politics of Poverty in Postwar Philadelphia* (Chapel Hill: University of North Carolina Press, 2009).
56 Beverly Guy-Sheftall, ed., *Words of Fire: An Anthology of African-American Feminist Thought* (New York: The New Press, 1999).
57 Roth, *Separate Roads to Feminism*; Paula Giddings, *When and Where I Enter: The Impact of Black Women on Race and Sex in America* (New York: Bantam Books, 1985); Deborah Gray White, *Too Heavy a Load: Black Women in Defense of Themselves, 1894–1994* (New York: W.W. Norton, 1999); Nancy Naples, *Grassroots Warriors: Activist Mothering, Community Work, and the War on Poverty* (New York: Routledge, 1998); Kimberly Springer, "Black Feminist Organizations and the Emergence of Interstitial Politics," in *Modern American Queer History*, ed. Allida M. Black (Philadelphia: Temple University Press, 2001), Kimberly Springer, *Living for the Revolution: Black Feminist Organizations, 1968–1980* (Durham, NC: Duke University Press, 2005).
58 "Virginia Slims American Women's Opinion Poll."
59 Roth, *Separate Roads to Feminism*, 11.
60 NOW Papers.
61 Freeman, *Politics of Women's Liberation*, 88.
62 Ibid., 87.
63 Arlie Hochschild, *The Second Shift* (New York: Viking, 1971).
64 "Report of informal meeting of NOW members from Illinois, Indiana, and Wisconsin," January 21, 1967, quoted in NOW papers.
65 Memo from Kathryn Clarenbach to Board of Directors, June 14, 1967, quoted in Barakso, *Governing NOW*, 163, n. 41.
66 By 1967, seven task forces were formed to address the following issues: equal employment opportunity, legal and political rights, women in poverty, education, image of women, family, women and religion. See Letter, Betty Friedan to NOW Member, March 14, 1967, Carabillo/Mueli Files, archived by David Dinsmore, Los Angeles. David Dinsmore has kept incredibly rich records of NOW activism, as recorded in Toni Carabillo and Judith Mueli's papers and in major newspapers. My thanks to him for generously sharing his archive and commitment to feminist history of the women's movement.
67 Memo, Kathryn Clarenbach to Board of Directors, June 14, 1967, quoted in Barakso, *Governing NOW*, 163, n. 41.
68 Interview with Dolores Alexander, April 22, 2002.

69 "Dollars and Sense of Revolution," *NOW Acts* 3, no. 1 (winter 1970).

70 Sociologist Jo Reger has written extensively on New York City NOW. See Jo Reger, "Social Movement," Jo Reger, "More than One Feminism: Organizational Structure, Ideology, and the Construction of Collective Identity," in *Social Movements: Identity, Culture, and the State*, ed. David S. Meyer, Nancy Whittier, and Belinda Robnett (New York: Oxford University Press, 2002), and Jo Reger, "Organizational Dynamics and the Construction of Multiple Feminist Identities in the National Organization for Women," *Gender and Society* 16, no. 5 (2002): 710–27.

71 Reger, "More than One Feminism," and Jo Reger, "Organizational 'Emotion Work' through Consciousness-Raising: An Analysis of a Feminist Organization," *Qualitative Sociology* 27, no. 2 (2004): 205–22. Reger indicates that, as of 2000, the Consciousness-Raising Committee was still the largest and most active task force in the NYC NOW chapter.

72 Freeman, *Politics of Women's Liberation*, 86.

73 Interview, Dolores Alexander, April 22, 2002.

74 Interview, Del Martin and Phyllis Lyon, March 22, 2002.

75 Letter to Inka O'Hanrahan from Del Martin, March 18, 1968, from personal files of Del Martin and Phyllis Lyon, copy in author's possession.

76 Letter to Del Martin from Inka O'Hanrahan, March 20, 1968, from personal files of Del Martin and Phyllis Lyon, copy in author's possession.

77 Letter from Kay Clarenbach to Del Martin, March 6, 1970, personal files of Del Martin and Phyllis Lyon, copy in author's possession.

78 Letter from Del Martin to Dolores Alexander, July 29, 1970, personal files of Del Martin and Phyllis Lyon, copy in author's possession.

79 Stephanie Gilmore and Elizabeth Kaminski, "A Part and Apart: Lesbian and Straight Feminists Negotiate Identity in a Second-Wave Organization," *Journal of the History of Sexuality* 16 (1) 2007: 95–113. I thank and acknowledge Elizabeth Kaminski, my coauthor, and the *Journal of the History of Sexuality* for allowing me to cite this work here.

80 Karla Jay, *Tales of the Lavender Menace: A Memoir of Liberation* (New York: Basic Books, 1999); Rita Mae Brown, "Reflections of a Lavender Menace," *Ms.* (July–August 1975): 40–47; and Evans, *Tidal Wave*, esp. 48–50.

81 NOW Press release, December 17, 1970, Carabillo/Mueli Files.

82 Ibid.

83 Betty Friedan, "Up from the Kitchen Floor," *New York Times Magazine*, March 4, 1973, 32.

84 NOW, *NOW Acts*, Fall 1971.

85 Letter, Rita Laporte to Jean Stapleton, Los Angeles "NOW News," October 1971.

86 Roth, *Separate Roads to Feminism*, 5; Kaplan, *Crazy for Democracy*. Kaplan points out that the media often pursues the "stars" of a movement, but activists often focus on the day-to-day work of activism and the pursuit of progressive change.

87 Paul Wilkes, "Mother Superior to Women's Lib," 1970, reprinted in *Conversations with Betty Friedan*, ed. Janann Sherman (Jackson: University Press of Mississippi, 2002), 21.

88 See, for example, Lisa Hammel, "They Meet in Victorian Parlor to Demand 'True Equality'—NOW," *New York Times*, November 22, 1966, 44. I acknowledge that publishing such details about Friedan's home and surroundings was likely an attempt to discredit her and would not have been an unusual journalist ploy.

89 Wilkes, "Mother Superior to Women's Lib," 17.

90 "Friedan Scolds Steinem, Abzug," *Los Angeles Times*, July 19, 1972, 7; Friedan, "Up from the Kitchen Floor;" "Betty Friedan Links Chauvinists, Scandal," *Los Angeles Times*, August 28, 1973, 16.

91 "National Day of Demonstration, December 14," memo from Betty Friedan to board members and chapter conveners, December 1, 1967, Carabillo/Mueli Files.

92 NOW Press Release, December 14, 1967, Carabillo/Mueli Files; and Marilyn Bender, "The Feminists are on the March Again," *New York Times*, December 14, 1967, 56.
93 Martha Weinman Lear, "What do These Women Want? The Second Feminist Wave," *New York Times Magazine*, March 10, 1968, 22.
94 "Public Relations Guidelines for NOW Members and Chapters," passed by the National Board of Directors, September 15, 1968, Carabillo/Mueli Files.
95 Quotation from Charlotte Curtis, "Miss America Pageant Picketed by 100 Women," *New York Times*, September 7, 1968, 81. On Colgate-Palmolive strike, see NOW, "Colgate-Palmolive Boycott," *NOW in the News*, 2, in Carabillo/Mueli Files. On the Miss America protest, see Curtis, "Miss America Pageant Picketed by 100 Women;" and Judith Duffett, "WLM vs. Miss America: Atlantic City is a Town with Class— They Raise Your Morals While They Judge Your Ass," *Voice of the Women's Liberation Movement*, (October 1968), 1. On the fast and support for the Poor People's Campaign, see Memo, Kay Clarenbach to NOW Chapters, May 18, 1968, Carabillo/Mueli Files.
96 "'Young, Black and Beautiful' Organize," *Los Angeles Times*, October 31, 1968, part 4, 4.
97 Letter, Mimi Kaprolat to Aileen Hernandez and the Western Regional Division of NOW, December 6, 1968, Carabillo/Mueli Files.
98 NOW News Release, December 10, 1968, Carabillo/Mueli Files.
99 Nancy Baltad, "Women Stage Protest Demonstration in Bar: Claim Female Discrimination," *Hollywood (CA) Citizen-News*, February 19, 1969.
100 "A General protest against hypocrisy which celebrates 'mother's day' one day a year and exploits her year round," flyer advertising protest on May 11, 1969, Los Angeles, CA, Carabillo/Mueli Files. See also Andrea Estepa, "Taking the White Gloves Off: Women Strike for Peace and 'the Movement,' 1967–73," in Gilmore, *Feminist Coalitions*, 84–112; and Amy Swerdlow, *Women Strike for Peace: Traditional Motherhood and Radical Politics in the 1960s* (Chicago: University of Chicago Press, 1993).
101 Barakso, *Governing NOW*, chapter 3, 39–46.
102 "Highlights of NOW's national membership conference, 7–8 December 1968," *NOW Acts*, 1969.
103 Freeman, *Politics of Women's Liberation*, 85.
104 Dolores Alexander, "An Editorial," *NOW Acts*, 1969.
105 Verta Taylor and Nella Van Dyke, "Get Up, Stand Up: Tactical Repertoires of Social Movements," in *The Blackwell Companion to Social Movements*, ed. David Snow, Sarah Soule, and Hanspeter Kriesi (New York: Blackwell, 2004), 262–93.
106 Memphis NOW Newsletter, November 1975, 4–6.
107 Betty Friedan, "How NOW Began," a background memorandum on NOW from Betty Friedan, President, October 29, 1966, Carabillo/Mueli Files.

3 Feminist Activism in Memphis: Beyond the Liberal/Radical Divide

1 Material in chapter 3 was gleaned, in part, from Stephanie Gilmore, "The Dynamics of Second-Wave Feminist Activism in Memphis, 1971–82: Rethinking the Liberal/Radical Divide." *NWSA Journal* 15, no. 1 (2003): 94–117.
2 Mary Cashiola, "Cosmetology to Car Care: The Southern Girl Convention is Covering All Bases," *Memphis Flyer,* August 2, 1999, accessed online: http://weeklywire.com/ww/08-02-99/memphis_socvr.html.
3 On the Southern Girl (and, later, Girls) Convention, see its website: http://southern girlsconvention.org

4 Cashiola, "Cosmetology to Car Care."
5 http://southerngirlsconvention.org
6 Newsletter, National Organization for Women, Memphis Chapter (hereafter Memphis NOW), 27 September 1970, Box 1, folder 6, Memphis NOW papers, Special Collections, Ned McWherter Library, University of Memphis (hereafter Memphis NOW papers).
7 Newsletter, Memphis NOW, November 16, 1970, Box 1, folder 6.
8 Ibid.
9 Daneel Buring uses "sleepy little river town" to refer to Memphis in her work, *Lesbian and Gay Memphis* (New York: Garland, 1997), 17.
10 Dewey Grantham, "History," *Encyclopedia of Southern History* (Baton Rouge: Louisiana State University Press, 1979).
11 Buring, *Lesbian and Gay Memphis*.
12 Memphis NOW Newsletter, April 1974, Box 1, folder 7, Memphis NOW Papers.
13 For more on the PAW in Memphis, see Jocelyn Wurzburg's papers (hereafter Wurzburg Papers) Special Collections, Ned R. McWherter Library, the University of Memphis.
14 Roth, *Separate Roads to Feminism*.
15 Giddings, *When and Where I Enter*; White, *Too Heavy a Load*; and Hartmann, *The Other Feminists*.
16 Evelyn Brooks Higginbotham, "African-American Women's History."
17 Memphis NOW Newsletter, October 1972, Box 1, folder 6, Memphis NOW Papers.
18 Memphis NOW Newsletter, August 1973, Box 1, folder 6, Memphis NOW Papers.
19 Roth, *Separate Roads to Feminism*; Giddings, *When and Where I Enter*; White, *Too Heavy a Load*; and Springer, *Living for the Revolution*.
20 Art Gilliam, "Few Black Faces in Women's Lib Crowd," Memphis *Commercial Appeal*, June 7, 1971.
21 Giddings, *When and Where I Enter*, 307.
22 Gilliam, "Few Black Faces in Women's Lib Crowd."
23 Roth, *Separate Roads to Feminism*.
24 Press release, "United Sisters and Associates," 1972, Wurzburg Papers.
25 "Old Doubts Deter Feminists," Memphis *Commercial Appeal*, August 7, 1973.
26 For other examples of local, interracial alliance-building, see Nancy Naples, *Grassroots Warriors*; Anne Valk, *Radical Sisters: Second-Wave Feminism and Black Liberation in Washington, DC* (Urbana: University of Illinois Press, 2010); and Stephanie Gilmore, ed., *Feminist Coalitions: Historical Perspectives on Second-Wave Feminism in the United States* (Urbana: University of Illinois Press, 2008).
27 Martha Allen, "One Woman Thinking Things Through," Memphis NOW Newsletter, April 1974, Box 1, folder 7, Memphis NOW Papers.
28 Memphis NOW Newsletter, January 1976, Box 1, folder 7, Memphis NOW Papers.
29 Memphis NOW Newsletter, March 1976, Box 1, folder 7, Memphis NOW Papers.
30 Michael A. Conley, "Blacks Defend Scant Support of Feminism," Memphis *Commercial Appeal*, April 7, 1976.
31 Memphis NOW Newsletter, November 1979, Box 1, folder 8, Memphis NOW Papers.
32 DeHart, "Second Wave Feminism(s) and the South," 283.
33 Memphis NOW Newsletter, December 1970, Box 1, folder 6, Memphis NOW papers.
34 Mathews and DeHart, *Sex, Gender, and the Politics of ERA*; see also Mansbridge, *Why We Lost the ERA*; and Berry, *Why ERA Failed*.
35 Tennessee House Journal, March and April 1972; Tennessee Senate Journal, April 1972.

36 Schlafly, *The Power of the Positive Woman* (New Rochelle, NY: Arlington House, 1977); Berry, *Why ERA Failed*; Mansbridge, *Why We Lost the ERA*; and Mathews and DeHart, *Sex, Politics, and the Politics of ERA*. See also Brown, *For A "Christian America"*; Williams, *God's Own Party*; and Hodgson, *The World Turned Right Side up*.

37 "Tennessee's First Miss America, Barbara Walker Hummel, dies," Nashville *Tennessean*, June 9, 2000.

38 Ibid.

39 Jim Willis, "Some Reports Termed False on Equal Rights Amendment," Memphis *Press-Scimitar*, March 6, 1973; and Memphis NOW Newsletter, January 1974, Box 1, folder 7, Memphis NOW Papers.

40 "Women's Rights Supporters Take Floor," Memphis *Press-Scimitar*, 1974.

41 Memphis NOW Newsletter, March 1974, Box 1, Folder 7, Memphis NOW Papers.

42 "NOW Women Sell Blood to Finance Campaign," Memphis *Commercial Appeal*, 6 April 1973; Memphis NOW Newsletter, January 1973 and March 1973, Box 1, folder 7, Memphis NOW Papers. In January 1973, the chapter raised money for a woman who could not afford an abortion to have one. When the woman changed her mind, the chapter voted to turn the money over to the "blood-money" campaign. In Chicago, where it was illegal to sell blood, the NOW chapter sold Bloody Marys instead at fundraising cocktail parties. Memphis NOW Newsletter, March 1973.

43 Memphis NOW Newsletter, April 1974, Box 1, folder 6, Memphis NOW Papers.

44 Memphis NOW Newsletter, January 1974, Box 1, folder 7, Memphis NOW Papers.

45 Ibid.

46 "Legislators Vote to Rescind ERA Ratification," Memphis *Commercial Appeal*, April 24, 1974.

47 "Loaf of Bread, Talk with Senators Aim at Keeping Women in 'Place,'" Memphis *Commercial Appeal*, August 10, 1978.

48 Interview, Lynda Dolbi, March 6, 1996.

49 "Memphians Go to Illinois to Urge ERA Ratification," Memphis *Press-Scimitar*, May 10, 1980.

50 Memphis NOW Newsletter, February 1982, Box 1, folder 8, Memphis NOW Papers.

51 See, for example, Mathews and DeHart, *Sex, Gender, and the Politics of ERA*.

52 Memphis NOW Newsletter, March 1979, Box 1, folder 8, Memphis NOW Papers.

53 Memphis NOW Newsletter, August 1972, Box 1, folder 6, Memphis NOW Papers. NOW records do not indicate how long MWPC lasted in this first incarnation, but it was resurrected when the NOW chapter split in 1982. Interview with Paula Casey, April 20, 1996.

54 "Wife abuse" is the term Memphis NOW members used to describe domestic violence in which a man abused a woman, whether she was a wife or lover. It did not apply to abuse against female children or siblings.

55 Echols, *Daring to Be Bad*; Whittier, *Feminist Generations*; and Evans, *Tidal Wave*.

56 Memphis NOW Newsletter, January 1973 and February 1973, Box 1, folder 6, Memphis NOW papers.

57 Interview with Lynda Dolbi, March 6, 1996.

58 Whittier and Echols suggest that such coalition or umbrella structures were the province of radical feminist groups. However, NOW has a history, largely untold, of coalition building, especially at the local level but also encouraged and fostered from the national level. See Whittier, *Feminist Generations*; and Echols, *Daring to Be Bad*.

59 "The Wheel," newsletter of the Memphis Women's Resource Center, March 1974, MVC Periodicals, Special Collections, Ned R. McWherter Library, The Univeristy of Memphis (hereafter "The Wheel").

60 "Women's Resource Center of Memphis, Inc.," June 1977, in Wurzburg Papers.

61 "The Wheel," October 1982.
62 "The Comprehensive Rape Crisis Program," n.d. [1975], Memphis NOW Papers.
63 Alayne Barry Adams, "Memphis' Badge of Infamy," Memphis *Commercial Appeal*, May 23, 1975.
64 "NOW Members Protest Violence against Women," Memphis *Commercial Appeal*, 27 August 1975.
65 Memphis NOW Newsletter, September 1974, Box 1, folder 7, Memphis NOW Papers.
66 "The Wheel," July 1978.
67 Memphis NOW Newsletter, August 1975, Box 1, folder 7, Memphis NOW Papers.
68 Michael Conley, "Task Force Looks at Wife Beating," Memphis *Press-Scimitar*, September 8, 1976.
69 Anna Byrd Davis, "Memphis Group Offers Help to Wives," Memphis *Press-Scimitar*, July 2, 1976.
70 Conley, "Task Force Looks at Wife Beating."
71 Memphis NOW Newsletter, August 1979, Box 1, folder 8, Memphis NOW Papers.
72 "The Wheel," June 1978.
73 Memphis NOW Newsletter, November 1978, Box 1, folder 8, Memphis NOW Papers.
74 "The Wheel," February 1979.
75 Memphis NOW Newsletter, November 1978, Box 1, folder 8, Memphis NOW Papers.
76 Ibid.
77 Thomas Fox, "Acting, Fakery in 'Snuff' Should Bring its Well-Deserved Demise," Memphis *Commercial Appeal*, September 27, 1977.
78 Chapter newsletter insert, "Enough SNUFF," n.d. [1977], Box 1, folder 7, Memphis NOW Papers.
79 Fox, "Acting, Fakery in 'Snuff' Should Bring its Well-Deserved Demise."
80 Ibid.
81 For more on NOW and the "lavender menace," see Gilmore and Kaminski, "Apart and A Part."
82 Other studies on lesbian communities include Susan Kathleen Freeman, "From the Lesbian Nation to the Cincinnati Lesbian Community"; Buring, *Lesbian and Gay Memphis*; Elizabeth Lapovsky Kennedy and Madeline Davis, *Boots of Leather, Slippers of Gold: The History of a Lesbian Community* (New York: Routledge, 1993); and Brett Beemyn, ed., *Creating a Place for Ourselves: Lesbian, Gay, and Bisexual Community Histories* (New York: Routledge, 1997).
83 Buring, *Lesbian and Gay Memphis*.
84 Memphis NOW Newsletter, June 1974, Box 1, folder 7, Memphis NOW Papers.
85 Memphis NOW Newsletter, July 1974, Box 1, folder 7, Memphis NOW Papers.
86 Memphis NOW Newsletter, December 1974, Box 1, folder 7, Memphis NOW Papers.
87 "Local Task Force," *Gaiety*, August 1975.
88 Memphis NOW Newsletter, June 1975, Box 1, folder 7, Memphis NOW Papers.
89 "Local Task Force," *Gaiety*, August 1975, 2.
90 Buring, *Lesbian and Gay Memphis*, 168.
91 Ibid.
92 Buring, *Lesbian and Gay Memphis*; and Lillian Faderman, *Odd Girls and Twilight Lovers: A History of Lesbian Life in Twentieth-Century America* (New York: Penguin Books, 1991) are two scholars who discuss the centrality of softball in terms of lesbian community building. For more on this in Memphis, see Buring, *Lesbian and Gay Memphis*.
93 Buring, *Lesbian and Gay Memphis,* 155.
94 Interview, Betty Sullivan, October 21, 1995.

95 Buring, *Lesbian and Gay Memphis*, 156.
96 Ibid., 165.
97 Interview, Lynda Dolbi, March 6, 1996.
98 Ibid.
99 Buring, *Lesbian and Gay Memphis*, 167.
100 Interview, Paula Casey, April 20, 1996.
101 For theoretical development and various studies on oppositional communities and cultures, see Jane Mansbridge and Aldon Morris, eds., *Oppositional Consciousness: The Subjective Roots of Social Protest* (Chicago: University of Chicago Press, 2001).
102 Unattributed "quotable quote," Memphis NOW Newsletter, August 1975.

4 Feminist Theorizing, Feminist Activisms in Columbus

1 For more information on the Feminist Avengers, see their website: http://feminista-vengers.blogspot.com.
2 Kitty McConnell, "Someone Was Raped Here: Radical Feminism is Back in Columbus, But Is It Doing Any Good?" *The Other Paper*, April 23, 2009. Accessible online at http://www.theotherpaper.com/news/article_2921c9a3-f8d8–50a3–919d-0a8f02bf67dd.html.
3 Mary Bridgman, "Revolution Proves Costly to 'Gahanna Five' Women," *Columbus Dispatch*, June 14, 1979.
4 Ibid.
5 Verta Taylor and Leila J. Rupp, "Women's Culture and Lesbian Feminist Activism: A Reconsideration of Cultural Feminism," *Signs* 19, no. 1 (1993): 32–61, quotation on 39. On WAC, see Whittier, *Feminist Generations*.
6 Interview, Barbara Wood, December 3, 2004.
7 Whittier, *Feminist Generations*, esp. 35–38; Right NOW, Columbus NOW Newsletter, Columbus NOW Papers, Ohio Historical Society, October 1973 (hereafter Columbus NOW).
8 Interview, June Sahara. Whittier (*Feminist Generations*, 38) refers to this action as "courtwatch."
9 Angela Taylor, "The Rape Victim: Is She Also the Unintended Victim of the Law?" *New York Times*, 15 June 1971, 52. On the numbers of rapes in the state, see the FBI, Uniform Crime Reports, 1970, 1971, 1972, 1973, 1974, 1975, 1976, 1977, 1978, 1979, and 1980, accessible through www.disastercenter.com/crime/ohcrime.htm.
10 Interview, Barbara Wood, December 3, 2004.
11 Bridgman, "Revolution Proves Costly to 'Gahanna Five' Women."
12 See Whittier, *Feminist Generations*; and Kathleen Laughlin, "Sisterhood, Inc.: The Status of Women Commission and the Rise of Feminist Coalition Politics in Ohio, 1964–74," *Ohio History* 108 (spring 1999): 39–60.
13 Ann Fisher, "From Clubroom to Network: As Women's Status has Evolved, so Have Their Associations." *Columbus Dispatch*, December 26, 1999.
14 Verta Taylor, "Social Movement Continuity." See also Rupp and Taylor, *Survival in the Doldrums*; Hartmann, *The Other Feminists*, and Harrison, *On Account of Sex*.
15 Fisher, "From Clubroom to Network."
16 For more on the YWCA historically, see Nina Mjackij, *Men and Women Adrift: The YMCA and YWCA in the City* (New York: New York University Press, 1997); Daphne Spain, *How Women Saved the City* (Minneapolis: University of Minnesota Press, 2000).
17 Fisher, "From Clubroom to Network."
18 Ibid.
19 Ibid. For more on submerged networks as a sociological term of analysis, see Taylor, "Social Movement Continuity"; and Carol Mueller, "Conflict Networks and the

Origins of Women's Liberation," in *New Social Movements: From Identity to Ideology*, ed. Enrique Larana, Hank Johnston, and Joseph R. Gusfield (Philadelphia: Temple University Press, 1994), 234–63.

20 Fisher, "From Clubroom to Network." On feminist peace activism, see Estepa, "Taking the White Gloves Off," and Swerdlow, *Women Strike for Peace.*

21 Fisher, "From Clubroom to Network."

22 Ibid.

23 Whittier, *Feminist Generations*, 28.

24 On PCSW, see Harrison, *On Account of Sex.*

25 Laughlin, "Sisterhood, Inc.," 40.

26 Ibid., 41.

27 Ibid., 55–56, and *Columbus Citizen Journal*, August 21, 1970.

28 Fisher, "From Clubroom to Network." The definitive study of WAC is Whittier, *Feminist Generations.*

29 Whittier, *Feminist Generations*, 34–35.

30 Whittier, *Feminist Generations*, outlines how WAR received CETA funding for the rape crisis center, making it the financial hub of the collective.

31 There are few studies on women's feminist bookstores; on Fan the Flames, see Whittier, *Feminist Generations*; see also Saralyn Chestnut and Amanda Gable, "Women Ran It: Charis Books and More and Atlanta's Lesbian-Feminist Community," in *Carryin' On in the Lesbian and Gay South*, ed. John Howard (New York: NYU Press, 1997): 241–84; and Enke, *Finding the Movement: Finding the Movement: Sexuality, Contested Space, and Feminist Activism* (Durham, NC: Duke University Press, 2007). For more on other cities that incorporated various feminist-generated institutions into the city government, see Stephanie Gilmore, "The Dynamics of Second-Wave Feminist Activism in Memphis, Tennessee, 1971–82: Rethinking the Liberal/Radical Divide," *NWSA Journal* 15, no. 1 (2003): 94–117; and Judith Ezekiel, *Feminism in the Heartland* (Columbus: Ohio State University Press, 2002).

32 Whittier, *Feminist Generations.*

33 Interview, Janet Burnside, November 26, 2004.

34 On the importance of appearance and the "look" among lesbian feminists, see Taylor and Whittier, "Collective Identity in Social Movement Communities."

35 Interview, Janet Burnside, November 26, 2004. She later became "politically savvy" as an elected member of the Ohio Supreme Court.

36 Ibid. Others corroborated this statement, including many interviewed for Whittier, *Feminist Generations*; Interview, June Sahara (Gretchen Dygert), November 11, 2004; Interview, Susan Bader, November 11, 2004; and Interview, Barbara Wood, December 3, 2004.

37 Whittier, *Feminist Generations*; Interview, Barbara Wood, December 3, 2004; Interview, Gretchen Dygert, November 11, 2004. Susan Bader suggests that, in 2004, many lesbians are active in Columbus NOW. Interview, Susan Bader, November 11, 2004. See also, Taylor and Rupp, "Women's Culture and Lesbian Feminist Activism"; and Taylor and Whittier, "Collective Identity in Social Movement Communities."

38 *Right NOW*, January 1972.

39 *Right NOW*, January 1972.

40 Interview, Janet Burnside, November 26, 2004.

41 Interview, Barbara Wood, December 3, 2004.

42 *Right NOW*, March 1972, featured an interview with Browning.

43 See, for example, *Right NOW*, April 1972. In this newsletter, Saunier discussed her interest and efforts at bringing women's groups together in the city to discuss common ground, strategies, and perspectives. For more on Saunier, see Judith Ezekiel, *Feminism in the Heartland*, esp. 218–20.

44 Laughlin, "Sisterhood, Inc."

45 Ibid.
46 Ibid. See also, on Memphis, Gilmore, "The Dynamics of Second-Wave Feminist Activism in Memphis, 1971–82"; on North Carolina, see Mathews and DeHart, *Sex, Gender, and the Politics of ERA*.
47 Right NOW, January 1972.
48 Right NOW, April 1972.
49 Right NOW, June 1972.
50 Laughlin, "Sisterhood, Inc."
51 Right NOW, June 1972.
52 Ibid.
53 Interview, Mary Miller, conducted by Mary Irene Moffitt for Rupp and Taylor, *Survival in the Doldrums*, Sophia Smith Collection, Smith College, Northampton, MA; Laughlin, "Sisterhood, Inc."; and Interview, Janet Burnside, November 26, 2004.
54 Whittier, *Feminist Generations*, 28.
55 Interview, Janet Burnside, November 26, 2004.
56 Laughlin, "Sisterhood, Inc.", 39.
57 Interview, Janet Burnside, November 26, 2004.
58 Ibid.
59 Ibid.
60 Right NOW, October 1972.
61 Right NOW, April 1973.
62 Ibid.
63 Ibid.
64 Laughlin, "Sisterhood, Inc.," 59; and Cleveland *Plain Dealer*, January 13, 1974.
65 Right NOW, January 1974.
66 Laughlin, "Sisterhood, Inc." 39; *Columbus Dispatch*, February 21, 1973; see also Mathews and DeHart, *Sex, Gender, and the Politics of ERA*.
67 Laughlin, "Sisterhood, Inc.," 59; and *Columbus Dispatch*, February 7, 1974.
68 On STOP ERA in Columbus, see Laughlin, "Sisterhood, Inc." On STOP ERA in a national context, see Brown, *For a "Christian America"*; and Marjorie Julian Spruill, "Gender and America's Right Turn," in *Rightward Bound: Making America Conservative in the 1970s*, ed. Bruce Schulman and Julian Zelizer (Cambridge, MA: Harvard University Press, 2008); Mansbridge, *Why We Lost the ERA*; and Mathews and DeHart, *Sex, Gender, and the Politics of ERA*. On the shift in labor from anti-ERA to neutral or even supportive of the ERA, see Gabin, *Feminism in the Labor Movement*; Hartmann, *The Other Feminists*; and Cobble, *The Other Women's Movement*.
69 Interview, Barbara Wood, December 3, 2004.
70 Interview, Janet Burnside, November 26, 2004.
71 James Bradshaw, "Questions Hinge on Red Door," *Columbus Dispatch*, July 30, 1972.
72 Right NOW, June 1972.
73 Right NOW, July 1972.
74 Interview, Janet Burnside, November 26, 2004.
75 Bradshaw, "Questions Hinge on Red Door."
76 Ibid. For more on contemporary cases of reverse discrimination, see Dennis Deslippe, "Do Whites Have Rights? White Detroit Policemen and Reverse Discrimination," *Journal of American History* 91, no. 3 (2004).
77 Interview, Janet Burnside, 26 November 2004; June Sahara supported this idea, though from the perspective that "respectability" was very important to NOW and not so important to WAC. Interview, June Sahara, November 11, 2004.
78 Interview, Barbara Wood, December 3, 2004.
79 Ibid.
80 Interview, Janet Burnside, November 26, 2004.
81 Ibid.

82 Ibid.
83 Ibid.
84 Interview, Barbara Wood, December 3, 2004.
85 Ibid.
86 Interview, June Sahara, November 11, 2004; see also Whittier, *Feminist Generations*.
87 Karen J. Lewis, Jon Shimabukuro, and Dana Ely, "Abortion: Legislative Response," *Congressional Research*, Library of Congress, November 22, 2004.
88 Right NOW, January 1977 (in this newsletter, Saunier offered a brief history of the lawsuit as it stood at the time); "Suit Challenges 3 Police Tests," *Columbus Dispatch*, June 17, 1975.
89 "Suit Challenges 3 Police Tests"; "Findings of Fact," *Youla Brant, et al. v. City of Columbus* (1978 U.S. Dist., 15109).
90 Right NOW, January 1977.
91 Thomas Sheenan, "Police Suit Defendants Told To Pay Damages," *Columbus Dispatch*, October 6, 1978.
92 Right NOW, January 1977.
93 "Findings of Fact," *Youla Brant, et al. v. City of Columbus* (1978 U.S. Dist., 15109).
94 Ibid.
95 Interview, Barbara Wood, December 3, 2004.
96 Sheenan, "Police Suit Defendants Told to Pay Damages."
97 Interview, Barbara Wood, December 3, 2004.
98 Whittier, *Feminist Generations*, 36.
99 Interview, Barbara Wood, December 3, 2004.
100 Ibid.
101 Right NOW, January 1972.
102 Right NOW, March 1972.
103 Ibid.
104 For more on the importance of publishing and the variety of journals and "rags" published among radical feminists, see Barbara Crow, *Radical Feminism*; and Susan Brownmiller, *In Our Time: Memoir of a Feminist Revolution* (New York: Vintage, 2000). Chicago Women's Liberation Union features a variety of feminist publications on their website: <http://www.cwluherstory.org/CWLUArchive/classic.html>
105 Whittier, *Feminist Generations*.
106 Jane O'Reilly, "Click! A Housewife's Moment of Truth," *Ms.* (spring 1972).
107 Right NOW, June 1972.
108 Ibid.
109 Ibid.
110 Interview, Barbara Wood, December 3, 2004. April 1972 marked the first adverstised woman-only CR group, but they appeared consistently through the newsletters in the 1970s.
111 Right NOW, July 1972.
112 Right NOW, August 1972.
113 Ibid.
114 On the development of *Ms.*, see Amy Farrell, *Yours in Sisterhood: Ms. Magazine and the Promise of Popular Feminism* (Chapel Hill: University of North Carolina Press, 1998). On the takeover at *Ladies Home Journal*, see Brownmiller, *In Our Time*, 83–93; Ruth Rosen, *The World Split Open*, 300–301 and 309–10.
115 Right NOW, August 1972.
116 Ibid.
117 Ibid.
118 Taylor and Rupp, "Women's Culture and Lesbian Feminist Mobilization"; Echols, *Daring to Be Bad*; Whittier, *Feminist Generations*.
119 Right NOW, August 1972.

120 NOW, Statement of Purpose, 1966.
121 Interview, Barbara Wood, December 3, 2004; Interview, June Sahara, November 11, 2004.
122 Interview, Barbara Wood, December 3, 2004.
123 Interview, Janet Burnside, November 26, 2004.
124 Ibid.
125 Right NOW, April 1973.
126 Right NOW, February 1977.
127 Right NOW, April 1973.
128 Ibid.
129 Ibid.
130 *Columbus Dispatch*, November 28, 1976, J18.
131 Right NOW, December 1976.
132 *Columbus Dispatch*, November 28, 1976.
133 Interview, Barbara Wood, December 3, 2004.
134 Ibid.
135 Ibid.
136 Right NOW, December 1980.
137 Interview, Barbara Wood, December 3, 2004.
138 Ibid.
139 Right NOW, December 1980.
140 Right NOW, January 1981.
141 Ibid.
142 Ibid.
143 Right NOW, December 1979; Right NOW, August 1981.

5 A Liberal Feminist Front of Progressive Activism in San Francisco

1 For a history of the Women's Building and a list of the organizations it hosts at present, see http://womensbuilding.org/content/index.php/about-us/history; http://womensbuilding.org/content/index.php/affiliated-organizations/in-house-organizations.
2 Janine Kahn, "Feminists Unite at the Racial Women Conference," October 7, 2008, SF Weekly, online at http://blogs.sfweekly.com/thesnitch/2008/10/last_weekend_the_radical_women.php.
3 Shirley Bernard, "How to Attract and Retain Members by Promoting Various Action Projects," n.d., Box 9, folder 35 "Chapter structural plan, 1970–75," NOW Papers. Although this particular memo is undated, Bernard was Western Regional Director for NOW from 1971 to 1973.
4 Bernard, "How to Attract and Retain Members by Promoting Various Action Projects."
5 Richard Edward DeLeon, *Left Coast City: Progressive Politics in San Francisco, 1975–1991* (Lawrence: University of Kansas Press, 1992).
6 Nan Alamilla Boyd, *Wide Open Town: A History of Queer San Francisco to 1965* (Berkeley: University of California Press, 2003). Other histories of San Francisco in the context of activism and community include William Issel and Robert W. Cherney, *San Francisco 1865–1932: Politics, Power, and Urban Development* (Berkeley: University of California Press, 1986); Douglas Henry Daniels, *Pioneer Urbanites: A Social and Cultural History of Black San Francisco* (Philadelphia: Temple University Press, 1980); John H. Mollenkopf, *The Contested City* (Princeton, NJ: Princeton University Press, 1980); Roger W. Lotchin, *The Bad City in the Good War: San Francisco, Los Angeles,*

Oakland, and San Diego (Bloomington: Indiana University Press, 2003); James Brook, Chris Carlsson, and Nancy J. Peters, eds., *Reclaiming San Francisco: History, Politics, Culture* (San Francisco: City Lights Books, 1998) Chester Hartman, *City for Sale: The Transformation of San Francisco*, rev. ed. (Berkeley: University of California Press, 2002); Frederick M. Wirt, *Power in the City: Decision Making in San Francisco* (Berkeley: University of California Press, 1974); Manuel Castells, *The City and the Grassroots: A Cross-Cultural Theory of Urban Social Movements* (Berkeley: University of California Press, 1983); Deborah Wolf, *The Lesbian Community* (Berkeley: University of California Press, 1979); John D'Emilio, *Sexual Politics, Sexual Communities: The Making of a Homosexual Minority in the United States, 1940–1970*, 2nd ed. (Chicago: University of Chicago Press, 1998); and DeLeon, *Left Coast City*.

7   Boyd discusses this phenomenon in the context of gay and lesbian politics and culture in *Wide-Open Town*. See also Anne Enke, "Smuggling Sex Through the Gates: Race, Sexuality, and the Politics of Space in Second-Wave Feminism," *American Quarterly* 55 (2003): 635–55; Enke, *Finding the Movement*.

8   San Francisco NOW Newsletter, December 1970, Box 54, folder 50, Del Martin and Phyllis Lyon Papers, GLBT Historical Society, San Francisco (hereafter SF NOW; all SF NOW papers, unless otherwise noted, are from this collection). The quotation is a reference to a day-long "Women's Conference for Liberation and Peace," which SF NOW hosted and sponsored with local affiliates of WILPF, Women for Peace, Women's Liberation, YWCA, Democratic Women's Forum, and Women With a Purpose.

9   Report of Women's Coalition Meeting, 27 September 1969, from the personal files of Del Martin and Phyllis Lyon, copies in author's possession.

10 Ibid.

11 Ibid.

12 Ibid.

13 Ibid.

14 For more on women in labor unions and labor disputes, see Cobble, *The Other Women's Movement*; Gabin, *Feminism in the Labor Movement*; Hartmann, *The Other Feminists;* and Herr, *Women, Power, and AT& T* (Boston: Northeastern University Press, 2003).

15 Report of the Second Bay Area Women's Coalition (untitled), February 9, 1970, SF NOW Papers.

16 "Report of the Women's Coalition Meeting," September 27, 1969.

17 SF NOW Newsletters, n.d. 1969 and May 1970. Unlike national NOW and other local chapters, SF NOW refers to its task forces as "committees" until the mid-1970s.

18 SF NOW Newsletter, August/September 1970; October 1970.

19 SF NOW Newsletter, October 1970.

20 "Skirting the Capitol," April 1971, Box 56, folder 18, Martin and Lyon Papers.

21 SF NOW Newsletter, April 1971.

22 SF NOW Newsletter, August 1971.

23 Ibid.

24 Ibid.

25 LMU went on to garner other successes and face battles differently. See also Del Martin and Phyllis Lyon, *Lesbian/Woman*, 20th anniversary edition (New York: Volcano Press, 1992); and Daniel Rivers, "Radical Relations: A History of Lesbian and Gay Parents and their Children," Ph.D. dissertation, Stanford University, 2010.

26 SF NOW Newsletter, August 1972.

27 Fousekis, *Demanding Child Care*.

28 SF NOW Newsletter, May 1973. (It is perhaps no coincidence that, in this same issue, the chapter encouraged members to "show your appreciation" for Mother's Day by purchasing "Fuck Housework" posters.)

29 SF NOW Newsletter, June 1973.
30 SF NOW Newsletter, July 1973.
31 Ibid.
32 Ibid.
33 SF NOW Newsletter, December 1973.
34 Ibid.
35 "Report of the Women's Coalition," September 27, 1969.
36 SF NOW Newsletter, May 1969.
37 SF NOW Newsletter, December 1969.
38 SF NOW Newsletter, April 1970.
39 Ibid.
40 SF NOW Newsletter, May 1970.
41 Ibid.
42 SF NOW Newsletter, June 1970.
43 SF NOW Newsletter, August 1970.
44 SF NOW Newsletter, December 1970.
45 SF NOW Newsletter, January 1971.
46 Ibid.
47 SF NOW Newsletter, September 1971.
48 SF NOW Newsletter, June 1971.
49 Ibid.
50 ARAL Letter, inserted in SF NOW Newsletter, June 1971.
51 SF NOW Newsletter, July 1971.
52 SF NOW Newsletter, October 1971.
53 Ibid.
54 Ibid.
55 SF NOW Newsletter, September 1969.
56 SF NOW Newsletter, December 1969.
57 "Report of the Women's Coalition," 27 September 1969.
58 SF NOW Newsletter, December 1969.
59 SF NOW Newsletter, January 1970. For more on the particulars of feminists' fight against AT&T, and for a chapter on NOW and AT&T, see Herr, *Women, Power, and AT&T*.
60 SF NOW Newsletter, May 1970.
61 SF NOW Newsletter, October 1970.
62 SF NOW Newsletter, January/February 1969.
63 SF NOW Newsletter, November 1969.
64 SF NOW Newsletter, December 1969.
65 Ibid.
66 SF NOW Newsletter, January 1970.
67 On January 26, 1970, for the first time and with no mention elsewhere in the newspaper, the *Oakland Tribune* listed all help-wanted advertisements in alphabetical order.
68 Robinson, "Two Movements in Pursuit of Equal Opportunity." See also Hartmann, *From Margin to Mainstream.*
69 SF NOW Newsletter, December 1970.
70 SF NOW Newsletter, February 1971.
71 On FEPC, see Albert S Broussard, *Black San Francisco, : The Struggle for Racial Equality in the U.S. West, 1900–1954* (Lawrence: University Press of Kansas, 1994), esp. 146.
72 SF NOW Newsletter, July 1971.
73 SF NOW Newsletter, May 1972.
74 *San Francisco Chronicle*, April 11, 1972, D22.
75 "The Unmentionable Help-Wanted Ad," editorial, *San Francisco Chronicle*, A8.

76 SF NOW Newsletter, May 1972.

77 Ibid.

78 Letter, Aileen Hernandez to Eve Norman, April 29, 1971, Box 169, folder 20 "Western Region, 1970–76," NOW Papers.

79 SF NOW Newsletter, June 1970.

80 SF NOW Newsletter, May 1972.

81 SF NOW Newsletter, March 1973.

82 SF NOW Newsletter, May 1973.

83 SF NOW Newsletter, July 1973.

84 SF NOW Newsletter, November 1974.

85 SF NOW Newsletter, December 1973.

86 Interview, Del Martin and Phyllis Lyon, March 22, 2002. Corroborated in interview with Aileen Hernandez, August 12, 2002.

87 Interview, Martin and Lyon, March 22, 2002.

88 SF NOW Newsletter, December 1973.

89 SF NOW Newsletter, March 1971.

90 SF NOW Newsletter, October 1973.

91 For more on prostitution and the women's movement, see Jill Nagle, ed. *Whores and Other Feminists* (New York: Routledge, 1997); Frederique Delacoste and Priscilla Alexander, eds., *Sex Work: Writings by Women in the Sex Industry* (San Francisco: Cleis Press, 1998); and Ronald Weitzer, *Sex for Sale: Prostitution, Pornography, and the Sex Industry* (New York: Routledge, 2000). On the sex wars in general, see Lisa Duggan and Nan Hunter, *Sex Wars: Sexual Dissent and Political Culture* (New York: Routledge, 2000).

92 GG NOW Newsletter, September 1974.

93 BAWC Statement of Purpose, n.d. [July 1974], from the personal files of Del Martin and Phyllis Lyon, copies in author's possession.

94 Ibid; Interview, Martin and Lyon, March 22, 2002.

95 BWAC Statement of Purpose. These ideas are reiterated in the "Working Paper: Commissioners Appointed by the Women's Coalition," n.d., from the personal files of Del Martin and Phyllis Lyon, copies in author's possession.

96 On the history of the PCSW and other state commissions on the status of women, see Harrison, *On Account of Sex.*

97 Keith Power, "Commission on Women Urged," *San Francisco Chronicle*, 4 December 1974.

98 Carol Kroot, "New Commission Will Eye Women's Status," *San Francisco Progress,* January 11, 1975, 5.

99 Ibid.

100 "Statement of the Bay Area Women's Coalition in Regard to the Ordinance to Establish a Commission on the Status of Women," n.d., from the personal papers of Del Martin and Phyllis Lyon, copies in author's possession; and "Women Upset over S.F. Panel," *San Francisco Chronicle*, January 18, 1975, 14.

101 BAWC, Newsletter, March 1975, from the personal papers of Del Martin and Phyllis Lyon, copies in author's possession.

102 Interview, Aileen Hernandez, August 12, 2002.

103 Interview, Martin and Lyon, March 22, 2002.

104 Del Martin, *Battered Wives* (San Francisco: Volcano Press, 1975).

105 SF NOW Newsletter, November 1970.

106 SF NOW Newsletter, July 1971.

107 SF NOW Newsletter, August 1971.

108 Ibid.

109 SF NOW Newsletter, May 1972.

110 SF NOW Newsletter, June 1972.

111 SF NOW Newsletter, October 1972.
112 SF NOW Newsletter, November 1972.
113 SF NOW Newsletter, November 1977.
114 Ibid.
115 SF NOW Newsletter, December 1977.
116 NOW Newsletter, January 1978.
117 SF NOW Newsletter, May 1979.
118 SF NOW Newsletter, August 1979.
119 SF NOW Newsletter, February 1980.
120 Ibid.
121 SF NOW Newsletter, May 1980.
122 SF NOW Newsletter, July 1980.
123 Ibid.
124 SF NOW Newsletter, May 1981.
125 SF NOW Newsletter, January 1969.

6 Learning from Grassroots Activisms in the Past

1 This survey was conducted online at http://columbusnow.homestead.com/Annual Survey~ns4.html, accessed March 12, 2002, Bold emphasis in the original.
2 Right NOW, June 1972, 1.
3 Nancy A. Naples, "Women's Community Activism: Exploring the Dynamics of Politicization and Diversity," in *Community Activism and Feminist Politics: Organizing across Race, Class, and Gender*, ed. Nancy A. Naples (New York: Routledge, 1998), 327–50, quotation on 337.
4 Mansbridge, *Why We Lost the ERA*; Berry, *Why ERA Failed*; Mathews and DeHart, *Sex, Gender, and the Politics of ERA*.
5 "Memphians Go to Illinois to Urge ERA Ratification," Memphis *Press-Scimitar*, May 10, 1980.
6 Right NOW, October 1980.
7 Email correspondence, Barbara Winslow to Stephanie Gilmore, 8 March 2005.
8 Brown, *For a "Christian America"*; Jean Hardisty, *Mobilizing Resentment: Conservative Resurgence from the John Birch Society to the Promise Keepers* (Boston: Beacon Press, 2000); Sara Diamond, *Roads to Dominion: Right Wing Movements and Political Power in the United States* (New York: Guilford Press, 1995); and Rebecca Klatch, *A Generation Divided: The New Left, the New Right, and the 1960s* (Berkeley: University of California Press, 1999) explore the rise of the Right in opposition to the ERA and other progressive legislation and use gender to explain, at least in part, the successful mobilization of the Right at the grassroots. See also McGirr, *Suburban Warriors*; Williams, *God's Own Party*; and Critchlow and Maclean, *Debating the American Conservative Movement*.
9 Interview with Myrtle Kelly conducted by Ruth Murray Brown, October 13, 1981, in Brown, *For a "Christian America,"* 15.
10 Interview, Paula Casey, April 20, 1995.
11 "ERA Song," Box 1, folder 10 "Ephemera and Printed Material/pamphlets, flyers, promotions," Carolyn Nuban Papers, Social Protest Collection, Bancroft Library, University of California, Berkeley.
12 Interview, Janet Burnside, November 26, 2004.
13 Interview, Aileen Hernandez, August 12, 2002.
14 Interview, Janet Burnside, November 26, 2004.
15 Interview, Barbara Wood, December 3, 2004.
16 The term "white-hot mobilization" is from John Lofland, "White-Hot Mobilization: Strategies of a Millenarian Movement," in *The Dynamics of Social Movements*, ed.

Mayer N. Zald and John D. McCarthy (Cambridge, MA: Winthrop Publishers, 1979): 157–66.

17 Membership rosters 1977 and 1978, in Columbus NOW Papers.

18 Interview, Betty Sullivan, April 21, 1995.

19 Stephanie Gilmore and Elizabeth Kaminski, "A Part and Apart: Implementing Inclusivity in a Second-Wave Feminist Organization," *Journal of the History of Sexuality* 16, no. 1 (2007): 97–113.

20 On the problems of "outreach" and the perspectives of women of color who resisted such an idea, see, for example, Gloria Anzaldua and Cherrie Moraga, eds., *This Bridge Called My Back: Writings by Radical Women of Color* (Boston: Kitchen Table Press, 1987); Gloria T. Hull, Patricia Bell Scott, and Barbara Smith, eds., *But Some of Us Were Brave* (New York: Feminist Press, 1993). Other analyses include, but are not limited to, Benita Roth, *Separate Roads to Feminism*, and Beverly Guy-Sheftall and Johnetta Cole, *Gender Talk: The Struggle for Women's Equality in African American Communities* (New York: Ballantine, 2003).

21 "Is Feminism Dead?" *Time*, June 29, 1998; Courtney Martin, "The End of the Women's Movement," *American Prospect*, March 27, 2009, available online: http://www.prospect.org/article/end-womens-movement.

22 Mary Hawkesworth, "The Semiotics of Premature Burial: Feminism in a Postfeminist Age," *Signs* 29, no. 4 (2004): 961–86.

23 Phyllis Chesler, *Letters to a Young Feminist* (New York: Seal Press, 1997). Older feminists lamenting the absence of young feminists in a movement or organization is not new; see Leila J. Rupp, "Is Feminism the Province of Older (or Middle-Aged) Women?" *Journal of Women's History* 12, no. 4 (2001): 164–73.

24 Martin, "The End of the Women's Movement."

25 Jennifer Baumgardner and Amy Richards, *Manifesta: Young Women, Feminism, and the Future* (New York: Farrar, Straus, and Giroux, 2000); Ednie Kaeh Garrison, "Are We on a Wavelength Yet? On Feminist Oceanography, Radios and Third-Wave Feminism" in *Different Wavelengths: Studies of the Contemporary Women's Movement*, ed. Jo Reger (New York: Routledge, 2005), 312–34. All of the chapters in *Different Wavelengths* invite readers to reconsider the idea that feminism of any strand simply happened.

26 Jo Reger, *Everywhere and Nowhere*: Contemporary Feminism in the United States (New York: Oxford University Press, 2012).

27 Clare Hemmings, "Telling Feminist Stories" *Feminist Theory* 6 (2005) 115–39; Susan Faludi, "America's Electra: Feminism's Ritualistic Matricide," *Harper's Magazine*, October 2010, available online: http://www.harpers.org/archive/2010/10/0083140.

28 Gerda Lerner, *Why History Matters: Life and Thought* (New York: Oxford University Press, 1997), 211.

29 Stephanie Gilmore, "Marcha de las Putas: Slutwalking Crosses Global Divides," *On the Issues* (fall 2001). Available online at http://www.ontheissuesmagazine.com/2011fall/2011fall_gilmore.php.

30 Ray, *Fields of Protest*, 166.

31 Kaplan, *Crazy for Democracy*, 6.

32 Interview, Linda Raiteri, February 21, 1996.

33 See http://www.now.org/chapters.

34 "Ladies Against Women" maintains a website, www.ladiesagainstwomen.com, where it offers photographs of various demonstrations and its "Ladyfesto." This campy style of street protest employs hyperbolic and mocking images of womanhood to draw attention to sexism and gender discrimination; various LAW actions have also raised awareness of poverty and welfare, environmental issues, and reproductive rights.

BIBLIOGRAPHY

Interviews

All interviews conducted by the author, unless otherwise noted.

Alexander, Dolores. Phone interview, April 22, 2004.

Bader, Susan. Phone interview, November 11, 2004.

Booth, Heather. Phone interview, April 7, 2004.

Burnside, Janet. Phone interview, November 26, 2004.

Casey, Paula, Interview, Memphis, TN, April 20,1995.

Dolbi, Lynda, Interview, Memphis, TN, March 6, 1996.

Glenn-Rodgers, Deborah. Interview, San Francisco, CA, February 25, 2002.

Grieco, Helen. Phone interview, March 24, 2002.

Harrison, Cynthia. Email correspondence, January 25, 2002.

Hernandez, Aileen. Interview, San Francisco, CA, August 12, 2002.

Hester, Leslie, Interview, Memphis, TN, March 5, 1996.

Hughes, Patti Squeo. Phone interview, March 20, 2005.

Lyon, Phyllis. Phone interview, February 22, 2002; interview, San Francisco, CA, March 22, 2002.

Mackenzie, Susan. Interview, Memphis, TN, March 20, 1996.

Martin, Del. Phone interview, February 22, 2002; interview, San Francisco, CA, March 22, 2002.

May, Audrey. Interview, Memphis, TN, August 21,1996.

Miller, Mary. Interview conducted by Mary Irene Moffitt, Rupp–Taylor collection of interviews, Sophia Smith Collection, Smith College, Northampton, MA, April 26, 1981.

Raiteri, Linda. Interview, Memphis, TN, February 21,1996.

Sahara, June (Gretchen Dygert). Phone interview, November 11, 2004.

Shea, Karen. Interview, Memphis, TN, April 20, 1996.

Sullivan, Betty. Interview, Columbus, MS, April 21, 1995.

Winslow, Barbara. Email correspondence, March 8, 2005.

Wood, Barbara. Phone interview, December 3, 2004.

Archives

Carolyn Nuban, Papers, Social Protest Collection, Bancroft Library, University of California, Berkeley, CA.
Columbus chapter of the National Organization for Women, Papers, Ohio Historical Society, Columbus, OH.
David Dismore, Los Angeles, CA. Available online at http://www.vfa.us/Dismore.htm.
Del Martin and Phyllis Lyon, Papers, Gay and Lesbian Historical Society, San Francisco, CA (includes papers of SF NOW and Golden Gate NOW).
Documenting the Midwestern Origins of the 20th Century Women's Movement. Oral History Project, directed by Gerda Lerner, Wisconsin Historical Society, Madison, WI.
Free Speech Movement, Papers, Bancroft Library, University of California, Berkeley, CA.
Jocelyn Wurzburg, Papers, Ned R. McWherter Library, University of Memphis, Memphis, TN.
Memphis chapter of the National Organization for Women, Papers, Ned R. McWherter Library, University of Memphis, Memphis, TN.
Memphis Women's Resource Center Papers, Ned R. McWherter Library, University of Memphis, Memphis, TN.
National Organization for Women, Papers of the National Organization for Women 1966–89, Schlesinger Library, Cambridge, MA.

Web Sources

Chicago Women's Liberation Union. www.cwluherstory.org
Feminist Avengers. www.feministavengers.blogspot.com
Free Speech Movement. www.bancroft.berkeley.edu/FSM
Ladies against Women. www.ladiesagainstwomen.com
Lesbian feminism. www.women-studies.osu.edu/araw/1970slf.htm
National Organization for Women. www.now.org
National Organization for Women chapters. www.now.org/chapters
Southern Girls Convention. www.southerngirlsconvention.org
Women's Building. www.womensbuilding.org

Other Primary Documents

Adams, Alayne Barry. "Memphis' 'Badge of Infamy,'" Memphis *Commercial Appeal*, August 27, 1975.
"Alliance is Formed by Ex-CORE Members," *New York Times*, October 21, 1968.
Baltad, Nancy. "Women Stage Protest Demonstration in Bar: Claim Female Discrimination," *Hollywood (CA) Citizen-News*, February 19, 1969.
Bender, Marilyn. "The Feminists are on the March Again," *New York Times*, December 14, 1967, 56.
"Betty Friedan Links Chauvinists, Scandal," *Los Angeles Times*, August 28, 1973, 16.
Bradshaw, James. "Questions Hinge on Red Door," *Columbus Dispatch*, July 30, 1972.
Bridgman, Mary. "Revolution Proves Costly to 'Gahanna Five' Women," *Columbus Dispatch*, June 14, 1979.
Caldwell, Earl. "CORE to Tighten its Organization," *New York Times*, July 4, 1968.
Caldwell, Earl. "Wilkins, in Talk to CORE, Seeks to Close Negro Rift," *New York Times*, July 6, 1968.
Caldwell, Earl. "CORE Dissenters Quit Convention," *New York Times*, July 8, 1968.
Cashiola, Mary. "Cosmetology to Car Care: The Southern Girl Convention is Covering All Bases." *Memphis Flyer*, August 2, 1999.

Conley, Michael. "Blacks Defend Scant Support of Feminism." Memphis *Commercial Appeal,* April 7, 1976.

Conley, Michael. "Task Force Looks at Wife Beating," Memphis *Press-Scimitar*, September 8, 1976.

Curtis, Charlotte. "Miss America Pageant Picketed by 100 Women," *New York Times*, September 7, 1968.

Davis, Anna Byrd. "Memphis Group Offers Help to Wives," Memphis *Press-Scimitar*, July 2, 1976.

"Disturbance in Columbus," *New York Times*, September 21, 1967.

Faludi, Susan. "America's Electra: Feminism's Ritualistic Matricide." *Harper's Magazine*. October 2010.

"Findings of Fact," *Youla Brant, et al. v. City of Columbus* (1978 U.S. Dist., 15109).

Fisher, Ann. "From Clubroom to Network: As Women's Status has Evolved, so Have Their Associations," *Columbus Dispatch*, December 26, 1999.

Fox, Thomas. "Acting, Fakery in 'Snuff' Should Bring its Well-Deserved Demise," Memphis *Commercial Appeal*, September 27, 1977.

Friedan, Betty. *The Feminine Mystique*. New York: W. W. Norton, 1963.

Friedan, Betty. "Up from the Kitchen Floor," *New York Times Magazine*, March 4, 1973.

"Friedan Scolds Steinem, Abzug," *Los Angeles Times*, July 19, 1972, 7.

Gilliam, Art. "Few Black Faces in Women's Lib Crowd," Memphis *Commercial Appeal*, June 7, 1971.

Hammell, Lisa. "They Meet in Victorian Parlor to Demand 'True Equality'—NOW," *New York Times*, November 22, 1966, 44.

Kahn, Janine. "Feminists United at the Radical Women Conference," *SF Weekly*. October 7, 2008.

Kroot, Carol. "New Commission will Eye Women's Status," *San Francisco Progress*, January 11, 1975.

"Lady Objects to 'Maude' Episode," *Los Angeles Times*, November 21, 1972, 16.

Lear, Martha Weinman. "What do These Women Want? The Second Feminist Wave," *New York Times Magazine*, March 10, 1968, 22.

"Legislators Vote to Rescind ERA Ratification," Memphis *Commercial Appeal*, April 24, 1974.

"Loaf of Bread, Talk with Senators Aim at Keeping Women in 'Place,'" Memphis *Commercial Appeal*, August 10, 1978.

"Local Task Force," *Gaiety*, August 1975.

Martin, Courtney. "The End of the Women's Movement." *American Prospect*, March 27, 2009.

Martin, Del. "Goodbye, My Alienated Brothers." *Advocate*, May 1970.

Martin, Del. *Battered Wives*. San Francisco: Volcano Press, 1975.

Martin, Del and Phyllis Lyon. *Lesbian/Woman*. San Francisco: Glide Publications, 1972.

McConnell, Kitty. "Someone Was Raped Here: Radical Feminism is Back in Columbus, But Is It Doing Any Good?" *The Other Paper*. April 23, 2009.

"Memphians Go to Illinois to Urge ERA Ratification," Memphis *Press-Scimitar*, May 10, 1980.

"Notes on People," *New York Times*, November 25, 1972, 13.

"NOW Members Protest Violence against Women," Memphis *Commercial Appeal*, August 27, 1975.

"NOW Suit over Maude Abortion Show Denied," *New York Times*, November 25, 1972, 3.

"NOW Women Sell Blood to Finance Campaign," Memphis *Commercial Appeal*, April 6, 1973.

"Old Doubts Deter Feminists," Memphis *Commercial Appeal*, August 7, 1973.

O'Reilly, Jane. "Click! A Housewife's Moment of Truth," *Ms.* (spring 1972).

Power, Keith. "Commission on Women Urged," *San Francisco Chronicle*, December 4, 1974.

Roe v. Wade (410 U.S. 113). 1973.
"Seven Shot, Guard Called in Ohio State U. Riot," *New York Times*, April 30, 1970.
Sheenan, Thomas. "Police Suit Defendants Told to Pay Damages," *Columbus Dispatch*, October 6, 1978.
"Suit Challenges 3 Police Tests," *Columbus Dispatch*, June 17, 1975.
"Tennessee's First Miss American, Barbara Walker Hummel, Dies," Nashville *Tennessean*, June 9, 2000.
"The Unmentionable Help Wanted Ad," editorial, *San Francisco Chronicle*, November 13, 1968, A8.
"Virginia Slims American Women's Opinion Poll," March 24, 1972.
Williams, Sherri. "Civil Rights Act of 1964 Culminated Long Struggle," *Columbus Dispatch*, July 2, 2004, 1A.
Willis, Jim. "Some Reports Termed False on Equal Rights Amendment," Memphis *Press-Scimitar*, March 6, 1973.
"Women Upset over S.F. Panel," *San Francisco Chronicle*, January 18, 1975, 14.
"Young, Black, and Beautiful Organize," *Los Angeles Times*, October 31, 1968, 4.
"Youth on Board of Urban League," *New York Times*, August 30, 1968.

Secondary Sources

Anderson, Zoe. "Queer(ing) History: Queer Methodologies, Pedagogies, and Interventions in the Discipline of History." *Student Engagement* (2007).
Armstrong, Elizabeth A. *Forging Gay Identities: Organizing Sexuality in San Francisco, 1950–1994*. Chicago: University of Chicago Press, 2002.
Baker, Jean H., ed. *Votes for Women: The Struggle for Suffrage Revisited*. New York: Oxford University Press, 2002.
Barakso, Maryann. *Governing NOW: Grassroots Activism in the National Organization for Women*. Ithaca, NY: Cornell University Press, 2004.
Basu, Amrita, ed. *Women's Movements in the Global Era: The Power of Local Feminisms*. Boulder, CO: Westview Press, 2010.
Baumgardner, Jennifer and Amy Richards. *Manifesta: Young Women, Feminism, and the Future*. New York: Farrar, Straus, and Giroux, 2000.
Baxandall, Rosalyn and Linda Gordon, eds. *Dear Sisters: Dispatches from the Women's Liberation Movement*. New York: Basic Books, 2002.
Becker, Howard S., ed. *Culture and Civility in San Francisco*. Chicago: Aldine, 1971.
Beemyn, Brett, ed. *Creating a Place for Ourselves: Lesbian, Gay, and Bisexual Community Histories*. New York: Routledge, 1997.
Beifuss, Joan Turner. *At the River I Stand: Memphis, the 1968 Strike, and Martin Luther King Jr.* Brooklyn, NY: Carlson Press, 1985.
Berger, Dan, ed. *The Hidden 1970s*. New Brunswick, NJ: Rutgers University Press, 2010.
Berkeley, Kathleen C. *The Women's Liberation Movement in America*. New York: Greenwood Press, 1999.
Bernstein, Mary. "Celebration and Suppression: The Strategic Uses of Identity by the Lesbian and Gay Movement." *American Journal of Sociology* 103 (1997): 531–65.
Bernstein, Mary. "Identities and Politics: Toward a Historical Understanding of the Lesbian and Gay Movement." *Social Science History* 26 (2002): 531–81.
Berry, Mary Frances. *Why ERA Failed: Politics, Women's Rights, and the Amending Process of the Constitution*. Bloomington: Indiana University Press, 1986.
Berube, Allan. *Coming Out Under Fire: The History of Gay Men and Lesbians in World War II*. Chicago: University of Chicago Press, 1995.
Boyd, Nan Alamilla. *Wide-Open Town: A History of Queer San Francisco to 1965*. Berkeley: University of California Press, 2003.

Boyle, Kevin. *Organized Labor and American Politics, 1894–1994: The Labor-Liberal Alliance.* New York: SUNY Press, 1998.

Brook, James, Chris Carlsson, and Nancy J. Peters, eds. *Reclaiming San Francisco: History, Politics, Culture.* San Francisco: City Lights Books, 1998.

Broussard, Albert S. *Black San Francisco: The Struggle for Racial Equality in the U.S. West, 1900–1954.* Lawrence: University Press of Kansas, 1994.

Brown, Rita Mae. "Reflections of a Lavender Menace," *Ms.* (July–August 1975): 40–47.

Brown, Ruth Murray. *For a 'Christian America': A History of the Religious Right.* Amherst, NY: Prometheus Books, 2002.

Brownmiller, Susan. *In Our Time: A Memoir of a Feminist Revolution.* New York: Vintage, 2000.

Buechler, Steven. *Women's Movements in the United States.* New Brunswick, NJ: Rutgers University Press, 1990.

Buring, Daneel. *Lesbian and Gay Memphis: Building Communities behind the Magnolia Curtain.* New York: Garland, 1997.

Burner, David. *Making Peace with the Sixties.* Princeton, NJ: Princeton University Press, 1996.

Carabillo, Toni, Judith Mueli, and June Bundy Cisca. *Feminist Chronicles, 1953–1993.* Los Angeles: Women's Graphics, 1993.

Castells, Manuel. *The City and the Grassroots: A Cross-Cultural Theory of Urban Social Movements.* Berkeley: University of California Press, 1983.

The Castro. Videocassette, dir. Peter L. Stein. San Francisco: KQED Public Television, 1998.

Center for Research on Women, The University of Memphis. "Profiles: A Report on Women and Girls in Greater Memphis." Memphis: Center for Research on Women, 1997.

Chappell, Marisa. "Rethinking Women's Politics in the 1970s: The National Organization for Women and the League of Women Voters Confront Poverty," *Journal of Women's History* 13, no. 4 (2002): 155–79.

Chappell, Marisa. "Demanding a New Family Wage: Feminist Consensus in the 1970s Full Employment Campaign," in *Feminist Coalitions: Historical Perspectives on Second-Wave Feminism in the United States*, ed. Stephanie Gilmore. Urbana: University of Illinois Press, 2008: 252–81.

Chappell, Marisa. *The War on Welfare: Family, Poverty, and Politics in Modern America.* Philadelphia: University of Pennsylvania Press, 2009.

Chesler, Phyllis. *Letters to a Young Feminist.* New York: Seal Press, 1997.

Chestnut, Saralyn and Amanda Gable, "Women Ran It: Charis Books and More and Atlanta's Lesbian-Feminist Community," in *Carryin' on in the Lesbian and Gay South*, ed. John Howard. New York: NYU Press, 1997: 241–84.

Clarke, Danielle. "Finding the Subject: Queering the Archive." *Feminist Theory* 5, no. 1 (2004): 79–83.

Cobble, Dorothy Sue. *The Other Women's Movement: Workplace Justice and Social Rights in Modern America.* Princeton, NJ: Princeton University Press, 2005.

Cohen, Lizabeth. *Making a New Deal: Industrial Workers in Chicago, 1919–1939.* New York: Cambridge University Press, 1990.

Cohen, Robert and Reginald E. Zelnik, eds. *The Free Speech Movement: Reflections on Berkeley in the 1960s.* Berkeley: University of California Press, 2002.

Cole, Andrew C. *A Fragile Capital: Identity and the Early Years of Columbus, Ohio.* Columbus: Ohio State University Press, 2001.

Conley, Michael A. "Blacks Defend Scant Support of Feminism." Memphis *Commercial Appeal*, April 7, 1976.

Coontz, Stephanie. *A Strange Stirring: The Feminine Mystique and American Women at the Dawn of the 1960s.* New York: Basic Books, 2011.

Critchlow, Donald and Nancy Maclean. *Debating the American Conservative Movement.* Lanham, MD: Rowman and Littlefield, 2009.

Crow, Barbara, ed. *Radical Feminism: A Documentary Reader.* New York: NYU Press, 2000.

Cunningham, David. *There's Something Happening Here: The New Left, the Klan, and FBI Counterintelligence.* Berkeley: University of California Press, 2004.

Dailey, Jane, Glenda Elizabeth Gilmore, and Bryand Simons, eds. *Jumpin' Jim Crow: Southern Politics from the Civil War to Civil Rights.* Princeton, NJ: Princeton University Press, 2000.

Daniels, Douglas Henry. *Pioneer Urbanites: A Social and Cultural History of Black San Francisco.* Philadelphia: Temple University Press, 1980.

Davis, Flora. *Moving the Mountain.* Urbana: University of Illinois Press, 1999.

DeHart, Jane Sherron. "Second Wave Feminism(s) and the South: The Difference that Difference Makes," in *Women of the American South: A Multicultural Reader,* ed. Christie Anne Farnham. New York: NYU Press, 1997.

Delacoste, Frederique and Priscilla Alexander, eds. *Sex Work: Writings by Women in the Sex Industry.* San Francisco: Cleis Press, 1998.

DeLeon, Richard Edward. *Left Coast City: Progressive Politics in San Francisco, 1975–1991.* Lawrence: University of Kansas Press, 1992.

D'Emilio, John. *Sexual Politics, Sexual Communities: The Making of a Homosexual Minority in the United States, 1940–1970,* 2nd ed. Chicago: University of Chicago Press, 1998.

D'Emilio, John. "Gay Politics and Community in San Francisco since World War II," in *Hidden From History: Reclaiming the Gay and Lesbian Past,* ed. Martin Duberman, Martha Vicinus, and George Chauncey, Jr. New York: Penguin Books, 1989: 456–76.

D'Emilio, John. "Gay Politics, Gay Community: San Francisco's Experience," in *Making Trouble: Essays on Gay History, Politics, and the University,* ed. John D'Emilio. New York: Routledge, 1992: 74–95.

Deslippe, Dennis. *Rights, Not Roses: Unions and the Rise of Working-Class Feminism, 1945–1980.* Urbana: University of Illinois Press, 1998.

Deslippe, Dennis. "Do Whites Have Rights? White Detroit Policemen and Reverse Discrimination," *Journal of American History* 91, no. 3 (2004).

Diamond, Sara. *Roads to Dominion: Right Wing Movements and Political Power in the United States.* New York: Guilford Press, 1995.

Douglas, Susan J. *Enlightened Sexism: The Seductive Message that Feminism's Work is Done.* New York: Times Books, 2010.

Duffett, Judith. "WLM vs. Miss America: Atlantic City is a Town with Class—They Raise Your Morals While They Judge Your Ass." *Voice of the Women's Liberation Movement,* October 1968, 1.

Duggan, Lisa. *Sapphic Slashers: Sex, Violence, and American Modernity.* Durham, NC: Duke University Press, 2001.

Duggan, Lisa and Nan Hunter. *Sex Wars: Sexual Dissent and Political Culture.* New York: Routledge, 2000.

DuPlessis, Rachel and Ann Snitow, eds. *The Feminist Memoir Project: Voices from Women's Liberation.* New Brunswick, NJ: Rutgers University Press, 2007.

Echols, Alice. *Daring to Be Bad: Radical Feminism in America, 1967–1975.* Minneapolis: University of Minnesota Press, 1989.

Enke, Anne. *Finding the Movement: Sexuality, Contested Space, and Feminist Activism.* Durham, NC: Duke University Press, 2007.

Enke, Anne. "Smuggling Sex Through the Gates: Race, Sexuality, and the Politics of Space in Second-Wave Feminism." *American Quarterly* 55 (2003): 635–55.

Ensler, Eve. *The Vagina Monologues.* New York: Dramatists Play Service, 2000.

Estepa, Andrea. "Taking the White Gloves Off: Women Strike for Peace and 'The Movement'," in *Feminist Coalitions: Historical Perspectives on Second-Wave Feminism,* ed. Stephanie Gilmore. Urbana: University of Illinois Press, 2008: 84–112.

Evans, Sara. *Personal Politics: The Roots of the Women's Liberation in the Civil Rights Movement and the New Left.* New York: Vintage, 1980.

Evans, Sara. *Tidal Wave: How Women Changed America at Century's End.* New York: Free Press, 2003.

Ezekiel, Judith. *Feminism in the Heartland.* Columbus: Ohio State University Press, 2002.

Faderman, Lillian. *Odd Girls and Twilight Lovers: A History of Lesbian Life in Twentieth-Century America.* New York: Penguin Books, 1991.

Faludi, Susan. *Backlash: The Undeclared War against American Women.* New York: Anchor, 1992.

Farrell, Amy. *Yours in Sisterhood: Ms. Magazine and the Promise of Popular Feminism.* Chapel Hill: University of North Carolina Press, 1998.

Ferree, Myra Marx and Beth Hess. *Controversy and Coalition: The New Feminist Movement Across Four Decades of Change.* New York: Routledge, 2000.

Findlen, Rebecca, ed. *Listen Up: Voices from the Next Generation.* New York: Seal Press, 1995.

Fink, Gary M. and Merl Reed, eds. *Race, Class, and Community in Southern Labor History.* Tuscaloosa: University of Alabama Press, 1994.

Fonow, Mary Margaret. *Union Women: Forging Feminism in the United Steelworkers of America.* Minneapolis: University of Minnesota Press, 2003.

Fousekis, Natalie. *Demanding Child Care: Women's Activism and the Politics of Welfare, 1940–1971.* Urbana: University of Illinois Press, 2011.

Franzen, Trisha. "Differences and Identities: Feminism and the Albuquerque Lesbian Community," *Signs,* 18, no. 4 (1993): 891–906.

Freedman, Estelle. *No Turning Back: The History of Feminism and the Future of Women.* New York: Ballantine Books, 2002.

Freeman, Jo. "The Origins of the Women's Liberation Movement," *American Journal of Sociology* 78 (1973): 792–811.

Freeman, Jo. *The Politics of Women's Liberation.* New York: Longman, 1975.

Freeman, Jo(reen). "The Bitch Manifesto," in *Radical Feminism: A Documentary Reader,* ed. Barbara Crow. New York: NYU Press, 2000: 226–32.

Freeman, Jo. *At Berkeley in the Sixties: The Education of an Activist, 1961–1965.* Bloomington: Indiana University Press, 2003.

Freeman, Susan Kathleen. "From the Lesbian Nation to the Cincinnati Lesbian Community: Moving toward a Politics of Location." *Journal of the History of Sexuality* 9, no. 1–2 (2000): 137–74.

Friedan, Betty. *Life So Far.* New York: Simon and Schuster, 2000.

Fuentes, Sonia Pressman. *Eat First—You Don't Know What They'll Give You: The Adventures of an Immigrant Family and Their Feminist Daughter.* New York: Xlibris, 1999.

Gabin, Nancy. *Feminism in the Labor Movement: Women and the United Auto Workers, 1935–1975.* Ithaca, NY: Cornell University Press, 1990.

Garrison, Ednie Kaeh. "Are We on a Wavelength Yet? On Feminist Oceanography, Radios and Third-Wave Feminism," in *Different Wavelengths: Studies of the Contemporary Women's Movement,* ed. Jo Reger. New York: Routledge, 2005: 312–34.

Giddings, Paula. *When and Where I Enter: The Impact of Black Women on Race and Sex in America.* New York: Bantam Books, 1985.

Gilmore, Stephanie. "Marcha de las Putas: Slutwalking Crosses Global Divides." *On the Issues* (fall 2001). Available online at http://www.ontheissuesmagazine.com/2011fall/2011fall_gilmore.php.

Gilmore, Stephanie. "The Dynamics of Second-Wave Feminist Activism in Memphis, 1971–82: Rethinking the Liberal/Radical Divide," *NWSA Journal* 15, no. 1 (2003): 94–117.

Gilmore, Stephanie. "Bridging the Waves: Sex and Sexuality in a Second-Wave Organization," in *Different Wavelengths: Contemporary Perspectives on the Women's Movement in America,* ed. Jo Reger. New York: Routledge, 2005.

Gilmore, Stephanie, ed. *Feminist Coalitions: Historical Perspectives on Second-Wave Feminism in the United States.* Urbana: University of Illinois Press, 2008.

Gilmore, Stephanie, and Elizabeth Kaminski. "A Part and Apart: Lesbian and Straight Feminists Negotiate Identity in a Second-Wave Organization," *Journal of the History of Sexuality* 16, no. 1 (2007): 95–113.

Ginsburg, Fay. *Contested Lives: The Abortion Debate in an American Community.* Berkeley: University of California Press, 1989.

Gordon, Linda and Rosalyn Baxandall, eds. *Dear Sisters: Dispatches from Women's Liberation.* New York: Basic Books, 2001.

Grantham, Dewey. "History." *Encyclopedia of Southern History.* Baton Rouge: Louisiana State University Press, 1979.

Greene, Julie. *Pure and Simple Politics: The American Federation of Labor and Political Activism, 1881–1917.* Cambridge: Cambridge University Press, 2006.

Guy-Sheftall, Beverly. "Response from a 'Second Waver' to Kimberly Springer's 'Third Wave Black Feminism?'" *Signs* 27, no. 4 (2002): 1091–94.

Guy-Sheftall, Beverly, ed. *Words of Fire: An Anthology of African-American Feminist Thought.* New York: The New Press, 1999.

Hall, Jacquelyn Dowd. "The Long Civil Rights Movement and the Political Uses of the Past." *Journal of American History* 91 (2005): 1233–63.

Haraway, Donna. *Simians, Cyborgs, and Women: The Reinvention of Nature.* London: Free Association Press, 1991.

Hardisty, Jean. *Mobilizing Resentment: Conservative Resurgence from the John Birch Society to the Promise Keepers.* Boston: Beacon Press, 2000.

Harrison, Cynthia. *On Account of Sex: The Politics of Women's Issues, 1945–1968.* Berkeley: University of California Press, 1989.

Hartman, Chester. *City for Sale: The Transformation of San Francisco,* rev. ed. Berkeley: University of California Press, 2002.

Hartmann, Susan M. *From Margin to Mainstream: American Women and Politics since 1960.* New York: Knopf, 1980.

Hartmann, Susan M. *The Other Feminists: Activists in the Liberal Establishment.* New Haven, CT: Yale University Press, 1998.

Hartmann, Susan M. "Pauli Murray and the 'Juncture of Women's Liberation and Black Liberation.'" *Journal of Women's History* 14, no. 2 (2002): 74–77.

Hawkesworth, Mary. "The Semiotics of Premature Burial: Feminism in a Postfeminist Age." *Signs* 29, no. 4 (2004): 961–86.

Hemmings, Clare. "Telling Feminist Stories." *Feminist Theory* 6 (2005): 115–39.

Herr, Lois. *Women, Power, and AT&T.* Boston: Northeastern University Press, 2003.

Hesse-Biber, Sharlene and Patricia Leavy. *The Practice of Qualitative Research.* Thousand Oaks, CA: Sage, 2010.

Hewitt, Nancy, ed. *No Permanent Waves: Recasting Histories of U.S. Feminism.* New Brunswick, NJ: Rutgers University Press, 2010.

Heywood, Leslie and Jennifer Drake. *Third Wave Agenda: Being Feminist, Doing Feminism.* Minneapolis: University of Minnesota Press, 1997.

Higginbotham, Evelyn Brooks. "African American Women's History and the Metalanguage of Race." *Signs* 17, no. 4 (1992): 251–74.

Hochschild, Arlie. *The Second Shift.* New York: Viking, 1971.

Hodgson, Godfrey. *The World Turned Right Side up: A History of the Conservative Ascendancy in America.* New York: Mariner Books, 1996.

Holloway, Harry. *The Politics of the Southern Negro: From Exclusion to Big City Organization.* New York: Random House, 1969.

Horowitz, Daniel. *Betty Friedan and the Making of the Feminine Mystique: The American Left, the Cold War, and Modern Feminism.* Amherst: University of Massachusetts Press, 1998.

Howard, John, ed. *Carryin' on in the Lesbian and Gay South.* New York: NYU Press, 1997.

Hull, Gloria T., Patricia Bell Scott, and Barbara Smith, eds. *But Some of Us Were Brave.* New York: Feminist Press, 1993.

Hurtado, Albert L. "Settler Women and Frontier Women: The Unsettling Past of Western Women's History." *Frontiers* 22, no. 3 (2001): 1–5.

Issel, William and Robert W. Cherney. *San Francisco 1865–1932: Politics, Power, and Urban Development.* Berkeley: University of California Press, 1986.

Isserman, Maurice and Michael Kazin, *America Divided: The Civil War of the 1960s.* New York: Oxford University Press, 2000.

Jay, Karla. *Tales of the Lavender Menace: A Memoir of Liberation.* New York: Basic Books, 1999.

Jayawardena, Kumari. *Feminism and Nationalism in the Third World.* London: Zed Books, 1986.

Kalpagam, U. "Perspectives for a Grassroots Feminist Theory," *EPW Perspectives* 37 (November 2002): 4686–93.

Kaplan, Caren and Inderpal Grewal, eds. *Scattered Hegemonies: Postmodernity and Transnational Feminist Practice.* Minneapolis: University of Minnesota Press, 1996.

Kaplan, Temma. *Crazy for Democracy: Women in Grassroots Movements.* New York: Routledge, 1996.

Kennedy, Elizabeth Lapovsky and Madeline Davis. *Boots of Leather, Slippers of Gold: The History of a Lesbian Community.* New York: Routledge, 1993.

Kitchell, Mark. *Berkeley in the Sixties.* Videocassette. New York: First Run Features, 1990.

Klatch, Rebecca. *A Generation Divided: The New Left, the New Right, and the 1960s.* Berkeley: University of California Press, 1999.

Lapp, Rudolph M. *Blacks in Gold Rush California.* New Haven, CT: Yale University Press, 1997.

Laughlin, Kathleen. "Sisterhood, Inc.: The Status of Women Commission and the Rise of Feminist Coalition Politics in Ohio, 1964–74." *Ohio History* 108 (spring 1999): 39–60.

Lavrin, Ascunsion. *Women, Feminism, and Social Change in Argentina, Chile, and Uruguay, 1890–1940.* Lincoln: University of Nebraska Press, 1995.

Lerner, Gerda. "Midwestern Leaders of the Modern Women's Movement: An Oral History Project." *Wisconsin Academy Review* 41, no. 1 (1994–95): 11–15.

Lerner, Gerda. *Why History Matters: Life and Thought.* New York: Oxford University Press, 1997.

Levenstein, Lisa. *A Movement without Marches: African American Women and the Politics of Poverty in Postwar Philadelphia.* Chapel Hill: University of North Carolina Press, 2009.

Lewis, Karen J., Jon Shimabukuro, and Dana Ely. "Abortion: Legislative Response." *Congressional Research*, Library of Congress, November 22, 2004.

Liechtenstein, Nelson. *State of the Union: A Century of American Labor.* Princeton, NJ: Princeton University Press, 2003.

Lofland, John. "White-Hot Mobilization: Strategies of a Millenarian Movement," in *The Dynamics of Social Movements*, ed. Mayer N. Zald and John D. McCarthy. Cambridge, MA: Winthrop Publishers, 1979: 157–66.

Lotchin, Roger W. *The Bad City in the Good War: San Francisco, Los Angeles, Oakland, and San Diego.* Bloomington: Indiana University Press, 2003.

Luker, Kristin. *Abortion and the Politics of Motherhood.* Berkeley: University of California Press, 1988.

Maclean, Nancy. *Behind the Mask of Chivalry: The Making of the Second Ku Klux Klan.* New York: Oxford University Press, 1994.

Maclean, Nancy. *Freedom is Not Enough: The Opening of the American Workplace.* Cambridge, MA: Harvard University Press, 2008.

Mansbridge, Jane. *Why We Lost the ERA.* Chicago: University of Chicago Press, 1986.

Mansbridge, Jane and Aldon Morris, eds. *Oppositional Consciousness: The Subjective Roots of Social Protest*. Chicago: University of Chicago Press, 2001.

Mathews, Donald and Jane Sherron DeHart. *Sex, Gender, and the Politics of the ERA: A State and a Nation*. New York: Oxford University Press, 1990.

McBride, Genevieve, ed. *Women's Wisconsin: From Native Matriarchs to the New Millennium*. Madison: Wisconsin Historical Society, 2005.

McCaffrey, Dawn and Jennifer Keys. "Competitive Framing Process in the Abortion Debate: Polarization-Vilification, Frame Saving, and Frame Debunking." *Sociological Quarterly* 41, no. 1 (2000): 41–61.

McGirr, Lisa. *Suburban Warriors: The Origins of the New American Right*. Princeton, NJ: Princeton University Press, 2002.

Meyerowitz, Joanne, ed. *Not June Cleaver: Women and Gender in Postwar America, 1945–1960*. Philadelphia: Temple University Press, 1994.

Mikell, Gwendolyn. *African Feminism: The Politics of Survival in Sub-Saharan Africa*. Philadelphia: University of Pennsylvania Press, 1997.

Miller, Byron. *Geography and Social Movements: Comparing Antinuclear Activism in the Boston Area*. Minneapolis: University of Minnesota Press, 2000.

Mjackij, Nina. *Men and Women Adrift: The YMCA and the YWCA in the City*. New York: NYU Press, 1997.

Mollenkopf, John H. *The Contested City*. Princeton, NJ: Princeton University Press, 1980.

Molyneux, Maxine. *Women's Movements in International Perspective*. New York: Palgrave, 2001.

Montgomery, David. *The Fall of the House of Labor: The Workplace, the State, and American Labor Activism, 1895–1925*. Cambridge: Cambridge Univeristy Press, 1989.

Moraga, Cherríe and Gloria Anzaldúa, eds. *This Bridge Called My Back: Writings by Radical Women of Color*. Boston: Kitchen Table Press, 1987.

Mueller, Carol. "Conflict Networks and the Origins of Women's Liberation," in *New Social Movements: From Identity to Ideology*, ed. Enrique Larana, Hank Johnston, and Joseph R. Gusfield. Philadelphia: Temple University Press, 1994: 243–63.

Murphy, Lucy Eldersveld and Wendy Hamand Vanet, eds. *Midwestern Women: Work, Community, and Leadership at the Crossroads*. Bloomington: Indiana University Press, 1997.

Murray, Gail S. "White Privilege, Racial Justice: Women Activists in Memphis," in *Throwing off the Cloak of Privilege: White Southern Women Activists in the Civil Rights Era*, ed. Gail S. Murray. Gainesville: University of Florida Press, 2004.

Murray, Pauli. "Pauli Murray's Notable Connections." *Journal of Women's History* 14 (summer 2002): 54–87.

Nadasen, Premilla. "Expanding the Boundaries of the Women's Movement: Black Feminism and the Struggle for Welfare Rights." *Feminist Studies* 28, no. 2 (2002): 271–301.

Nadasen, Premilla. "Black Feminism: Waves, Rivers, and Still Waters." *Feminist Formations* 22, no. 1 (2010): 98–105.

Nagle, Jill, ed. *Whores and Other Feminists*. New York: Routledge, 1997.

Naples, Nancy A. *Grassroots Warriors: Activist Mothering, Community Work, and the War on Poverty*. New York: Routledge, 1988.

Naples, Nancy A., ed. *Community Activism and Feminist Politics: Organizing across Race, Class, and Gender*. New York: Routledge, 1998.

Naples, Nancy, and Manisha Desai, eds. *Women's Activism and Globalization: Linking Local Struggles and Transnational Politics*. New York: Routledge, 2002.

No Secret Anymore. Videocassette. dir. Joan E. Biren, Joan E. Biren Productions.

Offen, Karen. *European Feminisms, 1700–1950: A Political History*. Stanford, CA: Stanford University Press, 1999.

Olcott, Jocelyn. *Revolutionary Women in Postrevolutionary Mexico.* Durham, NC: Duke University Press, 2005.

Payne, Charles. *I've Got the Light of Freedom: The Organizing Tradition and the Mississippi Struggle for Freedom.* Berkeley: University of California Press, 2000.

Radford-Hill, Sheila. "Keepin' it Real: A Generational Commentary on Kimberly Springer's 'Third Wave Black Feminism?'" *Signs* 27, no. 4 (2002): 1083–89.

Radicalesbians, "The Woman-Identified Woman," in *Radical Feminism,* ed. Barbara Crow. New York: NYU Press, 2000: 233–37.

Ray, Raka. *Fields of Protest: Women's Movements in India.* Minneapolis: University of Minnesota Press, 2001.

Redstockings, "Redstockings Manifesto," in *Radical Feminism: A Documentary Reader,* ed. Barbara Crow. New York: NYU Press, 2000: 223–25.

Reger, Jo. "Social Movement Culture and Organizational Survival in the National Organization for Women." Ph.D. dissertation, The Ohio State University, 1997.

Reger, Jo. "Motherhood and the Construction of Feminist Identities: Variations in a Women's Movement," *Sociological Inquiry* 71 (2001): 85–100.

Reger, Jo. "More than One Feminism: Organizational Structure, Ideology, and the Construction of Collective Identity," in *Social Movements: Identity, Culture, and the State,* ed. David S. Meyer, Nancy Whittier, and Belinda Robnett. New York: Oxford University Press, 2002.

Reger, Jo. "Organizational Dynamics and the Construction of Multiple Feminist Identities in the National Organization for Women." *Gender and Society* 16, no. 5 (2002): 710–27.

Reger, Jo. "Organizational 'Emotion Work' through Consciousness-Raising: An Analysis of a Feminist Organization." *Qualitative Sociology* 27, no. 2 (2004): 205–22.

Reger, Jo, ed. *Different Wavelengths: Studies of the Contemporary Women's Movement.* New York: Routledge, 2005.

Reger, Jo. *Everywhere and Nowhere: Contemporary Feminism in the United States.* New York: Oxford University Press, 2012.

Reger, Jo and Suzanne Staggenborg. "Patterns of Mobilization in Local Movement Organizations: Leadership and Strategy in Four National Organizations for Women Chapters." *Sociological Perspectives* 49 (2006): 297–323.

Reid-Pharr, Robert. "Extending Queer Theory to Race and Ethnicity." *Chronicle of Higher Education* 48 (2002): B7–B9.

Reps, John. *Cities of the American West: A History of Frontier Urban Planning.* Princeton, NJ: Princeton University Press, 1979.

Rich, Adrienne. "On the Politics of Location," *Bread, Blood, and Roses.* New York: Norton & Norton, 1989.

Rivers, Daniel. "Radical Relations: A History of Lesbian and Gay Parents and their Children." Ph.D. dissertation, Stanford University, 2010.

Robinson, Donald Allen. "Two Movements in Pursuit of Equal Opportunities." *Signs* 4, no. 3 (spring 1979): 413–33.

Rodgers, Andres D. *Noble Fellow William Starling Sullivant.* New York: G.P. Putnam and Sons, 1940.

Rosen, Ruth. *The World Split Open: How the Modern Women's Movement Changed America.* New York: Viking Press, 2000.

Roth, Benita. *Separate Roads to Feminism: Black, Chicana, and White Feminist Movements in America's Second Wave.* New York: Cambridge University Press, 2003.

Ruiz, Vicki. "Shaping Public Space/Enunciating Gender: A Multiracial Historiography of the Women's West, 1995–2000." *Frontiers* 22, no. 3 (2001): 22–25.

Rupp, Leila J. *Worlds of Women: The Making of an International Women's Movement.* Princeton, NJ: Princeton University Press, 1997.

Rupp, Leila J. "Is Feminism the Province of Older (or Middle-Aged) Women?" *Journal of Women's History* 12, no. 4 (2001): 164–73.

Rupp, Leila J. and Verta Taylor. *Survival in the Doldrums: The American Women's Movement, 1945 to the 1960s.* New York: Oxford University Press, 1987.

Rupp, Leila J. and Verta Taylor. *Drag Queens at the 801 Cabaret.* Chicago: University of Chicago Press, 2003.

Ryan, Barbara. *Feminism and the Women's Movement: Dynamics of Change in Social Movement Ideology and Action.* New York: Routledge, 1992.

Schechter, Patricia. *Ida B. Wells-Barnett and American Reform.* Chapel Hill: University of North Carolina Press, 2001.

Schlafly, Phyllis. *The Power of the Positive Woman.* New Rochelle, NY: Arlington House, 1977.

Schneir, Miriam, ed. *Feminism in Our Time: The Essential Writings, World War II to the Present.* New York: Vintage, 1994.

Schulman, Bruce and Julian Zelizer, eds. *Rightward Bound: Making America Conservative in the 1970s.* Cambridge, MA: Harvard University Press, 2008.

Scott, Anne Firor. *The Southern Lady: From Pedestal to Politics, 1830–1930.* Chicago: University of Chicago Press, 1970.

Sealander, Judith and Dorothy Smith. "The Rise and Fall of Feminist Organizations in the 1970s: Dayton as a Case Study." *Feminist Studies* 12, no. 2 (1986): 321–41.

Siebert, Wilbur. *The Mysteries of Ohio's Underground Railroad.* Columbus, OH: Long's College Book Co., 1951.

Sherman, Janann, ed. *Conversations with Betty Friedan.* Jackson: University of Mississippi Press, 2002.

Shoemaker, Nancy. *Negotiators of Change: Historical Perspectives on Native American Women.* New York: Routledge, 1994.

Small, Melvin. *Covering Dissent: The Media and the Anti-Vietnam War Movement.* New Brunswick, NJ: Rutgers University Press, 1994.

Smith, Andrea. *Conquest: Sexual Violence and Native American Genocide.* Boston: South End Press, 2005.

Solanis, Valerie. "SCUM Manifesto," in *Radical Feminism: A Documentary Reader,* ed. Barbara Crow. New York: NYU Press, 2000, 201–22.

Spain, Daphne. *How Women Saved the City.* Minneapolis: University of Minnesota Press, 2000.

Sprague, Joey. *Feminist Methodologies for Critical Researchers: Bridging Differences.* Thousand Oaks, CA: Sage, 2002.

Springer, Kimberly. "Black Feminist Organizations and the Emergency of Interstitial Politics," in *Modern American Queer History,* ed. Allida M. Black. Philadelphia: Temple University Press, 2001.

Springer, Kimberly. "Third Wave Black Feminism?" *Signs* 27, no. 4 (2002): 1059–82.

Springer, Kimberly. *Living for the Revolution: Black Feminist Organizations, 1968–1980.* Durham, NC: Duke University Press, 2005.

Spruill, Marjorie Julian. "Gender and America's Right Turn," in *Rightward Bound: Making America Conservative in the 1970s,* ed. Bruce Schulman and Julian Zelizer. Cambridge, MA: Harvard University Press, 2008.

Spruill, Marjorie. "Women for God, Country, and Family: Religion, Politics, and Antifeminism in 1970s America." Unpublished paper in author's possession.

Staggenborg, Suzanne. *The Pro-Choice Movement: Organization and Activism in the Abortion Conflict.* New York: Oxford University Press, 1991.

Stein, Marc. *Sisterly and Brotherly Love: Gay and Lesbian Movements in Philadelphia, 1948–1972.* New York: NYU Press, 2000.

Step by Step: Building a Feminist Movement, 1941–1977, dir. Joyce Follett. Women Make Movies, 1998.

Sugrue, Thomas. *The Origins of the Urban Crisis: Race and Inequality in Postwar Detroit.* Princeton, NJ: Princeton University Press, 1998.

Swerdlow, Amy. *Women Strike for Peace: Traditional Motherhood and Radical Politics in the 1960s*. Chicago: University of Chicago Press, 1993.

Taylor, Angela. "The Rape Victim: Is She Also the Unintended Victim of the Law?" *New York Times*, June 15, 1971, 52.

Taylor, Verta. "Social Movement Continuity: The Women's Movement in Abeyance." *American Sociological Review* 54 (1989): 761–75.

Taylor, Verta and Leila J. Rupp. "Researching the Women's Movement: We Make Our Own History, but Just Not As We Please," in *Beyond Methodology: Feminist Scholarship as Lived Research*, ed. Mary Margaret Fonow and Judith Cook. Bloomington: Indiana University Press, 1991.

Taylor, Verta and Leila J. Rupp. "Women's Culture and Lesbian Feminist Activism: A Reconsideration of Cultural Feminism." *Signs* 19, no. 1 (1993): 32–61.

Taylor, Verta and Nella Van Dyke. "Get Up, Stand Up: Tactical Repertoires of Social Movements," in *The Blackwell Companion to Social Movements*, ed. David Snow, Sarah Soule, and Hanspeter Kriesi. New York: Blackwell, 2004. 262–93.

Taylor, Verta and Nancy Whittier. "Collective Identity in Social Movement Communities: Lesbian Feminist Mobilization," in *Frontiers of Social Movement Theory*, ed. Aldon D. Morris and Carol McClurg Mueller. New Haven, CT: Yale University Press, 1992: 104–29.

Thompson, Becky. "Multiracial Feminism: Recasting the Chronology of Second Wave Feminism." *Feminist Studies* 28, no. 2 (2002): 337–55.

Tong, Rosemarie Putnam. *Feminist Thought: A More Comprehensive Introduction*, 2nd ed. Boulder, CO: Westview Press, 1998.

Turk, Katherine. "Out of the Revolution, Into the Mainstream: Employment Activism in NOW's Sears Campaign and the Growing Pains of Liberal Feminism." *Journal of American History* 97, no. 2 (2010): 399–423.

Valk, Anne. "Mother Power: The Movement for Welfare Rights in Washington, DC, 1966–72." *Journal of Women's History* 11, no. 4 (2000): 34–58.

Valk, Anne. *Radical Sisters: Second-Wave Feminism and Black Liberation in Washington, DC*. Urbana: University of Illinois Press, 2010.

Varon, Jeremy. *Bringing the War Home: The Weather Underground, the Red Army Faction, and Revolutionary Violence in the 1960s and 1970s*. Berkeley: University of California Press, 2004.

Walker, Rebecca, ed. *To Be Real: Telling the Truth and Changing the Face of Feminism*. New York: Anchor Books, 1995.

Weigers, Mary. "Beneath Those Charred Bras Revolution Smolders," *Washington Post*, March 8, 1970, G1.

Weitzer, Ronald. *Sex for Sale: Prostitution, Pornography, and the Sex Industry*. New York: Routledge, 2000.

Wheeler, Marjorie Spruill, ed. *One Woman, One Vote: Rediscovering the Woman Suffrage Movement*. Troutdale, OR: NewSage Press, 1995.

White, Deborah Gray. *Too Heavy a Load: Black Women in Defense of Themselves, 1884–1984*. New York: W.W. Norton, 1999.

Whittier, Nancy. *Feminist Generations: The Persistence of the Radical Women's Movement*. Philadelphia: Temple University Press, 1995.

Williams, Daniel. *God's Own Party: The Making of the Christian Right*. New York: Oxford University Press, 2010.

Wirt, Frederick M. *Power in the City: Decision Making in San Francisco*. Berkeley: University of California Press, 1974.

Wolcott, Victoria. *Remaking Respectability: African American Women in Interwar Detroit*. Chapel Hill: University of North Carolina Press, 1996.

Wolf, Deborah. *The Lesbian Community*. Berkeley: University of California Press, 1979.

Wright, Sharon D. *Race, Power, and Political Emergence in Memphis*. New York: Garland, 2000.

Wu, Judy. *Doctor Mom Chung of the Fair-Haired Bastards: The Life of a Wartime Celebrity.* Berkeley: University of California Press, 2005.

Yellin, Carol Lynn and Janann Sherman. *The Perfect 36: Tennessee Delivers Woman Suffrage.* New York: Iris Books, 1996.

Yung, Judy. *Unbound Feet: A Social History of Chinese Women in San Francisco.* Berkeley: University of California Press, 1995.

INDEX

Abzug, Bella 40
Adkins, Gail 60
AFL-CIO 76, 78, 104
Alexander, Dorothy 36
Allen, Gina 107
Allen, Martha 49
American Association of University
    Women 27, 77
American Women 24
American Women Are Richly Endowed
    (AWARE) 53, 54, 57
Ash, Marian 102
Atkinson, Ti-Grace 30, 41

Barnhill, Donna 109, 110
Bay Area Women's Coalition 99–102,
    119–21, 123, 125
Bell, Judy 75, 76, 81, 85
Bernard, Shirley 98
Black feminism 33
Blake, Jeri 54
Bodfish, Margaret 109–10
Booth, Heather 1
Bottini, Ivy 36
Boyer, Elizabeth (Gene) 1, 30
Brant, Youla 83, 84
Bratcher, Judy Copeland 112
Browning, Ruth 75
Brush, Brenda 101, 110, 113
Burnside, Janet 75, 78, 80–81, 82,
    90, 130

California Child Care Initiative
    Committee 103
Call Off Your Tired Old Ethics
    (COYOTE) 118, 121
Carney, Myra 83
Carroll, Betty 79, 87, 89, 91
child care 29, 34, 102–05, 130
Chisholm, Shirley 40
Civil Rights Act of 1964 24, 80, 100.
    See also Title II, Title VII
Clarenbach, Kathryn (Kay) 26, 28, 32, 34, 37
Clayton, Nancy 50
coalition politics among feminists. *See* Bay
    Area Women's Coalition; Women's
    Action Coalition; Women's Action
    Collective
Columbus NOW 2, 17, 20, 69–95,
    127, 129
Comprehensive Education and Training
    Administration (CETA) funding 59
Comprehensive Rape Crisis Program
    (Memphis) 60
Congress to Unite Women (1970) 26
Conroy, Catherine 26
consciousness raising (CR) 35, 73, 87
Counter-Commissioners Project 119–20
Cowart, Mary Jo 50, 64
cultural feminism 89

Daughters of Bilitis 36, 100, 118
Davis, Caroline 26, 27, 29

Dolbi, Lynda 56
domestic violence. *See* wife abuse
Duncan, Helen 48
Dygert, Gretchen 70

Eagle Forum 30, 52, 129
Eastwood, Mary 26, 27
Equal Employment Opportunity
   Commission (EEOC) 24, 25, 26, 27,
   40, 89, 109, 111. *See also* Title VII
Equal Pay Act 24
Equal Rights Amendment (ERA) 15, 18,
   24, 29, 30, 32, 46, 51, 52–58,
   66, 71, 74, 76–80, 84, 86, 90, 93–94,
   98, 100, 121–25, 129, 130;
   defeat of 130; extension campaign
   55–56; Message Brigade 55;
   rallies 56–57; rescission effort in
   Tennessee 54–55

Feminine Mystique, The 2, 25, 27,
   39, 89, 132
Feminist Avengers (Columbus) 69
Fox, Muriel 26
"Friedan mystique" 1, 22. *See also* Friedan,
   Betty; Havens, Mary
Fulcher, Patsy 117
Furness, Betty 26
Friedan, Betty 1, 2, 5, 14, 22,
   25, 26, 27, 32, 33, 44, 132.
   See also *The Feminine Mystique*

"Gahanna Five" 70–71, 92
Geiger, Dorothy 78
Gifford, Gayle 121
Gilliam, Art 48
Givens, V. 88
Glide Memorial Church 100, 107,
   118
Golden Gate (GG) NOW 117–20,
   125
Graham, Richard 26, 27
grassroots feminism 4, 7
"Great Wall of Gahanna" 70, 133
Grossinger, Tania 39
Gurner, Rowena 107

Haener, Dorothy 26
Hamlin, Marie 61
Harris, Lanna 71
Harris v. McRae (1980) 31
Hathaway, Virtue 118
Havens, Mary 89, 132

Hazen, Pam 59–60
Hensen, Carole 64
Hernandez, Aileen 1, 14, 26, 40, 114,
   117, 118, 120, 121, 131
Hersh, Rita 107
historiography, feminist, of women's
   movement 3–4, 6–7, 47–48, 73–74,
   134–35
Hooker's Convention 118
Howell, Julia 60
Hudson, Andrewnetta Hawkins 50
Hummel, Barbara Walker 53

Ikeda, Joanne 102, 103

Jensen, Cheriel 106
Jensen, Karen 91
job discrimination 29, 51, 80–81, 81–82,
   109–13, 130
Job Discrimination Committee
   (San Francisco) 109, 113

Keisker, Marion 60
Kennedy, Flo 15, 92
Knights of Columbus 31–32
Krapolat, Mimi 41

Lahr, Lorraine 104, 116
lavender menace 15, 26, 36–39, 64,
   66–67, 102
League of Women Voters 48
Lear, Norman 31
Legal Defense and Education Fund
   (NOW LDEF) 31
lesbian feminism 89
Lesbian Mothers Union (LMU) 103
lesbians in NOW. *See* National
   Organization for Women
liberal feminism 5, 11–12, 22, 28,
   29, 52, 63, 84, 125–26.
   See also liberal/radical divide
liberal/radical divide 5, 10–11,
   13–14, 18, 19, 22, 63, 67–68,
   74, 84, 125–26, 132–33, 134–35
Lightfoot, Judith 48
location, politics of 10, 16–17
Lyon, Phyllis 36–37, 117, 120.
   See also Martin, Del

Mackenzie, Nancy 79
Maginnis, Patricia 106–07
Maher v. Roe (1977) 31
Martin, Courtney 134

Martin, Del 36–37, 103, 117, 119, 120;
  bid for national board, 117–18.
  See also Daughters of Bilitis;
  Lyon, Phyllis
Marxist feminism 97
"Maude" 31
Meates, Susan 80–81
Memphis Gay Coalition 65
Memphis NOW 2, 17, 20, 45–68, 129
Memphis Women's Political Caucus 57,
  66, 67
Meyer, Adele 115
Miller, Mary 76, 77
Millett, Kate 38
Miss America Pageant protest 41
Morrison, Toni 48
Mosley, Mary 70
Ms. Magazine 86, 88
Murakami, Grace 81
Murray, Pauli 26

National Association for the Advancement
  of Colored People (NAACP) 28
National Black Feminist Organization
  13, 121
National Organization for Women
  (NOW): chapters 34–44; founding of 2,
  3, 21–28; lesbians within 36, 46, 64–67,
  90, 102, 133; statement of purpose
  28–30; women of color within 15,
  33–34, 47, 48–52, 117–19, 133. *See also*
  Columbus NOW; Golden Gate (GG)
  NOW; Memphis NOW; New York
  City (NYC) NOW; San Francisco
  (SF) NOW
National Sexual Violence Resource
  Center 69
National Welfare Rights Organization 13
National Women's Political Caucus
  40, 104
New York City (NYC) NOW 14,
  30, 35, 36
New York Radical Feminists 14
Norman, Eve 115

Ohio Civil Liberties Union 82
Ohio Commission on the Status of
  Women 17, 71, 73, 75, 77
Ohio State University 73, 86

Panel of American Women (PAW) 47, 49
People Against Rape (Memphis) 59–60
Peterson, Esther 27

Planned Parenthood of Pennsylvania v. Casey
  (1992) 31
pornography 62–63
Powell, Betty 70
President's Commission on the Status of
  Women 24, 27, 44
Pressman, Sonia (Sonny) 26
Proposition M 104–05

queer theory 4–5

Radicalesbians 14
radical feminism 11–12, 22, 58, 63,
  69–70, 71, 85–93
Radical Women 97
Raiteri, Linda 137
rape 51, 58, 59–60, 69, 91–92, 130
Red Door Tavern 80–81, 87, 128
Reeves, Helen 94
reproductive rights 29, 30, 32, 51,
  82–83, 101, 105–09, 120
Roe v. Wade (1973) 30, 54, 58
Rosen, Ronnie 86
Rossi, Alice 32, 34
Russo, Angie 60, 61

Sahara, June 89
St. James, Margo 121
San Francisco *Examiner-Chronicle*
  112–13, 128
San Francisco NOW 2, 17, 20,
  97–126, 129
San Francisco State College 101
Sanders, Marlene 26
Saunier, Anne 75, 76, 83
Schlafly, Phyllis 30, 52, 129
Seligman, Carole 124
Selmier, Vicki 106, 107, 111, 115
Sewell, Edie 61
Sexuality and Lesbianism Task Force
  (Memphis) 64–67
Shane, Johnette 64
SlutWalks 136
Smeal, Eleanor 55, 124
Smith, Dot 48
Smith, Merle 49
Snuff 62–63
Society for Humane Abortion 101,
  105–06
softball 65–66, 132
Southern Girl(s) Convention 45
Southern womanhood (trope) 15,
  47, 48, 63, 67, 129, 131

Squeo (Hughes), Patty 93
Steinem, Gloria 33, 40
STOPERA 52–58, 79,
  93–94, 129
Stout, Sandra 90–91
Strike for Women's Equality (also referred
  to as Women's Strike for Equality) 1, 2,
  14, 39, 43, 46
Sullivan, Betty 55

Take Back The Night 59, 73, 136
The Feminists 30
Thomas, Leathia 50
Title II 80, 81
Title VII 24, 26, 27, 42, 100, 111. *See also*
  Civil Rights Act of 1964; Equal
  Employment Opportunity Commission
  (EEOC)
Treseder, Anne 106
Trux, Nancy 79, 80

Union Women's Alliance to Gain
  Equality (WAGE) 122–23
United Auto Workers 26, 27, 29, 35
United Sisters and Associates (USA) 49
University of Memphis (formerly
  Memphis State University) 45, 65

Watson Diane 116, 123
waves, feminist model of 3–4, 8–9, 135

Webster v. Reproductive Health Services
  (1992) 31
Weston, Val 124
wife abuse 58, 60–62, 73
Wife Abuse Crisis Service
  (Memphis) 61
Women Against Rape (Columbus)
  70, 74, 91, 92
Women and Girls Employment Services
  (WAGES) 50
women of color in NOW.
  See National Organization
  for Women
Women's Action Coalition
  (WAC, Memphis) 45
Women's Action Collective
  (WAC, Columbus) 18, 70, 71,
  73–74, 77, 86
Women's Building (San Francisco) 97, 102
Women's Equity Action League
  (WEAL) 30
Women's International Terrorist
  Conspiracy from Hell (WITCH) 22
Women's Resource Center (Memphis)
  58, 59, 61–62
Wurzburg, Jocelyn 42
Wyatt, Addie 124

Young Women's Christian
  Association (YWCA) 73, 77